77-894

Over
PR
8753   Yeats, Joyce, and Beckett.
Y4

Date Due

JUL X X 2015

YEATS,
JOYCE,
AND
BECKETT

YEATS, JOYCE, AND BECKETT

New Light on Three Modern Irish Writers

Edited by Kathleen McGrory and John Unterecker

Lewisburg
Bucknell University Press

London
Associated University Presses

© 1976 by Associated University Presses, Inc.

Associated University Presses, Inc.
Cranbury, New Jersey 08512

Associated University Presses
108 New Bond Street
London W1Y OQX, England

Library of Congress Cataloging in Publication Data
Main entry under title:

Yeats, Joyce, and Beckett.

"Chronological bibliography of works by
William York Tindall": p. 183
Includes bibliographical references and index.
1. Yeats, William Butler, 1865–1939—Addresses,
essays, lectures. 2. Joyce, James, 1882–1941—
Addresses, essays, lectures. 3. Beckett, Samuel,
1906–   —Addresses, essays, lectures. 4. Tindall,
William York, 1903–   —Bibliography
I. McGrory, Kathleen. II. Unterecker, John
Eugene, 1922–
PR8753.Y4   820'.9'9415   74-4983
ISBN 0-8387-1465-X

PRINTED IN THE UNITED STATES OF AMERICA

For
WILLIAM YORK TINDALL

whose insights into the creative process and whose strict eloquence have helped hundreds of thousands of readers discover the structure and the strangeness and the art in works by Beckett, Joyce, and Yeats. Because a dedication is a good place for such things, this dedication is offered in gratitude and love.

Contents

Preface

WITH FIGURES LIKE Wilde, Shaw, O'Casey, Synge, Yeats, and Joyce cluttering the literary horizon, and with such impressive living writers as Samuel Beckett, Thomas Kinsella, and John Montague dominating the foreground, it is no wonder that students of twentieth-century English literature find themselves at one point or another remarking, "Whatever else English literature is, it's Irish."

Certainly most of those students would agree that Joyce is the major novelist and Yeats the major poet of the first half of this century, and many if not most of them would go on to name Beckett as the most important writer of the mid-century years.

It is easy to understand, then, that when we were approached by Bucknell University Press to get together a book of essays in honor of William York Tindall—"perhaps a Festschrift"—our first thought was that whatever we produced, it would focus on Irish literature. And in very short order, we also decided that what we really wanted was a Festschrift with a difference, a coherent collection of essays about the three most important Irish writers of this century. Instead of a miscellany, we wanted—whenever possible—commissioned work.

From the beginning we determined to produce a useful book: one that would offer a guide to the best work on Yeats and Joyce, one that would suggest something of the essential Irishness of all three writers, one that would offer new insights into hitherto-neglected aspects of their work, and one that would search out biographical material that had either little availability or no availability at all.

We also felt very strongly that we wanted to illustrate the material on each author with a set of photographs that would suggest something of the essential landscape of his work: for Joyce and Beckett the area in and around Dublin; for Yeats the open, vivid country in the west of Ireland where he had grown up, which dominated much of his work.

Though what we have finally produced is indeed a "Festschrift with a difference," we feel that it is a valid tribute to a great teacher. And though our bibliography of the works of William York Tindall seems to us woefully incomplete (Bill was adamant that none of his reviews be included), it does offer a good reading list, a good guide to the work of one of the major literary critics of our time.

Our gratitude for the contributions and the patience of our collaborators is unbounded. We are grateful also for the assistance of Colton Johnson and Michael and Grania Yeats in locating the photographs of W. B. Yeats and Anne Yeats, for the kindness of Mrs. Carola Giedion-Welcker in providing the photograph of James Joyce, and for Jack Coughlin's permission to use his splendid engraving of Samuel Beckett. We are also particularly grateful for the enthusiastic encouragement of Miss Frances Stelloff, whose Gotham Book Mart has for years been the meeting place of the James Joyce Society.

Most of all, we are grateful for the help and encouragement given us by Bill Tindall himself. Those honored by Festschrifts are not supposed to know what's going on when the book is being constructed, but they always do. We decided to announce the book early. Besides, we wanted to use some of Bill's hitherto-unpublished photographs of Joyce and Yeats landscapes. Once we had asked for them, it seemed only natural to consult him in regard to captions, bibliographical matters, and the nature of the Irish soul. Celia, his wife, encouraged our consultations and proved, as always before, hospitable, witty, and immensely kind. Bill once remarked that he hoped everything he had written would be helpful to the reader. In the same hope, we present this collection of essays and photographs.

Kathleen McGrory
John Unterecker

Acknowledgments

THE EDITORS THANK the following for permission to reprint copyrighted material:

Macmillan Publishing Co., Inc. for lines from William Butler Yeats, "The King of the Great Clock Tower." Reprinted with permission of Macmillan Publishing Co., Inc. from *Collected Poems* by William Butler Yeats. Copyright 1934 by Macmillan Publishing Co., Inc., renewed 1962 by Bertha Georgie Yeats; for lines from William Butler Yeats, "Under Ben Bulben." Reprinted with permission of Macmillan Publishing Co., Inc. from *Collected Poems* by William Butler Yeats. Copyright 1940 by Georgie Yeats, renewed 1968 by Bertha Georgie Yeats, Michael Butler Yeats and Anne Yeats; for lines from William Butler Yeats, "To Be Carved on a Stone at Thoor Ballylee." Reprinted with permission of Macmillan Publishing Co., Inc. from *Collected Poems* by William Butler Yeats. Copyright 1924 by Macmillan Publishing Co., Inc., renewed 1952 by Bertha Georgie Yeats; for lines from William Butler Yeats, "A Prayer on Going into My House" and "The Dawn." Reprinted with permission of Macmillan Publishing Co., Inc. from *Collected Poems* by William Butler Yeats. Copyright 1919 by Macmillan Publishing Co., Inc., renewed 1947 by Bertha Georgie Yeats. Also for quotations from William Butler Yeats, *Deirdre*. Reprinted with permission of Macmillan Publishing Co., Inc. from *Collected Plays* by William Butler Yeats. Copyright 1934, 1952 by Macmillan Publishing Co., Inc.

Shenandoah, for permission to reprint "An Interview with Anne Yeats" and Austin Clark's "Glimpses of W. B. Yeats: County Sligo." Copyright 1965 by *Shenandoah,* reprinted from *Shenandoah*: The Washington and Lee University Review with the permission of Anne Yeats, Austin Clarke, and the Editor.

A. P. Watt & Son Ltd. for English-language rights outside the U.S. to quote from "Alternative Song for the Severed Head" in "The King of the Great Clock Tower"; "Under Ben Bulben"; "To Be Carved on a Stone at Thoor Ballylee"; "The Dawn"; and "A Prayer on Going into My House," all from *The Collected Poems of W. B. Yeats;* also to quote from *Deirdre,* from *The Collected Plays of W. B. Yeats.* By permission of M. B. Yeats, Miss Anne Yeats, and Macmillan of London & Basingstoke.

Editors' Note

The following is a list of editions from which the texts accompanying the photographs have been drawn:

Yeats Landscape:
W. B. Yeats, *Collected Poems.* "Definitive Edition." New York: Macmillan, 1956.

W. B. Yeats, *Autobiographies.* New York: Macmillan, 1955.

Joyce Landscape:
James Joyce, *A Portrait of the Artist as a Young Man.* New York: Viking Press, 1962.

James Joyce, *Stephen Hero.* New York: New Directions Publishing Company, 1963.

James Joyce, *Ulysses.* New York: Random House, 1961.

James Joyce, *Finnegans Wake.* New York: Viking Press, 1958.

Beckett Landscape:
Samuel Beckett, *More Pricks Than Kicks.* London: Calder and Boyars, 1934.

Contributors

BERNARD BENSTOCK. Professor of English and Comparative Literature, University of Illinois at Urbana-Champaign. Author of *Joyce-again's Wake: An Analysis of Finnegans Wake* (1965) and *Sean O'Casey* (1970). Co-editor of *Approaches to Ulysses* (1970) and *Approaches to James Joyce's Portrait* (forthcoming). Articles on Joyce, O'Casey, Flann O'Brien, William Gaddis, and others.

AUSTIN CLARKE (1896–1974). Poet, friend of Yeats and other major figures of the Irish Literary Renaissance. Author of *The Vengeance of Finn* (1917), *Pilgrimage and Other Poems* (1928), *Poetry in Modern Ireland* (1951), *Collected Plays* (1963), *A Penny in the Clouds* (1968), *The Celtic Twilight and the Nineties* (1969), *Tiresias* (1972), *Collected Poems* (1974), and many other volumes of poetry, prose, and drama.

JOHN EICHRODT. Professor of English and Comparative Literature, Western Connecticut State College. Editorial Consultant, *The Connecticut Review*, author of articles on D. H. Lawrence, James Joyce, and five novels.

ADRIENNE GARDNER has taught at the University of Texas and is currently at the University of Pennsylvania. Author of articles on Yeats, Joyce, and John Fowles.

CAROLA GIEDION-WELCKER. Friend and patroness of Joyce in Zurich and Paris from 1929 until his death. Art historian and critic, author of books on Klee, Picasso, Arp, Brancusi, and other modern artists whom she knew personally. Her articles on Joyce have appeared in *Die Weltwoche* and *Neue Züricher Zeitung* (Zurich), and *Le Figaro* (Paris), among other periodicals. A selection of her articles on Joyce, Arp, Brancusi, Ernst, Picasso, and Schwitters has been published in *Schriften: Stationen zu einen Zeitbild 1926–1971* (1971).

NATHAN HALPER. Internationally known expert on *Finnegans Wake* and chess. Translator, author of *Early Work of James Joyce,* in the Columbia Essays on Modern Writers series, and numerous articles on Joyce in *Partisan Review, The Nation, James Joyce Quarterly, Wake Newslitter, Twelve and a Tilly,* and elsewhere.

SIGHLE KENNEDY. Professor of English and Comparative Literature, Hunter College of the City University of New York. Author of *Murphy's Bed: a Study of Real Sources and Sur-real Associations in Samuel Beckett's First Novel,* and a forthcoming study of *Watt* for which Mr. Beckett has given permission for use of facsimile reproductions of pages from his manuscripts now in collections of university libraries in the United States.

JACK MACGOWRAN (1919–1973). Irish actor and personal friend of Samuel Beckett. Internationally famous for his one-man Beckett show and for leading roles in plays by O'Casey and other Irish dramatists, and for his role as the Fool in the film version of *King Lear.* Samuel Beckett composed the play *Eh, Joe* for him, and has directed his performances of *Waiting for Godot* in London and Paris. Mr. MacGowran's sudden death in 1973 elicited tributes from Mr. Beckett and friends in the literary and theatrical world.

KATHLEEN MCGRORY. Associate Professor of English and Comparative Literature, Chairman of the Department of English, Composition, and Comparative Literature, Western Connecticut State College. Lecturer, author of articles on Joyce, Yeats, Lady Gregory, Synge, O'Casey, and Stephens in the *McGraw-Hill Encyclopedia of World Biography* (1972), "Medieval Aspects of Modern Irish Literature," in *Modern Irish Literature* (1973), articles and reviews in *Connecticut Review, Notre Dame English Journal, Eire/*

Ireland, and elsewhere. Co-author of second edition of Mabel Worthington's *Song in the Works of James Joyce* (forthcoming) and The James Joyce Cassette Series of recordings and commentary on songs in the works of Joyce.

RAYMOND J. PORTER. Professor of English, Iona College. Co-editor of *Modern Irish Literature* (1973). Author of *P. H. Pearse* in the Twayne series and *Brendan Behan* in the Columbia Essays on Modern Writers series, and of articles on Irish literature in scholarly periodicals.

RUBIN RABINOVITZ. University of Colorado. Author of *The Reaction Against Experiment in the English Novel: Iris Murdoch* and a full-length critical study of Samuel Beckett (forthcoming). Author of articles in *Columbia University Forum, Modern Fiction Studies, Modern Irish Literature,* reviews in the *New York Times Book Review* and *New York.*

MARGARET C. SOLOMON. Professor in English, Chairman, Graduate Studies in English, University of Hawaii. Author of *Eternal Geomater: The Sexual Universe of Finnegans Wake* (1969), numerous articles on Joyce in *Grain, The Celtic Master, A Wake Newslitter, Modern Fiction Studies, Ulysses: Cinquante Ans Après* (1974), *A Conceptual Guide to Finnegans Wake* (1974); Director of the Hawaii James Joyce Symposium 1974.

WILLIAM YORK TINDALL. Professor Emeritus, Columbia University. Dean of American Joyce criticism. Author of *A Reader's Guide to James Joyce* (1959), *A Reader's Guide to Finnegans Wake* (1969), *The Joyce Country* (1960), *James Joyce, His Way of Interpreting the Modern World* (1950), *Forces in Modern British Literature, 1885–1956* (1956), *The Literary Symbol* (1955), and numerous books, articles, and reviews. President of the James Joyce Society of New York.

JOHN UNTERECKER. Formerly Professor of English in the Graduate School, Columbia University; Visiting Professor at the University of Texas at Austin, 1974; presently Professor in English, University of Hawaii. Author of three books dealing with the works of William Butler Yeats and the prize-winning biography of Hart Crane, *Voyager;* of a children's book, *The Dreaming Zoo;* of numerous published poems including *Dance Sequence,* and of the soon-to-be-published *Stone.*

ANNE YEATS. Daughter of poet William Butler Yeats. Irish artist whose graphics and oils can be seen in many collections. She was for some time stage designer for the Abbey Theatre.

YEATS,
JOYCE,
AND
BECKETT

Part I

WILLIAM BUTLER YEATS

Photographs by John Unterecker

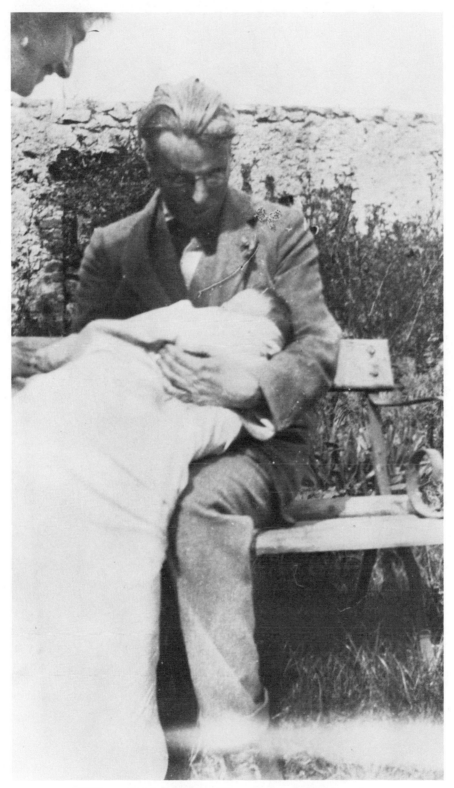

William Butler Yeats, Mrs. Yeats, daughter Anne. March 1919. *Courtesy of the Yeats family.*

William Butler Yeats and Anne. March 1935. *Courtesy of the Yeats family.*

Knocknarea, Maeve's Tomb. *Photo by Unterecker.*

Knocknarea is in Sligo, and the countrypeople say that Maeve, still a great queen of the western Sidhe, is buried in the cairn of stones upon it. (W. B. Yeats, notes to "The Hosting of the Sidhe," *Collected Poems*, p. 448)

Ben Bulben from Rosses Point. *Photo by Unterecker.*

"Saddle and ride," I heard a man say,
Out of Ben Bulben and Knocknarea,
What says the clock in the Great Clock Tower?
All those tragic characters ride
But turn from Rosses' crawling tide,
The meet's upon the mountain-side.
A slow note and an iron bell.
    (W. B. Yeats, "Alternative Song for the Severed
    Head in 'The King of the Great Clock Tower,' "
    Collected Poems, p. 279)

"Under bare Ben Bulben's head
In Drumcliff churchyard Yeats is laid . . ."
(W. B. Yeats, "Under Ben Bulben," *Collected
Poems*, p. 343)

**Graveyard, Drumcliff. (Note: Yeats's grave is in the
right foreground.)** *Photo by Unterecker.*

"Under bare Ben Bulben's head
In Drumcliff churchyard Yeats is laid.
An ancestor was rector there
Long years ago, a church stands near . . ."
　(W. B. Yeats, "Under Ben Bulben," p. 343)

**Round Tower and Church, Drumcliff. (Note: Church
and churchyard are in the distance.)** *Photo by Unterecker.*

The Celtic cross near Yeats's gravesite, Drumcliff.
Photo by Unterecker.

Under bare Ben Bulben's head
In Drumcliff churchyard Yeats is laid.
An ancestor was rector there
Long years ago, a church stands near,
By the road an ancient cross.
(W. B. Yeats, "Under Ben Bulben, p. 343)

Harbor at Rosses Point. *Photo by Unterecker.*

Jack Yeats's "Memory Harbour" was used as the frontispiece for the first edition of W. B. Yeats's *Reveries over Childhood and Youth.* Painted not far from this spot, it shows, as the poet explained, "the village of Rosses Point but with the distances shortened and the houses run together as in an old-fashioned panoramic map. . . . When I look at my brother's picture, *Memory Harbour . . .* I am full of disquiet and of excitement, and I am melancholy because I have not made more and better verses. I have walked on Sinbad's yellow shore and never shall another's hit my fancy." (*Autobiographies,* p. 52)

"... I would be ignorant as the dawn
That merely stood, rocking the glittering coach
Above the cloudy shoulders of the horses ..."
(W. B. Yeats, "The Dawn," *Collected Poems*,
p. 144)

Horses, Connemara. *Photo by Unterecker.*

Entrance to Yeats's tower, Ballylee. (Note: This photo was taken before the recent restoration of the tower, and long after the Yeats family had left it.) *Photo by Tindall.*

"I, the poet William Yeats,
With old mill boards and sea-green slates,
And smithy work from the Gort forge,
Restored this tower for my wife George;
And may these characters remain
When all is ruin once again."
  (W. B. Yeats, "To be Carved on a Stone at
  Thoor Ballylee," *Collected Poems,* p. 188)

"God grant a blessing on this tower and cottage
And on my heirs, if all remain unspoiled,
. . . and should some limb of the Devil
Destroy the view by cutting down an ash
That shades the road, or setting up a cottage
Planned in a government office, shorten his life,
Manacle his soul upon the Red Sea bottom."
  (W. B. Yeats, "A Prayer on Going into my
  House," *Collected Poems,* p. 160)

Yeats's tower, showing the cottages and garden below
it. *Photo by Unterecker.*

1

Deirdre: Yeats's Other Greek Tragedy

Adrienne Gardner

ALTHOUGH YEATS'S dramatizations of Irish heroic legends were composed in a self-conscious effort to revivify the sense of the past in which he felt Irish national identity to be rooted, *Deirdre,* his recounting of Conchubar's betrayal of Deirdre and her lover, Naoise, is more than a melodrama about love, jealousy, and treachery set in the Irish heroic age; it is a play in which Yeats's technical virtuosity is displayed through his dramatic melding of two generally divergent generic techniques: *Deirdre* is unified through the kind of sustained use of imagery that one is accustomed to look for in poetry, while Yeats's methods of heightening dramatic tension through understatement and irony are characteristic of Greek tragedy.

In describing the unity of George Eliot's later novels, Barbara Hardy once commented that they "depend for their full effect on the kind of slow and repeated attention to detail which we are more willing to give to the medium of poetry than to the medium of prose narrative."[1] The same might be said of *Deirdre;* much of the beauty of the play derives from an appreciation of the skillfully interwoven images—a perception one is likely to gain only through the close reading characteristically given poetry rather than the more subliminal apprehension of imagery one might enjoy during a dramatic performance. Yeats's appreciation of Greek tragedy and Noh drama reflects his strong interest in the verbal aspect of drama. In Greek tragedies most of the violent action takes place offstage; in Noh plays, as well as in Greek

drama, the actors wear masks—the element of facial expression is eliminated; in both, then, concentration is focused on the spoken word. In *Deirdre,* as in Greek tragedy, the violent deaths of the hero and heroine occur behind the scenes, while the tension culminating in this unseen violence is suggested onstage through irony and understatement. The sense of tragic inevitability is developed through the movement of the imagery that permeates the play.

The images are the underpinnings of the play, the trusses upon which its weight is supported and over which the forms of Greek tragedy are superimposed. The thematic tension between enclosure and wilderness, entrapment and freedom, convention versus chthonic loyalties is presented, in the main, through opposing images: night/day, house/forest, hunter/hunted. In imagery, as well as in values, Deirdre and Conchubar are the polar figures. Naoise, initially vacillating between these magnetic personalities but eventually impelled by the stronger pull of Deirdre's attraction, finally gravitates to her side.

Light imagery in *Deirdre* accomplishes two purposes simultaneously: while the pattern of fading light presents a visual parallel to the approaching deaths of Naoise and Deirdre, the imagery also serves as the symbolic vehicle for expressing the dichotomy between the light of reason and that darker, intuitive knowledge which is the thematic focus of *Deirdre.* As the light imagery in Shakespearian drama tends to move from bright to dark, paralleling the setting of the sun, so the sunlight wanes as Deirdre and Naoise move from the freedom of the forest to the enclosure of Conchu-

1. Barbara Hardy, "Imagery in George Eliot's Last Novels," *Modern Language Review* 50 (1955) : 14.

bar's guest house. Yeats's stage directions specify that the lighting at the play's opening should simulate "the sky dimming, night closing in."[2] Upon her entrance into the guest house, Deirdre pales; she must resort to rouge to bring the color back to her cheeks, a false blush that symbolizes the artificiality consistently associated with Conchubar throughout the play. Sensing the impending darkness of betrayal, Deirdre warns Naoise, "The gods turn clouds and casual accidents into omens" (p. 118). Naoise, blinded by the false light of Fergus's rationality, discounts Deirdre's intuitive knowledge: "It would ill become us,/ Now that King Conchubar has pledged his word,/ Should we be startled by a cloud or a shadow" (p. 118). Deirdre sees their fate more clearly: "though the day laughs, we shall be dead at cock-crow" (p. 119). Fergus, believing in the artificial light of reason, tries to reassure Deirdre: "I have believed the best of every man,/ And found that to believe it is enough/ To make a bad man show him at his best,/ Or even a good man swing his lantern higher" (p. 119). He doesn't see the darker side of human nature; the Musicians, being women, instinctively understand the impending tragedy; though they are forbidden on pain of death to voice their suspicions of Conchubar, their songs express their mistrust. Deirdre recognizes the bitter truth that the Musicians' words only thinly veil: "if they hint at all/ Their eyes and ears have gathered it so lately,/ That it is crying out in them for speech" (p. 110). Although Naoise clings to the ethic of rationality, "when we give a word and take a word/ Sorrow is put away, past wrong forgotten" (p. 121), his allegiance to Deirdre's pre-rational knowledge expresses itself (as is appropriate) through the involuntary paling of his cheek. Deirdre confronts him with the juncture between the spoken and the felt truth:

When we first came into this empty house
You had foreknowledge of our death, and even
When speaking of the paleness of my cheek
Your own cheek blanched.
. . . .
You speak from the lips out,
And I am pleading for your life and mine.
                                        (p. 121)

When the trap she has long feared is sprung and Naoise finally acknowledges, "So, then, it's treach-

ery," Deirdre speaks openly of their death in terms of darkness: "Praise the double sunset, for naught's lacking/ But a good end to the long, cloudy day" (p. 125).[3] Naoise tries to stave off the darkness a while longer with artificial light—an attempt certain to fail, since artificial light is associated with Conchubar: "Light the torches there and drive the shadows out/ For day's grey end comes up" (p. 125). The stage directions at this point reveal that "the light is almost gone from the wood, but there is a clear evening light in the sky" (p. 125); when the light has faded completely, Deirdre has gone to join Naoise behind that dark curtain through which no light penetrates and where they will "outsleep the cock-crow" (p. 133).

The opposing settings of forest and house reflect the antagonism between Deirdre and Conchubar, the conflict between intuitive and rational knowledge. Deirdre, whose chthonic wisdom is expressed through the animal imagery, is at a disadvantage when forced to debate those exponents of rationality, Naoise and Fergus, on their own grounds: Conchubar's guest house. Again, Yeats uses images to portray emotional states; Deirdre's initial discomfiture is displayed through the animal analogies she uses in describing her feelings. Forced at the play's beginning to put on jewels to appease Conchubar, Deirdre seems dragonish to herself—a wild beast, but an unattractive one. Her suspicion of Conchubar is discounted by Fergus as uncivilized: "It is but natural/ That she should doubt him, for her house has been/ The hole of the badger and the den of the fox" (p. 117). As the play progresses, however, the imagery becomes more flattering; though she is wary, associating enclosure with entrapment, her instinctive fears prove to be justified when Conchubar is revealed in his actual role, the hunter, whose house is his snare. Animals and wilderness come to be associated with freedom rather than, as they were initially, with naiveté.

While Deirdre is associated imagistically with animals and animal habitats, Conchubar is linked with the trappings of civilization: houses, especial-

2. William Butler Yeats, *The Collected Plays of W. B. Yeats* (New York: Macmillan Publishing Co., Inc., 1934), p. 112. All following page references to *Deirdre* are from this edition.

3. John Unterecker, author of *A Reader's Guide to William Butler Yeats*, suggested in conversation that the imagery Deirdre uses here, as elsewhere, parallels imagery in *Antony and Cleopatra*. Extending the analogy, one might point out parallels in characterization and thematic conflict: like Naoise, Antony wavers between two worlds, representing order and sensuality, whose principles cannot be harmonized; like Naoise, he chooses the latter, with the attendant consequences.

ly his royal house, symbolize his role as the embodiment of law and order in the land. Naoise is deceived by the external forms of justice; it is against his code to doubt a man's pledged word:

> . . . Such words and fears
> Wrong this old man who's pledged his word to us.
> We must not speak nor think as women do,
> That when the house is all abed sit up
> Marking among the ashes with a stick
> Till they are terrified.—Being what we are
> We must meet all things with an equal mind.
>
> (p. 118)

When he realizes that Conchubar does not intend to fight him man to man, as befits kings and is appropriate to the code, but intends to trap them like beasts, he is disgusted: "a prudent hunter, therefore, but no king" (p. 126). He plays into Conchubar's hand by running out in a "beast-blind rage," and is taken in a net "like a bird or a fish" (p. 128). Naoise is trapped because he is uncommitted to the values of either Deirdre or Conchubar; seeing both sides, he is unable to play either role wholeheartedly. Deirdre, however, undeceived about Conchubar's true intentions, is able to fly over his nets. Though Naoise despairs, "O my eagle! Why do you beat vain wings upon the rock/ When hollow night's above?" (p. 129), Deirdre is undismayed by impending death. Just as Conchubar has trapped the lovers by seeming to uphold standards of law and order, while in actuality capturing them by using animal trickery, Deirdre escapes his nets by employing Conchubar's weapons of conventionality against him. She threatens Conchubar that if he will not allow her to lay out Naoise's dead body, he will "have to drag [her] to his house by force. If he refuses he shall be mocked by all" (p. 132). She knows where he is vulnerable: the law may be respected, or it may be feared, but it must not be laughed at. Conchubar is forced to let her go. Though the hunter has arranged the table at his house with "the moorhen and the mallard and the speckled heathcock on a golden dish" (p. 118), he is unable to ensnare the eagle, wildest of the birds of prey, whose lofty aerie is reachable only by soaring flight. The Musicians speak the epitaph for Deirdre, describing her escape in the same images of eagle, cloud, and wilderness that have characterized her throughout the play:

> They are gone, they are gone.
> Whispering were enough.

Into the secret wilderness of their love.
> A high, grey cairn. What more is to be said?
> Eagles have gone into their cloudy bed.
>
> (p. 133)

The conflicting imagery—man/beast, house/forest, implements of entrapment/instruments of escape—creates a tension in Yeats's play similar to that evoked in Greek tragedy. There are other obvious structural parallels between *Deirdre* and, for example, the tragedies of Sophocles, that Yeats was later to render for the modern stage. The dramatic irony that Sophocles achieved by playing on his audience's knowledge of the Oedipus story Yeats injects into *Deirdre* by references to Ludaigh Redstripe and his wife, whose fate, the audience immediately understands, foreshadows that of Naoise and Deirdre. The sense of inevitability, which in Greek tragedy is evoked by a belief in the power of the gods or fate to determine the outcome of human events, is supplied in Yeats's play both by the foreshadowing and by the progression of the imagery: the inevitability of night's following day parallels death's following life; the outcome is foreordained. The role of the Musicians is similar, though not identical, to that of the Greek chorus; while the chorus in Sophocles' plays generally comprises the townspeople, who give voice to conventional community standards, in *Deirdre* the Musicians support the point of view of the heroine, while Naoise and Fergus are the spokesmen for Conchubar's.

The most striking parallel between Yeats's play and the plays of Sophocles, however, is not structural but thematic. Yeats seems to be working out in *Deirdre* some of the same themes that unify the Oedipus cycle. Yeats was obviously attracted to the plays of Sophocles; in the late 20s and early 30s he wrote modern stage versions of *Oedipus the King* and *Oedipus at Colonus*, but never offered a similar treatment of *Antigone*. One hypothesis to explain this omission is that he had already treated that material—twenty years previously in *Deirdre*. The characters fit: the old kings, Conchubar and Creon; the young queens, Deirdre and Antigone; the young kings and lovers, Naoise and Haemon. The conflict is the same too, the conflict between the principles of law and order and those older, chthonic loyalties whose claims, though unarticulated and intuitive, cannot safely be ignored. In both plays the old kings represent convention and their decisions are based on principles of rationality; Conchubar's justification for his actions in trying to reclaim Deirdre is that she was "most fitting to be queen" (p. 134). But people are not possessions, to be claimed by the highest bidder; Deirdre and Antigone uphold deeper, intuitive, sexual, pre-rational demands as having primary claims in determining actions. Yeats dramatizes the conflict between these two principles through a sexual dichotomy in *Deirdre*: the women represent intuitional knowledge; the men, rational. Naoise mocks "speaking or thinking as women do" (p. 118), but Naoise's belief in codified principles is undercut. Like Haemon, he is attracted to the male principles and tries to uphold them, but when forced to make a choice, he realizes their inadequacy and prefers death to a betrayal of love for life:

> O Eagle! If you were to do this thing,
> And buy my life of Conchubar with your body,
> Love's law being broken, I would stand alone
> Upon the eternal summits, and call out,
> And you could never come there, being banished.
>
> (p. 130)

Deirdre never would, of course, betray love's law—she is its spokeswoman. Naoise is deceived by the role she is playing, for in order to accomplish her true ends, Deirdre pretends to acquiesce to Conchubar's demands. At this point, Yeats's theory of masks explains the difference between his play and Greek tragedy. Creon and Antigone always uphold their principles, in speech as well as in actions. But Yeats believed that a person, to be most himself, had to adopt the mask antithetical to his true personality.[4] Thus when Conchubar, the exponent of rationality and institutionalized order, captures Naoise and Deirdre, it is through trickery; when Deirdre escapes his trap, it is through an appeal to conventionality, by threatening Conchubar with a loss of face. Yeats's preference for the principles of love over those of reason is obvious, yet he does not make Conchubar seem a bad man—simply limited. There is a place for each on the Tree of Life, but Yeats seems to suggest, at least metaphorically, that just as the eagle soars while the hunter plods along on the ground, so love is a higher good than order.

---

4. For a longer discussion of Yeats's doctrine of the Mask, see Unterecker's *Reader's Guide* (New York: Farrar, Straus & Giroux, 1959), pp. 15-18; for its effect on Yeats's own life, see Richard Ellmann's *Yeats: The Man and the Masks* (New York: E. P. Dutton & Co., Inc., 1948).

2

Interview with Anne Yeats

John Unterecker

WE ARE ACCUSTOMED in America to think of William Butler Yeats as a man deeply involved in national and literary matters; but we think of him all too often as a man isolated from that family of craftsmen, painters, and writers in which he grew up. That he was in fact, however, only the most vocal member of an extraordinarily creative family is obvious. His father, John B. Yeats, was a major portrait painter; and Jack Yeats, W. B. Yeats's brother, is now considered one of the finest painters Ireland has produced. Both Yeats's sisters were active in the arts, producing everything from water colors and embroidery to the beautifully printed and bound books of the Cuala Press. Since her father's death, W. B. Yeats's daughter, Anne, has also built a very solid reputation through paintings and drawings that are compelling, assured, and as uniquely her own as the work of her grandfather, father, or uncle is unique. It was about this family of artists and about the parallels and differences in their work that I spoke with her.

JU. I'd like to talk about some of the writers and painters—the workers in the arts—in your family and about your own career in the arts. I had wondered if you had thought much about it or if it was just that you got into painting by yourself?

AY. Well I got into the theatre first, really, largely I think because Father was connected with the Abbey.

JU. Was that with the production of *Purgatory?* Or was it before then?

AY. It was before that, actually. It was 1936. We went to Spain that year. Mother and Father were in Spain for some time and Michael and I went

out for a couple of months and it was when I came back from Spain in the summer that I went in. I went in as a sort of head cook/bottle washer, assistant to Tanya Moiseiwitsch.

JU. You were seventeen then, weren't you?

AY. I was sixteen then. From 1936 to 1940 I was her assistant with a break of four months when I went to Paris and then in 1940 I became designer but I think it was in 1938 and 1939 that I had a couple of trial runs.

JU. What did you do?

AY. I did *Purgatory* and I did—oh, some sort of non—but I'd better not say nondescript plays! Rather some class of play that was not of any great interest to anybody. I think probably I designed a kitchen or something like that.

JU. While you were doing *Purgatory* did you have much talk about the designs? Did you talk with your father about the designs before you worked on them, or did you just sit down with the manuscript?

AY. No, I more or less sat down with the play and then did a sketch and showed it to him and talked about it. I knew the kind of thing that he'd want.

JU. How did you do it? What kind of a sketch was it?

AY. It really could not have been simpler. It was just a bare whitish tree in the middle of the stage and a backcloth with the window cut out of it.

JU. Oh, you didn't try to build a solid set at all?

AY. No, because you see the facilities were limited and it was only a "one-acter" and there were plays to follow. It would have cost them far more money than they would have been prepared to spend to build a whole solid set and there was very little light on the scene anyway, because the only light was on the tree and on the window and probably a stray bit of light on, you know . . .

JU. On the actors?

AY. Yes. But mainly it was the tree; and the backcloth, I remember, was black and the window was dark blue—exceptionally dark. The tree was sort of "whitey." It was very simple. I haven't the remotest idea what clothes they dressed in, but obviously they came out of the Abbey wardrobe.

JU. What about the figures in the window?

AY. Well there was probably gauze in the window and they were probably very vague behind. I am sure there was gauze in the window. There would have had to be to keep it, you know, *straight.*

JU. Did you do designs for other plays by your father?

AY. I did *Baile's Strand* but I think that's the only one.

JU. That and *Purgatory?*

AY. That and *Purgatory,* yes.

JU. And then you went on to work in painting?

AY. I did free lance then—just in Ireland really until about 1945. And then gradually I found I was getting less satisfaction out of the theatre and I began to think—well, maybe I had better paint after all in spite of the uncles and grandfathers.

JU. That's what I was interested in. Was it really in spite of the uncles and grandfathers?

AY. Well pretty well! I started in water colors and waxes. I felt I was fairly safe, but it took a long time. . . . And it wasn't until I got really thoroughly dissatisfied with what I could get in the others that I went out into oils, because I felt that was really asking for trouble. It is very tricky in that way.

JU. Yes. I was just thinking that your father had had a similar experience. He had gotten into poetry rather than in painting for the same kind of a reason, don't you think?

AY. Yes, I hadn't thought of that. It's possible. He'd begun as an art student.

JU. Yes, he'd begun as an art student, and then there was this whole feeling of *Well, that's father's territory!*

AY. Unless he was put into it like I was put into the theatre.

JU. Were you just "stuck" into the theatre?

AY. No, but it was sort of announced that if I liked to go into the theatre I could do so.

JU. And it was available.

AY. It seemed to be a very good idea. I had no reason against it. And I had just spent three years drawing from the life for five hours a day; I thought it would be a nice change!

JU. Where were you doing that?

AY. The Hibernian Academy Schools here. They were very small, only about sixteen of us, but it was free and you got in because they thought you could draw. They did three hours' painting in the morning and two hours' drawing in the afternoon but they wouldn't let me paint. I do not know why, so I had to draw. A fantastic number of doodles went on around the board. You can imagine, five hours! Three hours every morning! They kept the blasted painting model for a fortnight in the same position! So that life was a little bit circumscribed as far as drawing went.

JU. When you moved out and did begin painting on your own you said that you took a while to get into oils. I don't know your early painting at all; I do know some of the recent ones.

AY. Well, when I began with water colors, color was usually the thing I was mainly interested in. And then I developed a method with waxes and inks which gave me more color, but I found that while I could get plenty of texture and plenty of color, I couldn't get an incisive line, and it was really that that decided me as much as anything else that it wasn't enough. I had to go and teach myself to paint in oils—which of course was what I had to do because, well, I had only about three lessons in oil painting, and those at the very end of the Academy Schools. They finally let me loose on a model. But by the time I had finished with the painting, it looked a bit risen from the dead! The color was so dirty; it was dark, dirty, putty colored—a terrible job! Oh, learning to work in oils took quite a while. And then for a long time I had no color at all—a lot of greys and whites—and now I'm gradually coming back to color—not with quite the same abandon yet, but I might!

JU. It seems to me that some people think of themselves really as designers, as people working in compositions of line and others do work, you know, from color. When you put a painting together, how do you go at it?

AY. I tend to work at it from line.

JU. Do you think of it as a composition first and then. . . .

AY. Yes, but I do find that increasingly the two are getting more nearly simultaneous. I find myself thinking sometimes in line and sometimes in pure shapes and colors and some day I hope they'll both meet.

JU. You had said that it was the fear of a kind of competition with your uncle's oil paintings that put you into water colors first. Yet he had had a similar development, hadn't he? That is, he'd started out very much in line.

AY. Yes, that's true.

JU. And then he moved toward a freer and freer use of color.

AY. And practically eliminating the line. He did it in water color, too. But I didn't know that, so I felt that was quite safe. I really didn't see an awful lot of Uncle Jack at that time.

JU. I was going to ask if you saw much of him at all.

AY. Not as children, not when we were growing up. Not until after I had started to paint, and my father had died. Then I used to go and see him quite a lot, and in the last few years of his life I used to go and see him about every week or ten days or so but didn't talk about painting much. He talked about almost everything else except painting.

JU. What was he inclined to talk about?

AY. Oh, memories of things that he'd done and seen—of circuses and people. Really, he talked rather *like* his paintings.

JU. I was going to say that his paintings are anecdotal.

AY. Yes, and rather like his books in a way.

JU. And always moving quite a ways back.

AY. Yes. Yes, it seems to go a long way back, very far. And yet he was by no means out of the present. He was very much on his feet in the present, too. But I think he preferred to be in the past in many ways.

JU. I was thinking also of your grandfather who was always painting what was in front of him, I suppose because of portraits, always portraits.

AY. Yes.

JU. But he was entirely concerned with the present. You don't get anything of the same quality in his son's work, in Jack Yeats's paintings.

AY. No.

JU. Jack Yeats's are so different, so different in tone.

AY. Yes. It is true. It really is. His characters are all—well, the characters of the West of Ireland long after he didn't live there any more. Yes they are all remembered life, really, aren't they?

JU. Yes, whereas John Butler Yeats's paintings are always straight on.

AY. Well, of course. Mind you, Grandfather was interested—if you think of his letters and things—

he was madly interested in his friends, what they did and said, and. . . .

JU. Yes, it was all in terms of personality wasn't it?

AY. Yes, very much.

JU. And that's in Jack Yeats, too, but with a very different quality.

AY. It is; it's very, very different. Three very different characters really.

JU. Yes, and your father too, who was also using personality, but using it in a different way.

AY. Yes.

JU. Did your father talk much about problems of the structure of a poem?

AY. No.

JU. Not at all?

AY. No, not to me anyway.

JU. That was private business.

AY. Exactly, yes. He . . . no, I don't think he did. But it was really only in the last few months of his life that I had any talk with him at all. I used to be sent in in the evening to talk to him. Mother thought that if I went in and talked to him, he wouldn't get so tired. So I went in one evening, and two evenings, and three evenings—and talked to him . . . and it was terribly heavy going for both of us. I couldn't think of a thing to say, and it was really awfully awkward. When I couldn't bear that any longer, I thought I'll make a sort of opening gambit of some sort; *I'll say something, and he'll be off.* And I used to start off to say something—anything—and he'd sit forward on the edge of his chair and he'd hold forth. And I honestly don't know what he held forth about now, unfortunately, which isn't much help. Probably all the things he was thinking of. And I don't think he wanted an answer. In fact, I'm sure he didn't want an answer. He just wanted an audience to do his thinking to. . . .

JU. Was that in France?

AY. No, I wasn't in France with him; this would have been Rathfarnham, before he went out to France. By the time he went to France I was in the Abbey.

JU. When you were at the Abbey—when you were just starting your own work, did you think much about yourself as part of a family, all of whom were engaged in the arts?

AY. No. No, I suppose not—except that you can't escape it, living in Dublin, I mean. I just feel that they got there first, and it's just too bad for me!

JU. How about growing up? When your father's

friends would be coming in. Of course, you probably were at school a good deal of the time, so you didn't . . .

AY. I didn't really see an awful lot of them—but some. They used to come and talk among themselves, and I would just sort of listen. Gogarty used to come quite a lot, and F. R. Higgins. They were going to take up golf together I think, at one moment. Fred Higgins took up golf because he got too fat, and he was encouraging Father to take up golf until he discovered he was getting much worse! The last day was worse than the first, because you got to the 18th hole and you ate it all on again or drank it all on again in the end—so it was just dropped. I really couldn't see Father playing golf.

JU. It would have been a marvelous sight though!

AY. Yes.

JU. Were you at all acquainted with Lady Gregory? You would have been quite young then. . . .

AY. Only in the sense that she'd be there when you went down to Coole. I have no really personal memories of her, except giving me milk and ginger biscuits if I had nightmares, and keeping my pet hoe for me and that kind of thing, letting me ride the donkey. . . . And she was a formidable old lady! And rather humorless, I gather. I don't remember, but apparently I brought a squeaky cushion and put it in the chair she used to sit in and she sat on it and it "squk" and she got up without a change of expression on her face —I must have been "so high"—and just took it out and put in on the floor and sat down again . . . and I thought that that was very unkind of her! But she was very nice to us I believe. She was very kind to us, even if she was rather formidable.

JU. Do you have memories of the Tower?

AY. Oh yes, quite a lot.

JU. You were . . .

AY. Nine, I think, the last time we went down there. I would have been nine I suppose the last time we went to Coole too, but I have many more memories of the Tower. I have memories of the places rather than the people. I can remember quite a lot about Coole. I can remember some of the rooms and the grounds and the high walled garden, which I hated, and, you know, things like the owl, the white owl in the shed in the stables, and things like that.

JU. A live white owl?

AY. A live white owl, and then in Ballylee in the Tower, I can remember quite a lot. Not such details as the colors of the rooms. I had been trying to remember those when they were restoring them, but I couldn't remember. I had forgotten the colors, but I remember the floods. I remember very well being carried out from the floods. They rose up in the spring. I suppose it would have been late spring.

JU. Spring and fall perhaps?

AY. No, only one flood a year.

JU. Only one?

AY. Only one. It was enough!

JU. But it could always be counted on?

AY. The floods could nearly always be counted on. I certainly remember at least two floods and I know there was one every year because Michael and I used to be sent up to Lady Gregory's and then Mother and Father would climb up, or Father would climb up to the first floor of the Tower and Mother would bring up the linen and the clothes and what have you, and they'd stay up there with food.

JU. Until the flood went down?

AY. Until the flood went down. Then she'd come down, sweep out the worms and things and then he'd come down and life would resume as usual.

JU. Did they live at the cottage at all next to it or was that never. . . .

AY. Yes, that was lived in. Mother and Father lived in the Tower and we lived in the cottages. Michael and I had rooms in the back cottage and Nanna, our nurse, had a room in the back cottage and the maid had a room in the front cottage. We weren't supposed to climb the Tower stairs. They are frightfully dangerous, you know. I mean they are really very very steep, and stone, and the shape of pieces of cheese. And they twist. The best possible stairs for children to fall down. So that we weren't supposed to go up the Tower unless we were taken.

JU. Did you go up?

AY. I did—naturally! But not very often. I wasn't let get up very often. But I did, I was up all right. We were allowed up if we were with somebody. But of course Father used to do a lot of writing on the flat roof, so childish voices weren't very popular.

JU. He'd climb out onto the roof?

AY. Yes, the stairs went up and then they came out actually on to the roof and they had made a flat cement terrace and then it had the high walls —about waist high around—and you could sit there in the chair and nobody would see you and nobody would know you were there.

JU. That would be very pleasant.

AY. It was very nice, yes.

JU. A good studio.

AY. You could see for miles. There was water. The river went more or less three sides round the Tower; we were almost on an island.

JU. When you were young, did you have any notion of what you wanted to do? Was it painting?

AY. No. I didn't somehow aspire to painting. It wasn't that I didn't think I'd be let paint, but it then seemed to be too improbable somehow that I'd ever get as far as that. I wasn't as ambitious as that somehow, but the only thing I liked doing was drawing. I enjoyed acting quite well but I didn't get very far with that because I could never speak loud enough. I used to get frightened and couldn't raise my voice.

JU. Did you ever act in any of your father's plays?

AY. No. I went through the School of Acting here because I thought that you should. You know. I had ideas that you ought to do everything if you were going to make the theatre your career, which it eventually was, and so I went through the School of Acting. I got as far as acting a bit, but only walk-ons: "the carriage is waiting" and "tea is served"—that kind of acting; but I was never in any of Father's plays.

JU. Did you have much to do with your aunts?

AY. Only in the sense that one of them taught me water color painting as a child.

JU. Which one?

AY. Elizabeth. She used to sit me down and make me paint flowers without drawing them first, which was her sort of "forte." I gather she was a pioneer in that kind of painting. And I used to go and visit them. But they were very much just "aunts."

JU. They lived in their separate world.

AY. As far as I was concerned, yes. And they impinged at Christmas. And you had to write them "thank you" letters for things you didn't want to get in the first place, which was very laborious. I was never very good at either writing or spelling.

JU. That runs in the family!

AY. I'm better now. Not very good mind you. But at least I don't spell *gas* with two s's, as my father once did . . . although I see no reason why it shouldn't have two s's!

JU. Were you in Italy on your father's trips to Rapallo?

AY. We were in Switzerland, Michael and I, a sort of kindergarten place, and we used to go to Rapallo for our holidays, so we had several Christmas and Easter holidays there, in the flat they had. And I must have met Ezra Pound, but I honestly don't remember.

JU. I thought that some time in those trips down you must have seen him.

AY. I must have seen him, I quite agree, but I remember very little of Italy except again the place—and being taken out and given ice cream by Father, which was a very great occasion. I didn't often go out alone with him. I think probably we were in bed by the time Ezra Pound and other people came. I would probably have only seen them in passing. We went to bed fairly early of course. We probably went to bed about half-past eight and they probably came about nine.

JU. Or they would be visited and you'd be left with nurse.

AY. Yes exactly.

JU. Did you know Ninette de Valois at all?

AY. No, I never met her.

JU. Because I cannot help feeling that her quality as a dancer was important to your father when he was doing those dance plays.

AY. Oh I think so, yes.

JU. I think hers and obviously that of the Japanese dancer, Mr. Ito.

AY. Oh I think they were, very. I think there is no doubt about that. I don't know how he came to see her dancing because he wasn't very interested in dancing as such I don't think. I don't know where the original contact would have come in.

JU. I think he'd seen her in London; I think that was it.

AY. Oh he'd been taken to see her, yes.

JU. Yes, and then thought that she would be an ideal dancer for the plays. She had said something about that in an interview once, that he came backstage and simply said: "Well, you're what we need at the Abbey!"

AY. That sounds right.

JU. You remember those firm announcements?

AY. That one has the stamp of truth about it!

JU. I wanted to talk also about your current feeling concerning painting, what you're really aiming at right now.

AY. Well it's hard to put into words. I've never really tried to put it into words. I don't think I've got a conscious aim in the sense of a message of any sort, if you know what I mean. At the moment I'm primarily interested in landscape but I think I will probably go back to people again. I'm interested in people as such, more or less continuously, but I don't know that I have any particular. . . . No, I find it very difficult to answer that question. If you were to ask me questions I might make a better stab at it.

JU. In terms of landscape then: do you feel that you are interested in an exterior landscape or a private one? I was thinking for instance of the drawings that you had in the show at the Municipal Gallery, the show that just closed.

AY. Oh, the Oireactas?

JU. Yes. You had three drawings there, didn't you?

AY. Three, yes.

JU. One, of course, was a portrait of a girl, and then one was of a cat.

AY. Oh, they put *The Cat* in, did they? I wonder why. Because in fact I sent *The Cat* in last year

"The Cat." *Painting by Anne Yeats.*

as well. They had it last year. And I didn't realize that until after I'd sent it in—because they put the title in Irish and I didn't recognize it.

JU. And then there was one other which I did think was landscape, but I wasn't sure—a landscape of stones in a brook, perhaps?

AY. Yes, it's basically landscape. It is, yes. I did a lot of stones and grasses and details—you know, small-scale landscape—and I did an awful lot of grasses, rather from the point of view of the cat or the mouse or something small looking through them, you know.

JU. Well that's in a way what I was getting at. It becomes public landscape but from a very special angle.

AY. It's from a special point of view I think, yes. It's not so much a picture of a particular landscape. I mean if I am looking at a piece of landscape I'm not interested in making a painting of that, that I could call by the name of that place, I'm only interested in getting out of it what I want to get out of it or what I find in it, which is perhaps a better way of putting it.

JU. Do you do the same with portraits?

AY. I find it more difficult to abstract people because I feel that people are people; you can't take the liberties with them that you can take with objects, you know. It is always a problem. I find continuously that while in theory I would very much like to be able to, as it were, "do a Picasso," if you know what I mean, I find that in practice. . . . It is not that I'm afraid of it. It's just that I think I have too much respect for people as such. I don't know what it is, but I find that they remain looking more or less—well, I mean, generally *less* rather than *more*—vaguely recognizable!

JU. Yes. That's what I felt about the portrait drawing in that show, and I thought that in a way the same was true of the stones.

AY. Yes.

JU. And *The Cat* was pretty well. . . .

AY. Well, I think I got the essential part of the cat. And I left out the bits that you don't need. But it was rather the reverse of the grasses. *The Cat* was done from the point of view of the mouse that has been more or less hypnotized by the cat. That is why it is looking straight out at you—and it's a curious effect that it has on people. They either like it or they can't bear it! I used to hang it up in the studio now and again and amuse myself by watching people's reactions when they ran into it. Some of them would turn their chairs so that they didn't look at it and still feel haunted! And others quite frankly didn't like it: it was a bad picture. Well, that was fair enough, that was a different thing; but I never met anybody who *really* liked it. It's not that it is a joke—I was quite serious when I did it—but I have had quite a lot of fun with it since. I am thinking of making a lithograph out of it actually at the moment. I have been doing lithography. A graphic studio opened, just across the street from me, about four years ago and I've belonged to it ever since, because I had been wanting to do lithography for a long time.

JU. What medium do you like to work in best?

AY. Oils. I find them fantastically difficult to do. But I find you can get more out of them. There is far more scope for color and texture and even line. Of course, they dry so damn slowly, but you can do almost anything with them, I find. I think it is probably mostly color and texture that interests me because those were what I missed so much in the water colors. And that is the kind of thing I'm aiming at in lithography, but I find that very difficult too. The amount of patience I've learned since I started lithography! You have no idea! I am not a patient person—I never have been very patient—but it took me the first year to discover that there was just no way out; you just had to be patient. If you got impatient you wrecked the whole thing. It's very good for the character but terribly hard on the nerves.

JU. Was Jack Yeats a patient person in his paintings? Did you ever watch him paint?

AY. Oh, no, nobody ever saw him painting. You could see the easel in his room but you never saw any signs of painting. I once did because I had to go around with a message in the morning, but otherwise nobody ever did and certainly his wife never saw him painting except when he painted her portrait. That was the only time that she ever saw him painting.

JU. Really? So he kept that all to himself?

AY. Oh yes, and once interrupted he was finished. He couldn't do any more work.

JU. I can understand that feeling.

AY. But there was never any smell of paint around the place. I think largely because he had a huge waste paper basket and he had a nice lady who lived downstairs who used to take it away every day so there was never any dirty paint hanging around. I mean, somebody else might have painted his pictures and brought them in for him for all the smell of paint there was in the room. And he used to keep them for six months when he finished them before letting them out.

JU. It's fair to say then, isn't it, that though you were all active in the arts, you all worked alone?

AY. Yes, I think that's true.

JU. True of your father, too?

AY. Yes, true of him. We'd hear him working—in his room, you know—but he never talked about what he was writing; and when he read to Michael and to me, it was always something like Scott's poetry—long narrative poems, *The Lay of the Last Minstrel*—eighty or ninety pages of it, a wonderful poem to listen to, because you knew the voice would just keep going on and you wouldn't have to say anything and you could think your own thoughts. I can't imagine why he chose that poem to read to us!

JU. Perhaps because his father had read it to him?

AY. Ah, yes, of course. That would be it. Of course.

3

Glimpses of W. B. Yeats

Austin Clarke

DURING MY early twenties I was tempted constantly by superstition and found it hard to resist its wiles. The discovery of our own mythology and epic stories by the poets of the Irish Literary Revival excited my imagination and I cycled with delight to many places associated with legend and enchantments—from the Glen of the Madmen in Co. Kerry to the Twelve Pins of Connemara and the Poisoned Glen in Donegal. The armies of Queen Maeve on the march, the defence of Ulster by Cuchullain—all these stories from the Táin obsessed me. In particular I was attracted by the earliest of our sages—the Intoxication of the Ulstermen, which tells how the Northern warriors, after a great banquet, drove—much the worse for drink—throughout the countryside and did not stop until they found themselves, to their bewilderment, in the enemy territory of the South and were locked in an oriental palace of iron, under which great fires were kindled. Equally fascinating were the tales of Fionn and his Fianna, hunting wild boar and deer through the great Munster Forest, pursuing them down wooded glens, along the slopes of the mountains or crossing to the Isle of Arran off Scotland. Moreover, there were the Songs and Lamentations of Oisin and his Colloquy with St. Patrick on his return, after three centuries, in Tir na nOg. These pagan figures of the heroic age became as real to me as the religious figures of my childhood, and the Celtic religion, of which vestiges had survived,

despite the care and toil of monks, had the appeal of a lost cause. I had become aware also of that invisible Ireland into which one might at any moment step. A few minutes there could be counted as a year here and the centuries passed there as quickly. So we have the story of Oisin, who was brought by Niamh across the ocean to the Land of the Ever Young. Nera, another poet, who ventured beyond the watchfires on the night of Samhain into the other land, stayed for a year there, married and returned. But he had only been a few seconds away for Maeve and her companies were still at feast.

With a headful of stories, I cycled about Co. Dublin, past ruined castles or Peel towers or over the Military Road by the Barracks, erected there by the British after the Rebellion of 1798, and still known incorrectly as the Hell Fire Club. When temptation took the form of two strange women, my difficulties were increased. The first whom I met was Ella Young. She was pale, ethereal, dressed in grey flowing silks, was about fifty years of age and looked like an ancient priestess or vestal virgin. She lodged in a small red-brick house in a terrace just beyond Harold's Cross and, on the first occasion when I came to see her in the afternoon, she lit a joss stick. I felt a dim, irreligious delight as the little haze of incense floated towards the ceiling. She was a devoted follower of A.E. and her poems, like those of Susan Mitchell, were of his kind. But though she, too, was a theosophist, her interests were quite different. A.E. was a student of the Sacred Books of the East. Ella Young concentrated on the Irish Cycle of Gods and Legends: her cold grey eyes became luminous and she was strangely remote as she spoke of the Tuatha Dé Dannan, the divine race, and her days seem to have been spent in visions. In particular, she was a devotee of Mannanaun Mac Lir but, being so serious herself, she never referred to his shape-changing and pranks as the God of Hilarity.

Often in the summer, when Ella Young was staying at Bahana in a small farmhouse in a hidden corner of Glencree, I cycled out to see her, sometimes by the Scalp and the woods of Enniskerry or over Killakee mountain and down the narrow Glencree road past the ancient oak-wood, in which Synge used to wander. In the little parlor, she spoke to me of the old beliefs and I found it difficult to resist the influence of her visionary ways and looks. She had come to lodge there because of an old story that in one of the upper glens of Djouce the children of Diarmuid and Grainne, those lovers who had been pursued by the jealous Fionn, had been fostered. There, of an evening, she listened to the elemental music and told me how she used to hear across the boglands of Donegal the distant sound of silver trumpets. When I left her, I was aware of all those forgotten multitudes of the past, as I cycled through the twilight by loose stone-walls, the rowan trees and the hillside heather.

In this way the temptation increased and, lying in the heather near the source of the Liffey under the morning lark-song or climbing past boulders into the upper glens and gullies of the Connemara Mountains, I was aware of our imaginative heritage.

II

One day I set out from the Lake Hotel at Glendalough and, crossing the narrow strip between the two lakes, went up between the trees past a water-fall near the ruins of a small ancient church. Below I could see, among the pine trees, the glitter of the lower lake and the water-fall above the western shore thinned by summer. After a short climb up the winding path, I came to the upper glen of Luggala and soon I was crossing over the last ridges. I looked down into the long, narrow Glenmalure, with its reedy flats and river winding its way towards Grianaun and the open hilly country beyond.

I came down by a brook which ran, with many little falls, towards the river and below in the glen I could see the figure of a tall woman, veiled and dressed in black, followed by a wolfhound. I remembered suddenly that Maud Gonne stayed sometimes at Glenmalure and I guessed that it must be she and that she was on a round of corporal acts of mercy. At last I came towards the first cottage in the glen. In recent years most of the people have left Glenmalure and their small farm houses are now melancholy ruins. I stopped at the half-door of the cottage to enquire where Madame Gonne McBride was staying, and a little old peasant woman came to it and replied, much to my surprise, in French. I knew instantly that I had come to the right house. As I replied in halting French, I heard inside the cottage an extraordinary medley of sounds as of a small menagerie and aviary: the chattering of a monkey, the wrangle of a parrot, the pretty twitters of canaries. The old woman brought me into a kitchen, bright and gay, for the white-washed walls were decorated with patterns of foxglove, buttercup and other wild flowers, and I knew that Maud Gonne or her son-in-law had painted them.

In a short time Maud Gonne returned and told me, as I had guessed, that she had been visiting the sick wife of a farmer who lived about a mile down the glen. I had met her first in her house in St. Stephen's Green and had dined there in a large room which was furnished like a kitchen with scrubbed dresser and table. The other guests were W. B. Yeats and Dermot O'Byrne, better known as the composer, Arnold Bax, who later became Master of the King's Musick. I met Arnold Bax on the landing while he waited with a humility and awe which surprised me, despite my own reverence for the great poet. Unfortunately, I cannot remember anything which Yeats said on that memorable evening—perhaps I was too shy to collect my thoughts.

On that night in Glenmalure, after supper, Maud Gonne talked to me late into the night. Much to my surprise, she spoke of the heroic past, of the visions she had seen often and of her awareness of the Invisible Ireland. She, too, like Ella Young, seemed to change. She was pale and wrinkled but her eyes, with their golden circles, were unusual and reminded me of the astonishing beauty of her early years. I remembered the many poems which Yeats had written about her and realised for the first time how greatly they had influenced one another. She had drawn him for a time into revolutionary politics, but he had lured her into the invisible land of the Ever Young.

There came into my mind that neglected poem of his, "The Old Age of Queen Maeve," which tells how the children of Maeve dug into an enchanted hill to rescue the blue-eyed Caer:

> And all that night, and all through the next day
> To middle night, they dug into the hill.
> At middle night great cats with silver claws,
> Bodies of shadow and blind eyes like pearls,
> Came up out of the hole, and red-eared hounds
> With long white bodies came out of the air
> Suddenly, and ran at them and harried them.

The poet turned from his narrative to tell of Maud Gonne:—

> Friend of these many years, you too had stood
> With equal courage in that whirling rout;
> For you, although you've not her wandering heart,
> Have all that greatness, and not hers alone,
> For there is no high story about queens
> In any ancient book but tells of you;
> And when I've heard how they grew old and died,
> Or fell into unhappiness, I've said,
> 'She will grow old and die, and she has wept!'
> And when I'd write it out anew, the words,
> Half crazy with the thought, She too has wept!
> Outrun the measure.

That night, as I drifted into sleep, I could hear the noise of the torrent outside and I struggled in vain against the superstition of Ella Young and Maud Gonne, for I seemed to catch within the waters the tinkle and running of many sweet sounds and chords.

The next morning, as we sat at breakfast and I was tapping with my spoon on a speckled egg, Maud Gonne told me how she had been aware in the night of those invisible beings she had known in the past. Much to my embarrassment, she thanked me for she was certain that my youth and eagerness had brought them around the cottage. I remained silent, knowing how desperately I had struggled against superstition, being determined to use those stories as an imaginative form and experiment since, in the poverty of our history, due to centuries of conquest, these were all that had been left to us. The day passed and, not wishing to spend another night so near to the fairy music, I pleaded an excuse and, saying farewell to my hostess, I got on my bicycle and cycled as fast as I could to the safety of the small hotel near the cataract at the end of Glenmalure.

III

During the early thirties, when I was earning my livelihood in London as a reviewer, I was asked by a publisher to write a biographical study of Yeats. Despite the reputation of the poet as a Nobel Prize-winner, only three studies of his work had appeared, the first, a short one, by an American writer, the other two by Irishmen, J. M. Hone, and the novelist Forrest Reid. The alert young director who interviewed me in the great office of the firm asked me whether the love affair between Maud Gonne and Yeats had been platonic or not, as this would give interest to the book. I said that I would question the poet himself and the director looked at me with such surprise that I realised at once the rashness of my promise. When I got back to Bricket Wood, a wooded corner of Herts near St. Albans, where I lived, I took down from the shelf *The Wind among the Reeds* and read it carefully in order to see if I could find out the truth from the poems themselves. These lyrics have the languorous, sensuous quality which the poets of the Nineties borrowed from Rossetti and his school. Certainly in some of them there were indications that the poet's relations with Maud Gonne had been immoral! He speaks of—

> Passion-dimmed eyes and long heavy hair
> That was shaken out over my breast

And again—

> White woman that passion has worn
> As the tide wears the dove-grey sands.

And in one of the later poems, "The Lover Speaks to the Hearers of his Songs in Coming Days," I was among those hearers as I read the line—

Bend down and pray for all that sin I wove in song.

I sat for a long time wondering over the character of Yeats and recalling various occasions on which I had met him.

When I was seventeen, I went frequently to the Abbey Theatre and sometimes saw Yeats sitting in the stalls beside Lady Gregory. When one of his verse plays was performed, he came always on to the stage afterwards and talked about it to the audience, a black lock falling over his brow, the long black ribbon of his pince-nez dangling. Tall and shadowy in a Celtic Twilight of his own, he would wave his arms as he chanted his chosen words. I met him some years later in a romantic way. I had gone down to Co. Sligo to see the Lake Isle of Innisfree, the cairn of Maeve between the town and the ocean, the little waterfall at Glencar and other places associated with his early poems. After that, I cycled down to Co. Galway and, on a sunny morning, stood outside the gates of Coole. I went into a field, climbed over a loose stone-wall and dropped into the Seven Woods. As I trespassed among them, I came after some time to the edge of the trees and, looking from my hiding place, saw, to my astonishment, the poet stalking across the lawn to Lady Gregory's mansion with fishing rod, basket and net, looking like one of the gentry. Shortly afterwards I was lunching with him in a small house outside the gate of Coole where he was staying after his marriage. He spoke to me at length of Donne, Vaughan, Herbert, Dryden and then of Landor, his voice rising and falling as he urged me to study their works and follow their austere example. As I was a lecturer in English Literature at the time in University College, Dublin, and still immersed in Gaelic mythology and poetry, his severe lecture chilled me and, like Joyce, I felt that I had met him a generation too late.

When Yeats returned to Dublin, I saw him every Thursday evening during the following winter at the house of Joseph O'Neill, Secretary to the Department of Education and a very original novelist. Yeats was then writing *A Vision*. Women crowded around him in that drawing-room, listening eagerly as he discussed the book with them. Across the room I could hear his monotonous tones: "One may regard the subjective phases as forming a separate wheel. It's phase 8 between phases 11 and 12 . . . of the larger wheel, it's phase 22 between phases 19 and 20 . . ." I turned to talk to others, but I could still hear that chanting voice: "The true *Creative Mind* of phase 27 I described as super sensual receptivity and it is derived from phase 3 as that phase is modified by its *Body of Fate*." I disliked astrology, horoscope casting and other follies of the past and so during that winter I carefully avoided the poet on these occasions. One night, however, I found myself walking home after midnight with him and Iseult, the beautiful daughter of Maud Gonne. They talked happily together and I felt an intruder as I kept up with their rapid pace for both were long-legged. As we were passing Harcourt Street Railway Station, I glanced at both of them furtively and they seemed so much alike that I could not help wondering whether the rumor that they were father and daughter were correct. Later

I learned that this literary legend of Dublin was completely false.

I wrote to Yeats asking whether he would approve of my wish to write a biographical study of him and asked if he would be kind enough to see me some time at his convenience, when I was over in Dublin. While I waited for a reply from him, I started to collect material for the work and went to the Reading Room of the British Museum three or four times a week. I piled the pretty books of the Nineties on the desk beside me and, as I read through them, I was surprised to find how alike the poets of that time were in tone and cadence. The graceful lines which Victor Plarr wrote about Mabel Beardsley, the sister of the artist, might well have inspired Yeats's later poem about her:

> Stand not uttering sedately
> Trite oblivious praise about her!
> Rather say you saw her lately
> Lightly kissing her last lover.
>
> Whisper not "There is a reason
> Why we bring her no white blossom":
> Since the snowy bloom's in season,
> Strow it on her sleeping bosom:
>
> Oh, for it would be a pity
> To o'erpraise her or to flout her:
> She was wild, and sweet, and witty—
> Let's not say dull things about her.

Ernest Dowson used the difficult Alexandrine measure with extraordinary skill and Yeats was surely influenced by him. An Epigram of his seems to have anticipated the austerity of the Irish poet in his middle period:

> Because I am idolatrous and have besought,
> With grievous supplication and consuming prayer,
> The admirable image that my dreams have wrought
> Out of her swan's neck and her dark, abundant hair:
> The jealous gods, who brook no worship save their own,
> Turned my live idol marble and her heart to stone.

I became interested in theosophy, dipped into Synnott's *Buddhism,* several books by Madame Blavatsky, explored Rosicrucianism and the nineteenth-century outbreak of Satanism in France. I read books by Maeterlinck, Loti and the early novels of Huysmans, Pierre Mac Orlan and others.

Six weeks had gone by and still I had not received a reply from Yeats but I did not worry for I knew that he was not a quick correspondent. When I had written my first verse play, then called *Black Fast,* I sent it to the Abbey Theatre, waited patiently for six months and then wrote to enquire about it. The comedy came back to me with a note from Lennox Robinson, who was then Manager of the Theatre, and a brief comment on it by Yeats. The comment was so badly typed that I suspect one or the other of them had poked it out on a machine which needed urgent repairs. The comment, which depressed me very much, was as follows:

"I return Austin Clarke's play. It has imagination, a sense of turbulent grotesque life, but it would not play. An audience would not understand the central idea and so it would lack coherence. I think that Austin Clarke has had two rival art forms competing with one another (1) the verse drama (2) the picturesque prose drama. I think that the play left to itself would have changed from (1) to (2). Open the play by chance at page 4, surely the natural rhythm here is prose rhythm and the line endings and the blank verse break up this rhythm without imposing their own. The very first words on the page prove my point—

'He was roaring in' (line ends)
The Kitchen.'

If he was to re-create in prose and disengage the central idea he might make an interesting play. I suppose the central idea is hunger as contrasted with the poet's dream or some dream but I am not sure. A work of art can have only one subject and there must be perfect clarity—at least to the subconscious mind—in the representation of the idea.
You can send any of this you like to Clarke."
I hasten to add that I had deliberately used a very free rhythm in parts of the play—which was produced later with reasonable success at the Cambridge Festival Theatre.

No reply to my second note had come and three months had almost elapsed. In despair, I called to see Robert Lynd, who was Literary Editor of the *Daily News* and gave me books to review.

"If it was a duchess who had written to him, a reply would have come to her at once," sneered Lynd. The sudden bitterness of so amiable an essayist surprised me for I had forgotten for the moment how many writers were irritated by the aloofness and aristocratic manner of Yeats. I decided to write once more to Dublin for I had to come to a decision about the biography. The re-

turn railway fare, third class, from Bricket Wood to Euston was 2s.6d., and my lunch at one of the small restaurants owned by polite elderly ladies or widows in the vicinity of Great Portland Street was usually 1s.11d. At this rate of expenditure, the fifty pounds advance on royalties promised to me by the publisher would not last too long. Elbows on desk, I had hurried through a hundred books about the period and was still searching confusedly for an explanation for the charm of the Nineties. How could so many literary movements in Europe have all appeared during the ten years of the *fin de siècle?* One happy morning, I received a note from the great man to tell me that he would be in London during the following week and would meet me in the Saville Club at four o'clock on the Tuesday afternoon of that week.

IV

In the sedate, gloomy lounge of the Saville Club, W. B. Yeats was seated alone at a small tea-table, already waiting for me. He got up at once, shook hands with me, and spoke at once.

"I am over in London for a few days to arrange about the publication of my new book, *A Vision,* which has taken me many years to write. I have no doubt that the critics and philosophers will not agree with what I have said in it, but I am sure that I am right in my theory of the universe."

He remained standing for a few moments, his head bowed in humility, looking so absurd that I could not help smiling secretly to myself. Somehow I could not believe in this new pose but I have no doubt that he felt a little anxious about the reception which the book would get because of its strange admixture of philosophy, astrology and abracadabra. He could not have guessed that in later years his theories would be analysed respectfully by professors and students with scant knowledge of the follies of the past. When he sat down, a waiter appeared immediately and the poet ordered tea. Then, much to my surprise, in a stern reproachful tone, he said:

"This is not an interview and on no account must anything I say be given to the press." He added, however, in a milder tone and with a smile, "When I was a younger writer, I frequently attacked the journalists, but since then I have learnt to tolerate them."

As I was only a book reviewer and much too impracticable to be a Fleet Street journalist, his suspicions made me uneasy—all the more so as I had before me the difficult problem of asking him about his relations with Maud Gonne.

We had scarcely begun to talk when, much to my alarm, I saw Sir John Squire, poet, critic, former editor of the *London Mercury,* and literary dictator, coming into the lounge. He hurried over to Yeats and began talking to him. After a minute or so he turned to me and asked agreeably, "How is your Celtic Empire getting on, Clarke?" For a moment I was puzzled and then I remembered the evening I had spent with him some years previously at his house in Chiswick. As we sat in his small, book-lined study upstairs drinking beer, he spoke unsympathetically of the Irish struggle for freedom. Provoked by his attitude and slightly intoxicated by the mild-and-bitter. to which I was not accustomed, I described rapidly a great Celtic Empire spreading to England, the Colonies and the United States of America. I had forgotten long since my horrible vision of a corrupting, powerful Tammany Hall—our contribution to modern civilisation. Fortunately, Yeats remained aloof and, seeing that he was not wanted, Sir John left us and strolled into the bar room.

We returned to our conversation and I mentioned Forrest Reid's book.

"I have forgotten it," intoned Yeats, gently waving away that invisible volume with his right hand, on which gleamed a large signet ring of silver made for him by Edmund Dulac. No doubt my own study would be forgotten as quickly, I thought, and my depression increased. He became cheerful again and said to me, as if by rote, "There are portraits of me in the National Gallery in Merrion Square, and also in the Dublin Municipal Art Gallery. There are others in the galleries of Liverpool, Birmingham, Bristol, Leicester and Edinburgh."

This was not very helpful but he mentioned soon afterwards that few critics had written about his plays and it was clear that he wished me to deal specially with them. As I had always admired his plays very much, I agreed with him about the critics. I would have liked to have told him of those early years when I had seen them at the Abbey Theatre, but I hesitated and the opportunity passed. There was a lull in our conversation and I knew the dire moment had come when I must ask about Maud Gonne. Carefully wrapping up my question in as many vague words as was possible, I said, "Mr. Yeats, I would like to discuss with you *The Wind among the Reeds,* a book which I have always liked immensely. It would help me very much in writing my study to have a general idea of your inclinations in those love-poems. Would it be too much to ask if there is any basis in actual fact for them?"

Yeats caught my implication at once. His manner changed and, looking down at me like an eminent Victorian, he exclaimed: "Sir, are you trying to pry into my private life?" Then, seeing my startled expression, he must have felt that he had gone too far for, in a trice, he had become confidential and, smiling pleasantly, continued with a vague wave of the hand. "Of course, if you wish to suggest something in your biography, you may do so, provided that you do not write anything that would give offense to any persons living."

As a Victorian, he wanted to have it both ways. Unfortunately, during this interview, I was sitting close to Yeats on the inner side of the small table and occasionally, as I turned to him, I could see behind the thick lens of his glasses a brown eye straining at its tiny muscles as if trying to peep into my very thoughts. It was the acute eye of a Sligo man and yet it seemed, somehow, to have an existence of its own. Every time I saw that small watcher, I turned away in embarrassment. About five o'clock he appeared fatigued and said the time had come for him to lie down and rest before dinner. He stood gazing into space as I put on my overcoat, took my hat and stick, and then said farewell to me at the entrance of the lounge.

I never wrote the book.

4

Scholarship Frowned into Littleness?

Kathleen McGrory

He had much industry at setting out,
Much boisterous courage, before loneliness
Had driven him crazed;
For meditations upon unknown thought
Make human intercourse grow less and less.
("All Souls Night"[1])

IN THE MORE than a century since Yeats's "setting out," the Yeats industry, like the Joyce industry, has become Big Business. And scholarly meditations upon much that is still unknown in Yeats's thought are still giving the lie to Auden's comment in his elegy for Yeats, "For poetry makes nothing happen." Yeats's poetry (to say nothing of his plays, prose, speeches, letters, and autobiographies) has made so much happen in the publishing business of the last two decades that it is little wonder a recent Yeats bibliography has been entitled, inevitably, *The Great Deluge.*[2]

So great has been the output of published books and articles on Yeats—many of them redundant—that several scholars recently surveying the state of Yeats scholarship in the period since the 1965 Centenary have used the occasion to deplore the misuse of scholarly publication in the service of strange gods, promotion and tenure committees. Currently, the case against the Yeats industry has been summed up by Hazard Adams:

The Yeats rituals have come to be the technique of cross-quotation and the adoption of a fervid tone which at once aligns the critic with *his* poet. Beyond this are the more vulgar academic quest-phrases,

the meeting with the thesis director, the search through the dark woods of bibliography for the object, confrontation with the 'white goddess' in several of her forms, including typist and thesis librarian; ultimately, after the trial of acceptance by the press, there is atonement with the father, better known as the associate professorship.[3]

Several years ago in the *Manchester Guardian*, Donald Davies complained that the Yeats industry, like the Shakespeare industry, had become "entirely an enterprise of interpretation" and source-hunting, with little attention to critical judgments upon the poem's worth as poetry.[4] Perhaps these dim views of scholarly activity are misdirected toward the younger members of the profession, but the point is well taken. There have been too many overlapping commentaries on Yeats lately. However, some of the most solid work of late has been produced by younger scholars flying in the face of at least one set of "fathers," their predecessors in the Yeats industry, and at least one major work on Yeats by an established scholar has disappointed young and old alike, as will be demonstrated.

William Butler Yeats is perhaps indirectly to blame for the critical logorrhea that has begun to characterize his industry: he authored the first commentaries on his own works, a factor whose solipsistic appeal has been hard to resist. "Reviewers find it easier to write if they have ideas to write about—ideas or a narrative like that in my Reveries," wrote Yeats in 1917; his career-long

---

1. *The Variorum Edition of the Poems of W. B. Yeats,* Peter Allt and Russell K. Alspach, eds. (New York: Macmillan, 1957), p. 473.
2. John E. Stoll, *The Great Deluge, A Yeats Bibliography* (Troy, N. Y.: Whitston, 1971).

3. "Scholarship and the Idea of Criticism: Recent Writing on Yeats," *Georgia Review* 26 (1972): 262.
4. Review of *In Excited Reverie, Manchester Guardian Weekly,* June 17, 1965.

series of elucidations to assist reviewers has made it easier for them to write about him. He would, perhaps, be surprised to find himself today playing, in the minds of iconoclastic critics (and their tribe has increased from Yvor Winters to Harold Bloom), the role he once assigned to "that vague Eastern pantheism" which, he told American audiences in 1932 and 1933, "made today's task seem nothing by setting vague immensities to frown it into littleness." However, in that same address, he called upon young men to "get busy making themselves perfect in some one of those trifling works." And men and women, young and old, have been busy ever since with Yeats's various forms, not all of them, however, trifling.

Because bibliographical overviews of Yeats criticism are as abundant in their own way as are the critical works they survey,[5] this essay will single out only those older works which, having stood the test of time and use, seem the really unavoidable books on Yeats; it will also attempt to provide information on the quality and content of resources published since 1960 or now in progress. Where the scholarship itself seems to indicate lacunae, an attempt will be made to indicate areas still in need of thoughtful critical attention.

Efforts are underway in several quarters to update Allan Wade's still basic *A Bibliography of the Writings of W. B. Yeats*, last revised and edited by Russell K. Alspach in 1968.[6] Klaus Peter Jochum has compiled an impressive list of additions in the *Bulletin of Bibliography* (1971)[7] and the editors of *Yeats Studies: an International Journal*, the first periodical devoted entirely to Yeats scholarship, have promised that with the exception of the first issue (1971), each number will contain a bibliographical section edited by Russell Alspach aimed at bringing the Wade-Alspach bibliography up to date.[8] However, the second issue (1972) has appeared without the promised bibliography.

Two bibliographies of Yeats criticism appeared in 1971: John Stoll's *The Great Deluge* and *A Bibliography of Yeats Criticism 1887–1965*, edited by K. G. W. Cross and R. T. Dunlop.[9] Cross and Dunlop's is by far the most complete and includes not only books, pamphlets, and articles but dissertations and theses on Yeats as well as reviews of Yeats's works by several generations of commentators. Stoll's work, though more limited in scope, may be of greater use to students whom he sends, first to the most easily accessible primary sources, then to secondary materials: general criticisms, esoteric and historical works, specialized critical and biographical books; three-quarters of the volume consists of an extensive listing of periodical materials on Yeats. The Dolmen Press's special Yeats issue of *The Irish Book* (1963) also contains Alspach's additions prior to his revision of Wade.[10]

The period of the 1960s and 1970s has been an auspicious one as far as editions of Yeats's own works are concerned and the end of this decade should see the completion of several projects involving as yet unpublished materials. It is regrettable that there are as yet no critical editions of most of the works recently reprinted by the Irish University Press[11] and Macmillan,[12] although

5. Cf. Hazard Adams, "Criticism, Politics and History: the Matter of Yeats," *Georgia Review* 24 (1970): 158-182; Adams, "Yeats Scholarship and Criticism: a Review of Research," *Texas Studies in Literature and Language* 3 (1962): 439-51; R. V. Adkinson, "Criticizing Yeats," *Revue des langues vivantes* (Brussels) 33 (1967): 423-30; John Brian, "Hurt into Poetry: Some Recent Yeats Studies," *Journal of General Education* 18 (1967): 299-306; Ian Fletcher, "History and Vision in the Work of W. B. Yeats," *Southern Review* 4 (1968): 105-26; George Mills Harper, "'All the Instruments Agree': Some Observations on Recent Yeats Criticism," *Sewanee Review* 74 (1966): 739-54; Harper, "'Sing Whatever Is Well Made': Recent Books About Yeats," *CEA Critic* 33 (1971): 29-35; A. N. Jeffares, "An Account of Recent Yeatsiana," *Hermathena* 72 (1948): 21-43; Norman Mackenzie, "The Yeats Canon and Recent Scholarship," *Queens Quarterly* 78 (1971): 462-64; Helen Vendler, "Assimilating Yeats," *Massachusetts Review* 7 (1966): 590-97. See also special Joyce issues: *Tri-Quarterly* 1 (1965); *Hermathena* 101 (1965); *University Review* 3 (1965); *James Joyce Quarterly* 3 (1965); *Southern Review* 5 (1969); *Ariel* (July 1972).
6. London: Rupert-Hart-Davis.
7. "Additions to the Yeats Bibliography" 28 (Oct.-Dec. 1971): 129-35.
8. Robert O'Driscoll and Lorna Reynolds, eds. (Shannon: Irish University Press).
9. London: Macmillan.
10. 2 (Autumn 1963).
11. *The Bounty of Sweden; The Cat and the Moon; The Death of Synge; Discoveries; Dramatis Personae; Essays, 1931-1936; Estrangement; Four Years; The Green Helmet and Other Poems; The Hour Glass; If I Were Four-and-Twenty; In the Seven Woods; The King of the Great Clock Tower; Last Poems and Two Plays; Michael Robartes and the Dancer; Mosada; New Poems; October Blast; On the Boiler; A Packet for Ezra Pound; Pages from a Diary Written in Nineteen Hundred and Thirty; Poems Written in Discouragement; Responsibilities; Reveries over Childhood and Youth; A Selection from the Love Poetry of W. B. Yeats; Seven Poems and a Fragment; Stories of Michael Robartes and His Friends; Stories of Red Hanrahan; Synge and the Ireland of his Time; Two Plays for Dancers; The Wild Swans at Coole; Words for Music Perhaps; The Words Upon the Window Pane.* (Facsimile editions of books originally published by the Dun Emer and Cuala Press.)
12. *Mythologies; Essays and Introductions; Explorations; A Vision* ("A Re-issue with the Author's Final Revisions," 1961).

these will undoubtedly widen the circle of popular acquaintance with Yeats. John Frayne's volume of early prose, *Uncollected Prose of W. B. Yeats: First Reviews and Articles 1886–1896* (1970),[13] incomplete in some respects, will be followed by a second volume edited by Colton Johnson in collaboration with Frayne. Donald R. Pearce has prepared a selection of Yeats's Senate speeches (1960)[14] and the late Curtis Bradford's first volume, *Reflections* (1971),[15] has made available previously unpublished sections of Yeats's important 1908–1914 Journals. The Journals and the first draft of the Autobiography have at last been transcribed and edited by Denis Donoghue in *Memoirs* (1972).[16] His edition contains the 246 entries from December 1908 through 1914, with irregular notes from November 1915 through October 1930.

Undoubtedly one of the most exciting manuscript projects now underway is the series of critical editions of the plays, under the general editorship of David R. Clark. The first volume, *Druid Craft: the Writing of "The Shadowy Waters"* (1971),[17] edited by Michael J. Sidnell, George P. Mayhew, and David R. Clark, supplies prepublication drafts, dating them in sequence, and includes synopses by Yeats, production design sketches, and several facsimile reproductions of the manuscripts in the Huntington and National Libraries. The second volume, *W. B. Yeats: The Writing of "The Player Queen"* (1974), has been edited by Curtis Bradford and other volumes in progress are *The Countess Cathleen,* edited by Michael J. Sidnell; *Deirdre,* edited by Virginia Rohan; *The Death of Cuchulain,* edited by Phillip Marcus; and *Yeats's Versions of Sophocles,* edited by David R. Clark and James Maguire. The Dolmen Press had previously published several early versions of *The Shadowy Waters* in a giftbook edition with illustrations by Leonard Baskin.[18]

Yeats's fiction has been the object of two studies

by Richard J. Finneran: his edition of the two early novelettes, *John Sherman and Dhoya* (1969)[19] and his monograph for the Dolmen Press New Yeats Papers series, *The Prose Fiction of W. B. Yeats: the Search for "Those Simple Forms"* (in press). The latter includes *The Speckled Bird,* the novel abandoned by Yeats in 1901, two portions of which had previously been published in Irish periodicals with notes by J. M. Hone and Curtis Bradford.[20] A two-volume edition of *The Speckled Bird,* edited by William O'Donnell, will be published as volumes 82 and 83 of the new Cuala Press series.

Of enormous service to scholars would be cooperative work on the ambitious projects suggested in the first number of *Yeats Studies,* the cataloguing of Yeats's unpublished works and the systematic publication of manuscript drafts of poems, plays, and prose. The first issue of the Journal has provided two such editions, Robert O'Driscoll's 'The Tables of the Law': a Critical Text"[21] and, on facing pages, two versions of the Red Hanrahan stories, edited by Michael J. Sidnell.[22]

One major area of need will be taken care of by the appearance of John Kelly and Eric Domville's definitive edition of the *Collected Letters.* Meanwhile, Allan Wade's fine collection, *The Letters of W. B. Yeats* (1954)[23] remains the major source. Two recent volumes have been added to the scattered collections of letters published in the 1940s and 1950s.[24] *Yeats and Patrick McCartan, a Fenian Friendship* (1967),[25] edited by John Unterecker, includes McCartan's address on Yeats the Fenian together with several letters from Eu-

13. New York: Columbia University Press.
14. *The Senate Speeches of W. B. Yeats* (Bloomington, Ind.: Indiana University Press).
15. Dublin: Cuala Press.
16. New York: Macmillan.
17. Amherst, Mass.: University of Massachusetts. At this writing, the University of Massachusetts has had to give up publication of the series for financial reasons. The Bradford edition has been published by Northern Illinois University Press, DeKalb, Ill.
18. *A Tower of Polished Black Stones* (Dublin: Dolmen Press, 1971).

19. Detroit: Wayne State University Press.
20. "The Speckled Bird, Part of a Chapter From an Unfinished Novel with Notes by J. M. Hone," *The Bell* (March 1941); "A Further Section from an Unfinished Novel, with a Note by Curtis Bradford," *Irish Writing* 31 (Summer 1955).
21. *Yeats Studies: an International Journal* 1 (1971): 87-118.
22. *Ibid.,* pp. 119-74.
23. New York: Macmillan.
24. Among the earlier collections of Yeats's letters, the following have proved to be of special interest to scholars and students: *Letters on Poetry from W. B. Yeats to Dorothy Wellesley,* ed. Kathleen Raine (New York: Oxford University Press, 1940 rpt. 1964); *Letters to Katharine Tynan,* ed. Roger McHugh (New York: McMullen Books, 1953); *Some Letters from W. B. Yeats to John O'Leary and his Sister, from Originals in the Berg Collection,* ed. Allan Wade (Folcroft, Pa.: Folcroft Press, 1953; rpt. 1969); *W. B. Yeats and T. Sturge Moore: Their Correspondence 1901-1937,* ed. Ursula Bridge (London: Routledge and Kegan Paul, 1953).
25. Dublin: Dolmen Press; no. 10, Dolmen Yeats Centenary Papers, 1965.

gene O'Neill, Shaw, and Gogarty. Roger Mc-Hugh's fine collection, *Ah, Sweet Dancer: W. B. Yeats, Margot Ruddock: a Correspondence* (1970),[26] concerns the poet's friendship with the beautiful young actress whom Yeats met when he was 69 and for whom he created speaking parts in *A Full Moon in March* and *The Player Queen.*

Another gap in epistolary materials will be filled by the projected *Letters to Yeats* under the general editorship of George Mills Harper in collaboration with William M. Murphy and Richard J. Finneran, to be published by Macmillan (London). The Yeats family letters to the poet will be edited by William M. Murphy.

With the abandonment of Denis Donoghue's authorized biography, Joseph Hone's *W. B. Yeats, 1865–1939* (1943; 2nd ed. 1962, rpt. 1965),[27] remains the only authorized source. However, as Curtis Bradford has pointed out, Hone has relied almost entirely on the first draft manuscript of the Autobiography, quoted liberally and verbatim without acknowledgment, in spite of the *carte blanche* issued him by Mrs. Yeats. Richard Ellmann's *Yeats, the Man and the Masks* (1948),[28] although not a biography in the formal sense, places equal emphasis on the life and the art of Yeats. In his "exposition of the development of Yeats's mind," Ellmann reveals Yeats as a man at the same time petty, timid, and heroic; the work does pose and answer significant questions about Yeats's family, his education, his friendships and loves, as these and other interests affected his mask as poet. Likewise, A. Norman Jeffares's *W. B. Yeats, Man and Poet* (1949)[29] deals fully with biographical materials supplied by Mrs. Yeats; Jeffares's work begins with pre-1700 backgrounds of the Yeats family and follows the poet's life and development through 1939.

Dublin's Dolmen Press produced several works on germane biographical materials in 1974: William M. Murphy's *The Yeats Family and the Pollexfens of Sligo* (1970), number one of the New Yeats Papers series, and George Mills Harper's *"Go Back to Where You Belong": Yeats's Return from Exile,* number 6 of the same series. Scheduled for publication in 1975 is William M. Mur-

phy's biography of the poet's father, tentatively entitled *Prodigal Father: the Life of John Butler Yeats,* by the Oxford Press (London). Additional works on John B. Yeats now in progress include *Letters from Bedford Park: a Selection from the Correspondence (1890–1901) of John Butler Yeats,* selected and edited by William M. Murphy, volume 81 of the new Cuala Press publications, and a John Butler Yeats issue of *Yeats Studies* (no. 5, 1976), under guest editorship of William M. Murphy. Liam Miller's *The Dun Emer and Later the Cuala Press,* no. 7 of the New Yeats Papers, will be published by the Dolmen Press with a preface by Michael B. Yeats.

Joseph Ronsley's *Yeats's Autobiography: Life as Symbolic Pattern* (1968)[30] provides useful information on the publishing history and composition of the *Autobiography,* describes the "exfoliative process" elucidated in *Reveries,* and deals extensively with *The Trembling of the Veil* and *Dramatis Personae.* The flavor of the *Autobiography,* with its color and disunity, eludes this singleminded search for consistency in the diffuse group of works originally entitled by Yeats, significantly, *Autobiographies.*

Having gone directly to the major sources, Yeats's *The Collected Poems* (1957, "Definitive Edition")[31] and *The Collected Plays* (1953, "New Edition"),[32] students and scholars have found their work made easier by a number of ancillary volumes. Nearly all that is known about Yeats's references to persons, places, and unfamiliar things may now be found neatly codified and chronologized in several single-volume reference works, which should be part of every Yeats library.

To accompany the poems, two indispensable volumes are *The Variorum Edition of the Poems of W. B. Yeats,* edited by Peter Allt and Russell K. Alspach (1957)[33] and Stephen Maxfield Parrish's *A Concordance to the Poems of W. B. Yeats* (1963).[34] George Brandon Saul's *Prolegomena to the Study of Yeats's Poems* (1957)[35] is an invaluable handbook for scholars and students; for each poem in *The Collected Poems* he supplies publication information and title changes, dates and significant facts of composition, identifications of

26. London: Macmillan.
27. New York: Macmillan. Hone's biography is also available in the new Pelican series of reprints (1971) of well-known biographical works.
28. New York: Macmillan.
29. New York: Barnes and Noble; 2d ed., 1966.
30. Cambridge: Harvard University Press.
31. New York: Macmillan.
32. Ibid.
33. Ibid.
34. "Programmed by James Allan Painter." Ithaca, N. Y.: Cornell University Press.
35. Philadelphia: University of Pennsylvania Press.

misprints in the final texts, and concise notes that point out related passages in other works as well as bits of information that help clear up obscurities and indicate influences. A. Norman Jeffares's *A Commentary on the Collected Poems of W. B. Yeats* (1968) [36] supplies in greater volume the kind of information that students need in order to feel more at home with the poems, using to good advantage relevant quotations from Yeats's prose, letters, and notebooks, together with snippets from other critics to indicate interpretations. While much of the information gathered here could be found elsewhere, it would take the uninitiated much more time to find it, so Yeatsians have been glad to find all between the covers of a single book.

John Untereckei's *A Reader's Guide to W. B. Yeats* (1959) [37] is still an excellent place to begin. Although the genre "reader's guide" has built-in weaknesses as well as strengths, the solid scholarship of this volume has not been challenged, even though later critics have occasionally differed on questions of interpretation; it still offers one of the best brief introductory essays on Yeats yet to appear. Similarly, M. L. Rosenthal's paperback edition, *Selected Poems and Two Plays of W. B. Yeats* (1962) [38] has deservedly become, as has A. Norman Jeffares's edition of the plays, *W. B. Yeats, Selected Plays* (1964),[39] a staple text for courses in modern Irish literature; in addition to the fine introductory essays and notes, Rosenthal's edition provides a glossary of names and places related to the 195 poems and two plays, *Calvary* and *Purgatory*.

To accompany *The Collected Plays, The Variorum Edition of the Plays of W. B. Yeats,* edited by Russell K. Alspach, assisted by Catherine Alspach (1966),[40] has been of assistance to scholars desirous of knowing more about the printed versions of the plays included in the definitive edition and of some not included in that final collection. George Brandon Saul's *Prolegomena to the Study of Yeats's Plays* (1958) [41] provides the same service for the plays as did his companion volume for the poems. In addition to full publication data for each of the plays, Saul supplies notes on first productions, dates of composition, corrections of dating errors, and suggests parallel passages in other plays as well as references to important critical commentaries.

Secondary materials on the plays have been handily codified and annotated by Klaus Peter Jochum in *W. B. Yeats's Plays: an Annotated Checklist of Criticism* (1966) .[42] Eric Domville's *Concordance to the Plays of W. B. Yeats* is still in preparation.

One of the best general treatments of Yeats, although now more than twenty years old, is Richard Ellmann's *The Identity of Yeats* (1954, reissued 1964) .[43] Ellmann has asserted definitively the fact that although Yeats spoke with many voices in his poems and plays—a performance of rhetorical shape-changing that has obscured his identity —he remains at the center of his work the same voice, "tenacious and solid," amid the shifting masks. Ellmann's study of the symbols is still one of the most useful and coherent expositions on the subject of Yeats's iconography.

Among Yeatsians, brevity has seldom been the soul of wit. Yet a number of distinguished scholars have produced excellent brief general works. The briefest, and certainly the wittiest, William York Tindall's monograph for the Columbia Essays on Modern Writers series, *W. B. Yeats* (1966),[44] contains the basic information within 48 pages. A. Norman Jeffares's *The Poetry of W. B. Yeats* (1961) ,[45] one of the Cambridge Studies in English Literature intended for use by "Sixth Formers" and university students, eschews the biographical or historical approach in favor of a critical commentary on the poetry from *The Wanderings of Oisin* through the *Last Poems*. Jeffares's later introductory study for students and general readers, *W. B. Yeats* (1971) ,[46] examines some 27 poems plus the group of love poems inspired by Maud Gonne, under thematic headings that include *A Vision*, biography, classicism, friendships, Ireland, and "heroic gesture." A. G. Stock's *W. B. Yeats, His Poetry and Thought* (1961) [47] introduces only the poems and *A Vision*, but touches

36. Stanford: Stanford University Press.
37. New York: Farrar, Straus & Giroux (Noonday).
38. New York: Macmillan (Collier).
39. London: Macmillan; U. S. edition, *Eleven Plays of W. B. Yeats* (New York: Macmillan; 2d ed. 1971).
40. New York: Macmillan.
41. Philadelphia: University of Pennsylvania Press.

42. Saarbrücken: Anglistisches Institut der Universität des Saarlandes.
43. New York: Oxford University Press.
44. New York: Columbia University Press; no. 15. Columbia Pamphlets on Modern Writers.
45. London: Edward Arnold Ltd.
46. London: Routledge and Kegan Paul (Profiles in Literature series).
47. Cambridge University Press.

upon Yeats's "disconcerting" thinking, his life-long preoccupation with his Irish inheritance, and the influence of Eastern thought. Denis Donoghue's *William Butler Yeats* (1971)[48] is not biography nor even "brief life," but is rather a unified brief study of Yeats with the focus on "sensibility"; Yeats's intense dedication to power, mastery, self-mastery, and delight in conflict as a mode of power are studied as these are manifested in his poems and plays. On a larger scale, Balachandra Rajan's *W. B. Yeats: a Critical Introduction* (1965; 2d ed. 1969)[49] goes beyond introductions to provide critical helps in a chronological approach to all the works. Since much of Yeats's poetic effect was visual, the introduction through picture and essay to be found in D. J. Gordon's *W. B. Yeats: Images of a Poet* (1961)[50] is not only appealing but appropriate. To a revised version of the mimeographed *Guide* that accompanied the University of Reading's 1957 photographic exhibit, co-authored by Gordon, Ian Fletcher, and Frank Kermode, this volume adds materials from the enlarged exhibit at Manchester and Dublin in 1961 and a descriptive essay and catalogue of the Yeats books and manuscripts by Robin Skelton.

Of the baker's dozen of collected essays on Yeats published or reissued since 1960, several are especially good. The Kennikat Press's reissue of Stephen Gwynn's earliest gathering, *William Butler Yeats: Essays in Tribute* (1965; originally published as *Scattering Branches* in 1940),[51] makes available once more eight impressions of Yeats by co-workers, friends, and fellows, among them Maud Gonne, Lennox Robinson, W. G. Fay, Edmund Dulac, F. R. Higgins and C. Day Lewis. *The Permanence of Yeats*, edited by James Hall and Martin Steinmann (1950; rpt. 1961),[52] its extensive bibliography still useful though outdated, reprints twenty-five classic early essays covering all phases of Yeats's career; the distinguished critics whose work is here reprinted without title include Edmund Wilson, T. S. Eliot, R. P. Blackmur, Allen Tate, William York Tindall, and Kenneth Burke.

The Centenary produced the inevitable tributes, several of superior quality. Ten pithy essays in *An Honoured Guest: New Essays on W. B. Yeats* (1965,[53] edited by Denis Donoghue and J. R. Mulryne, derive much of their appeal from their unified focus upon the middle and later Yeats. Beginning with a general essay on Yeats as poet (Charles Tomlinson), the volume proceeds in order through discussions of the poems by T. R. Henn, Graham Martin, Donald Davie, John Hollaway, and the editors, with single essays on the plays (Peter Ure) and the *Autobiographies* (Ian Fletcher). There is also a fine essay on *A Vision* by Northrop Frye. *In Excited Reverie: A Centenary Tribute to W. B. Yeats 1865–1939* (1965),[54] edited by A. Norman Jeffares and K. G. W. Cross, is an important collection of critical materials covering such topics as Yeats and Spenser, Yeats as anthologist, rhetoric and comedy, Yeats and the "felix culpa," and John Butler Yeats; the excellent bibliographical essay by K. G. W. Cross has already been alluded to above.[55] Another good collection of the "scattershot" variety is *W. B. Yeats 1865–1965: Centenary Essays on the Art of W. B. Yeats* (1965),[56] edited by D. E. S. Maxwell and S. B. Bushrui; of uneven quality, the essays treat influences (Shakespeare, Swift, Keats, Blake), Yeats's Irishness and nationalism, textual variants of several plays, two general essays on the drama, and notes on an incident at Lissadell. The volume includes an excellent bibliography of essays, books, and unpublished theses on Yeats. *The World of W. B. Yeats: Essays in Perspective* (1965),[57] edited by Robin Skelton and Anne Saddlemyer, is a record of the University of Victoria (British Columbia) Centennial Festival symposium; allowing for the raggedness such a format necessarily entails, Yeatsians have welcomed the information contained in this volume which, in addition to the usual focus on early Yeats, Celtic and occult influences, and the drama, brings to light often-ignored materials on the poet's artist-brother, Jack Yeats, and on T. Sturge Moore, Susan L. Mitchell, Gordon Craig, Charles Ricketts, and George Moore, as well as the better known figures of the Irish Renaissance. John Unterecker's *Yeats: A Collection of Critical Essays*

48. New York: Viking Press.
49. London: Hutchinson.
50. New York: Barnes and Noble.
51. Port Washington, N. Y.
52. New York: Macmillan.

53. London: Edward Arnold Ltd.; New York: St. Martin's Press.
54. New York: Macmillan.
55. See n9 above.
56. Ibadan, Nigeria: Ibadan University Press; U.S. distributors, International Publications Service, New York.
57. Victoria, British Columbia: University of Victoria; U.S. distributors, University of Washington Press, Seattle.

(1963),[58] one of the Prentice-Hall series of Twentieth Century Views, while not attempting a unified approach, reprints some of the best critical work that had appeared by the early 1960s; included are essays by Frank Kermode, Giorgio Melchiori, Hugh Kenner, William York Tindall, T. S. Eliot, R. P. Blackmur, Allen Tate, Richard Ellmann, and others, as well as Curtis Bradford's classic study of the two Byzantium poems.

Two collections of essays by single authors deserve special mention: the widespread influence of T. R. Henn's *The Lonely Tower: Studies in the Poetry of W. B. Yeats* (1950, 2d ed. rev. 1965, rpt. 1966)[59] can be seen in the number of acknowledgments of indebtedness by authors of works published since its first appearance. The eighteen essays touch all bases biography, shared Irish and political background, friends, the influence of early training in art, and the poetry and plays in all phases. Many of the issues raised and suggestions made by Henn have provoked later works by admirers of his scholarship as well as those not of his persuasion. A. Norman Jeffares's *The Circus Animals: Essays on W. B. Yeats* (1970)[60] is a wide-ranging group of distinguished essays on the mask, gyres, Yeats's public career and work as critic, women in Yeats, a biographical essay on John B. Yeats, and a critical evaluation of the poetry of Oliver St. John Gogarty. Patrick J. Keane's *William Butler Yeats: A Collection of Criticism* (1973)[61] is one of the finest minuscule collections to appear; it includes an annotated bibliography that beginning students of Yeats will find useful.

The first crop of works in what will undoubtedly be a popular genre of the Yeats industry of the future, the Casebook, has yielded two books of special interest to students and teachers of Yeats: Jon Stallworthy's *Yeats: Last Poems* (1968, rpt. 1970)[62] provides reviews of Yeats by his contemporaries and more recent studies of *Last Poems and Plays* by a distinguished array of critics. *William Butler Yeats: the Byzantium Poems* (1970),[63] edited by Richard J. Finneran, supplies texts of the two poems and relevant prose commentaries by Yeats, Gwynn, Henn, Unterecker, Vendler, and others, with the usual student apparatus for the research paper.

Attempts by scholars to devour and digest the Yeats canon whole seem doomed to produce either a smorgasbord or indigestion, but some have succeeded by narrowing the menu to bite size, focusing on such categories as Yeats's aesthetics, philosophy, history, myth, or period studies. The almost inevitable redundancy of such approaches when taken by writers unaware of each other's intentions can be seen in much that has been produced in the area of specialized studies.

One of the most provocative earlier studies on the subject of Yeats's poetics was Donald Stauffer's *The Golden Nightingale* (1949),[64] still recommended reading. Subtitled "Essays on Some Principles of Poetry in the Lyrics of William Butler Yeats," the book's primary emphasis is not upon Yeats as lyric poet but upon principles of poetry as these are exemplified in the lyrics of Yeats. Treating his subject from the point of view of aesthetics—the purpose of poetry, the reading of a lyric, the medium of poetry—Stauffer raised some necessary questions that have not yet been satisfactorily answered concerning the convictions, craftsmanship, and achievement of Yeats as a lyric poet. Two full-length studies of Yeats's aesthetics have appeared within the last decade: Edward Engelberg's *The Vast Design* (1964)[65] and Bernard Levine's *The Dissolving Image: the Spiritual-Esthetic Development of W. B. Yeats* (1970).[66] Engelberg's effort can be seen as an extension of Richard Ellmann's in sustaining, by carefully amassed details, the underlying unity of Yeats's approach to aesthetic problems in his craft, both the lyric and the drama. The result is a fine study of the emergence of the heroic image, the single controlling factor in what Engelberg describes as Yeats's "vast design" for a consistent aesthetics discernible not only in the poetry but in the scattered prose comments on his own work. He demonstrates that by 1918, with the publication of *Per Amica Silentia Lunae*, Yeats's aesthetic had been thoroughly explored and formulated as a "whole, self-consistent theory," to emerge again in the late 1930s when Yeats assumed the role of teacher for a younger poet; Yeats's metaphysic, his "System," took shape only after he had explored the problems of his craft. Levine, in a less well organized

58. Englewood Cliffs, N. J.: Prentice-Hall.
59. New York: Barnes and Noble.
60. Stanford, Calif.: Stanford University Press; London: Macmillan.
61. New York: McGraw-Hill (Contemporary Studies in Literature series).
62. London: Macmillan.
63. Columbus, Ohio: Charles E. Merrill Co.

64. New York: Macmillan.
65. Toronto: University of Toronto Press.
66. Detroit, Mich.: Wayne State University Press.

work, focuses not upon the image but upon the speaker of the poems as Self—the Daimon of *A Vision* and the true subject of the dozen or so poems studied. To show the underlying spiritual nature of Yeats's concern with aesthetics, Levine supplies close readings of the poems in which the concern for image gradually "dissolves into the gathering volume of words" and, in poems like "The Circus Animals' Desertion," leaves one with an awareness not of image but of the solitary presence of the speaker.

Robert Snukal in *High Talk: the Philosophical Poetry of W. B. Yeats* (1973) [67] is one of the first scholars to take Yeats the philosopher seriously. He locates Yeats in the Wordsworthian-Coleridgean tradition of English romanticism by way of Kant and Hegel. Even non-Yeatsians may be grateful for his early chapters elucidating the complex philosophy of Kant as this provided Yeats with a solid epistemology on which to base his romantic stance, a modified nontranscendental idealism. Professor Snukal holds that not only was Yeats's idealism in philosophy a respectable position but that his speculations on the subject were both coherent and intelligent, not outlandish. His thesis is that Yeats's thought was "all of a piece," the philosophy and the poetry coexisting in his mind at all times. Yeats himself would surely approve of this kind of ancillary reading of his prose speculations with his poetry, since he said himself that he required separate but equal channels for his different modes of expression: explaining why he wrote a second series of *Discoveries* along with *The Player Queen*, he admitted, " I find that my philosophical tendency spoils my playwriting if I have not a separate channel for it." If it is true, as Snukal argues, that earlier widespread rejection of Yeats's philosophical speculations was based on a prevailing critical prejudice that held anything outside the English empiricist tradition not worth considering, then future Yeats scholars may indeed demonstrate that Yeats's poetry was an early example of the shift away from an empiricist to a rationalist or idealist model.

Recalling Yeats's assertion that all history and knowledge are properly biography, Thomas R. Whitaker in *Swan and Shadow: Yeats's Dialogue with History* (1964)[68] has explored this assertion through an extended discussion of Yeats's "conversation" with history as double and anti-Self, a "mysterious interlocutor" through whose mediation Yeats transcended the fallen world in his greatest works. Whitaker's thesis, that vision (the "God's-eye view") and dramatic expression are Yeats's response to his view of history, combines in a nice dialectic (or dialogic) the earlier Yeatsian resolve, expressed in the 1906 letter to Florence Farr, that he would begin his "movement downward upon life" rather than continue the Shelleyan movement "upwards out of life." Much of his book is a commentary on *A Vision* and on the role of early literary influences and Irish history in Yeats's "subjective distortion" of history that moved his synthesis of vision-poetry and drama toward a universal history.

Peter Ure's *Towards a Mythology: Studies in the Poetry of W. B. Yeats* (1946; rpt. 1967) [69] discusses the role of myth as an ordering principle that would bring the "coherence of a metaphysic and the personalism of a religion" into Yeats's work. Beginning with Cuchulain, Ure shows how Yeats proceeded from readymade materials of Irish mythology to his own mythmaking, a personalized mythology woven out of strands of friendship, ancestors, and contemporaries, helping to bring order, tradition, comprehensibility, and unity to the poems. Morton Irving Seiden in *William Butler Yeats, the Poet as a Mythmaker 1865–1939* (1962) [70] approaches the area of myth and symbol from the perspective of *A Vision*, its early sources and analogues in Celtic and Greek myth, Blake, Shelley, Paracelsus, Boehme, Swedenborg, Cornelius Agrippa, theosophy, Joachim de Floris, Balzac, and Noh. Seeing *A Vision* as Yeats's attempt to create a private religious faith, Seiden studies the poems as "fragments of a great myth" based on that faith.

Alex Zwerdling's *Yeats and the Heroic Ideal* (1965)[71] is a historical exposition of the Yeatsian heroic ideal through several evolutionary forms— Irish epic hero, aristocrat, public hero, visionary. He provides a solid factual base in models that range from the Irish sagas to Castiglione and Lady Gregory's brothers. Yeats's anachronistic and nostalgic clinging to his ideal of a "public" hero as embodiment of ethical and moral values on their way to extinction in his country and his world is seen by Zwerdling as Yeats's vehicle for protest

67. Cambridge: Cambridge University Press.
68. Chapel Hill, N. C.: University of North Carolina Press.
69. Liverpool: University Press of Liverpool, 1946; London: Russell and Russell, 1967.
70. East Lansing, Mich.: Michigan State University Press.
71. New York: New York University Press.

against the religious, social, political, and cultural standards of his day. Somewhere between the Emersons, Carlyles, and Conor Cruise O'Briens there may be future Yeatsians who will produce the balanced critical evaluation needed to show Yeats's ideal of the hero in noble service to art as well as in the pernicious excesses to which it could lead ultra-conservative and fascist fanaticism—glorification of military force and violence.

Benjamin L. Reid's *W. B. Yeats: the Lyric of Tragedy* (1961) [72] is essentially an extended definition of tragedy as Yeats applied the concept to poetry, not drama. Treating first the theory and history of tragedy, then Yeats's application of this in the poems and prose, Reid concludes that the lyrics exemplify the cross-fertilization of formal and informal tragedy. His thesis (and his two complex hypotheses), that the poems of Yeats considered as a whole show substantially the same design as that of the Dionysus-mystery, the original of tragedy, has not provoked many critical follow-ups.

One of the few detailed studies of Yeats's eighteenth-century Anglo-Irish background is Donald Torchiana's *W. B. Yeats and the Georgian Influence* (1966),[73] which circumscribes Yeats as Protestant Irish (different from Irish Protestant), its emphasis being upon the intellectual and social, not religious, inheritance of Yeats from his "critical, detached and passionately cold" exemplars, Swift, Burke, and Berkeley.

Among major studies of Yeats's poetry, one of the first to take sides in the Great Debate over the relative merits of the early and later poems was Louis MacNeice's *The Poetry of W. B. Yeats* (1941; rpt. 1967).[74] MacNeice stated what was then the fashionable judgment of his day (still not unfashionable today), that the early poems showing the "languor of the late Victorian age" are less excellent and that the study of Yeats as poet is "a study in rejuvenation"—a view most recently countered by Harold Bloom. MacNeice took the hard critical stance toward Yeats possible only for one Irish poet to another, describing the master not as mystic but as a bit of a poseur and something of a fake—Yeats's belief in aristocracy leading him to fake an aristocratic family legend, his belief in mysticism leading to pretended mystical experience, and his belief in Ireland leading

to misrepresentations of Ireland in his poetry and plays; nevertheless, MacNeice saw Yeats's fabrications not as aberrations but as parts of a supreme fiction that is, in the last analysis, exactly what Yeats's life and work really were. Despite his reservations, MacNeice's final judgment was that Yeats wrote "the best poetry of his times."

Before 1965, one of the most neglected areas in critical work on the poetry was that of the early poems. Since then, a number of studies have appeared, some of them lamentably repetitive. Had there been some kind of creative cross-pollenation or collaboration, we might now have a series of contiguous works, each contributing to our better understanding of one or more of the nineteenth-century influences; instead, we now have more than a dozen books, each attempting to devote a chapter or less to ground covered by a contemporary. Instead of that "simplification through intensity" which Yeats himself desired, we have the equivalent in scholarship of the false mask, a dispersal and diffusion of analytical effort. No doubt the critical slipperiness of the entire problem of "influences" is partly to blame for the fact that a spate of works on the subject has added some information but few conclusions to the great deluge of recent works on Yeats's early poetry.

Among the better works, which avoid the extremes of mere "scrabbling for sources" and over-emphasis on personal enthusiasms or hostilities, is Thomas Parkinson's *W. B. Yeats: Self-Critic, a Study of His Early Verse* (1951; rpt. 1971).[75] Parkinson uses printed variants of early poems to show the effect of Yeats's writing for the theater on his lyric poetry, a task now made easier by the publication of the *Variorium Edition*. Parkinson's scholarly work, easily the best on the subject, traces the development of the poems through four phases from 1889 to 1933 and the final revisions. Harold Orel's monograph *The Development of William Butler Yeats: 1885–1900* (1968)[76] requests that serious attention be focused on what many earlier critics had dismissed as mere apprenticeship, the work of the fifteen-year period from 1885 (publication of the first poems in the *Dublin University Review*) and 1899 (*The Wind*

72. Norman, Okla.: University of Oklahoma Press.

73. Evanston, Ill.: Northwestern University Press.

74. London: Oxford University Press.

75. Berkeley and Los Angeles, Calif.: University of California Press. Reprinted with *W. B. Yeats: the Later Poetry* (1964) as a single volume, *W. B. Yeats: Self-Critic and the Later Poetry* (1971).

76. Lawrence, Kan.: University of Kansas Press (no. 39, Humanities Studies).

Among the Reeds). That these were years of intense intellectual activity is shown by Orel's discussions of Yeats as craftsman of playlets, newspaper correspondent, anthologist, and developing dramatist who, by the turn of the century, had succeeded in creating all the major types he had envisioned. Orel omits consideration of the Abbey Theatre experience and of Synge as being outside the limitations of a monograph, but he does treat Yeats's personal relations with theosophists, Rhymers, Edwin Ellis, A. E., Symons, and Maud Gonne.

Two fine studies of Yeats and his major Romantic models have brightened the horizon of "influence" books within the past two decades: Hazard Adams's *Blake and Yeats: the Contrary Vision* (1955; rpt. 1968)[77] is primarily a discussion of the relationship of Blake's symbolism and aesthetics to Yeats's, rather than a study of direct influence. Content with exposing the "systems" of Blake and Yeats, Adams leaves room for readers to make their own comparisons but shows the difference between the two poets to be basically an epistemological one without charging that "Yeats failed at Blake's game." In a 1968 preface he takes issue with Ellmann's *Identity* (which appeared after the original publication of Adams's work) to argue that Blake's vortex and its related images provide the main link between Blake and Yeats. Yeats's admission that Shelley shaped his life has provided the *raison d'être* for George Bornstein's *Yeats and Shelley* (1970).[78] The pervasive influence of Shelley is here presented in chronological phases: the youthful imitations, the weak verse plays of the 1880s and *The Wanderings of Oisin*, the young man's plays and poems about Intellectual Beauty, the mature works in which bitter attacks against Shelley are accompanied by continued borrowings of Shelleyan symbols and ideas, and the works of the late 1930s in which Yeats finally reinstated Shelley as a "lesser deity." Throughout his study, Bornstein, like Adams, permits Yeats poetic license in re-creating his model to suit his own differing aesthetic goals.

Scholars and students will find much helpful information on probable sources for Yeats in Blake, Shelley, and his Anglo-Irish predecessors in Harold Bloom's *Yeats* (1970).[79] But this iconoclastic study of nineteenth-century influences upon the Irish poet may come as something of a disappointment to those who have read with pleasure the author's fine objective contributions to Romantic scholarship. No doubt the plethora of enthusiastically uncritical books on Yeats in recent years is distressing to many, but the aim of Bloom's book, clearly stated ("This book sets itself against the prevalent critical idolatry of Yeats"), should forewarn readers that they may expect to find in Bloom's *Yeats* a work marred by the critical prejudice that obviously prefers a Shelley, a Blake, or a Wallace Stevens to a William Butler Yeats and that faults Yeats for his "misreading" of the great Romantics. Bloom's thesis, that the poet is necessarily revisionist, doomed to misread his predecessors in self-defense against their greatness, leaves little room for Yeats as creator of a system of his own. While there is abundant evidence in this work of the author's recognized excellence in recall and interpretation of Romantic verse, there are several badly remembered lines from major poems by Yeats[80] and at least one example of the way in which a little knowledge of early draft versions may be a dangerous thing when the final poem is studied not on its own merits as a poem but rather in the light of what we now know about earlier, more "logical" versions.[81] Naturally enough, Bloom sides with advocates of the early poems in the Great Debate, seeing those poems as superior where they follow most closely the central Romantic tradition and finding in the last poems evidence of Yeats's "growing inhumanity."

Dwight Eddins's *Yeats: the Nineteenth Century Matrix* (1971)[82] aimed to balance the opposing views of MacNeice and Bloom in the Great Debate, by giving evidence to support both MacNeice's stylistic condemnation and Bloom's affirmation of Romantic "vitalism" in the early

---

77. Ithaca, N. Y.: Cornell University Press.
78. Chicago: University of Chicago Press.
79. New York: Oxford University Press.
80. For example, in his discussion of "Adam's Curse," Bloom's "poets break their marrow-bones to a purpose" confuses line 7, "Better go down upon your marrow-bones," and the "break stones" of the next line, missing the point of the double reference to labor and prayer in the commonly used Irish idiomatic expression for the kneeling posture (p. 167); in agreeing with Sturge Moore that Yeats, in "Sailing to Byzantium," is "unjustified in asserting that he is 'out of nature' (p. 347), Bloom has neglected to go back to the final published version of the poem in which it is clear that the poet refers to a future state—"once out of nature I shall never take, etc."
81. Bloom's negative judgment of "The Second Coming" (pp. 317-25) is based not on the poem's merits as a poem but on what the drafts reveal of Yeats's "misuse" of Blakean and Shelleyan parallels.
82. University, Ala.: University of Alabama Press.

poems. He begins in a refreshing manner, by defining the terms *Romantic, Pre-Raphaelite,* and *Symbolist* before attempting to show the possible influence of the Elizabethans (Shakespeare), Romantics (Shelley), Rhymers' Club, French Symbolist poets, and Irish nationalism upon Yeats. He explains the developing tension between pictorial and dramatic modes in Yeats's work in terms of the poet's use of painting and drama as models, with emphasis on the positive influence of John B. Yeats upon the shaping of his son's mature aesthetic.[83] In Eddins's judgment, the reliance upon visual effects in the early poems represents a false direction for the poet, whose later lyrical impact would derive essentially from the force of dramatic speech. His essay on Yeats's "epitaphal coldness" is one of the first detailed studies of a puzzling and enduring quality of Yeats's best verse. Phillip L. Marcus's *Yeats and the Beginning of the Irish Renaissance* (1970)[84] covers much of the ground explored in Frayne's edition of the early prose but supplies additional facts concerning Yeats's nationalistic ideals for Irish literature, emphasizing his relationship with less well-known contemporaries, Katharine Tynan, Nora Hopper, John Todhunter, Lionel Johnson, and William Larminie, as well as A.E. and Douglas Hyde. He adds another good essay on the ways in which Irish myth and tradition were used by Yeats and the writers of the Irish Renaissance.

Yeats's later poems will most certainly be in for greater scrutiny in the future as the unpublished materials become available for general use. Since Vivienne Koch's *W. B. Yeats: the Tragic Phase. A Study of the Last Poems* (1951)[85]—a very personal reading of the poems and of Yeats's "wilful and exclusive ordering" of life in his "tawdry system" (*A Vision*)—left much to be done, it is surprising that only three works have since been devoted to this phase. Thomas Parkinson's *W. B. Yeats, the Later Poetry* (1964; rpt. 1971)[86] sheds enormous light upon Yeats's method of composition by examining the manuscripts of the later

poems. Parkinson's detailed exposition of the origins of "After Long Silence" and "Among School Children" and his study of Yeats's obsessive icons, swan, sun, and moon, might indicate the line future scholars should take in utilizing the manuscripts well. His concluding essay on Yeats's prosody contains conclusions drawn from the manuscript study, namely, that the poet's innate sense of linear measure led Yeats to use the stress line and syllabic line rather than the foot as his unit of measure. To the growing body of studies on the geriatric Yeats were recently added Arra M. Garab's *Beyond Byzantium: the Last Phase of Yeats's Career* (1969)[87] and Daniel Albright's *The Myth Against Myth: A Study of Yeats's Imagination in Old Age* (1972).[88] Garab's study is perhaps too enthusiastic and uncritical, but it nevertheless supplies useful information on the poems composed in the last ten years of the poet's life. Garab reads these last poems as counterstatements to the early theme of escape from the mortal condition and traces the development of this counterstance from the early romantic quest for essence to the more existential emphasis of the final poems, which reveal "postures appropriate to age." He contributes some valuable insights on Crazy Jane, Old Tom, and Ribh as they relate to the "tragic gaiety" of the last poems. Albright studies Yeats's self-criticism of the myth of the poet's search for immortality against a background of the limitations imposed by old age upon poetic powers, revealing that the final poems show Yeats's recognition of the "decay of apocalypse, the shrinking of millennium." Albright wisely narrows the focus of his study to four poems, "The Tower," "The Wanderings of Oisin," "News for the Delphic Oracle," and "The Circus Animals' Desertion," and reaches the same conclusion as earlier critics: that Yeats's construction of his own life was the only satisfactory myth, and that his final stance in poems like "The Circus Animals" was a recognition that the masks he had created to speak his poetry had no recognizable face but his own.

The Yeats industry has not yet produced the needed technical work on Yeats's prosody comparable in quality to Walter Jackson Bate's *The Stylistic Development of Keats* (1945) or M. R. Ridley's classic study, *Keats's Craftsmanship* (1933). The task is undoubtedly easier with a poet who died young and matured with convenient haste.

---

83. In contrast, Ellmann, Jeffares, Hone, Bloom and others have commented upon negative aspects of the influence of John B. Yeats; cf. James White, *John Butler Yeats and the Irish Renaissance* (Dublin: Dolmen Press, 1973), New Yeats Papers.

84. Ithaca, N. Y.: Cornell University Press.

85. London: Routledge and Kegan Paul, 1951; Baltimore: Johns Hopkins, 1952.

86. Berkeley and Los Angeles, Calif.: University of California Press. Reprinted with *W. B. Yeats: Self-Critic, a Study of His Early Verse* (1951) as a single volume, *W. B. Yeats: Self-Critic and the Later Poetry* (1971).

87. De Kalb, Ill.: Northern Illinois University Press.

88. New York: Oxford University Press.

Robert Beum's *The Poetic Art of William Butler Yeats* (1969),[89] admittedly not the technical study needed, treats the poetry from 1910 onward and is basically a discussion of Yeats's development of the octave from the quatrains of the earlier verse. His single chapter on the verse of the plays, while tantalizingly brief, does locate some of the areas in the drama also in need of prosodic analysis. Beum takes issue with Parkinson, asserting that Yeats was essentially an iambic poet with little intellectual interest in prosody in the abstract, content to use the traditional English metrical unit closest at hand. More than a third of Marjorie Perloff's *Rhyme and Meaning in the Poetry of Yeats* (1970),[90] an analysis of the sound features of the lyrics, is taken up by ninety-eight pages of tables showing the distribution of rhymed lines in each of the published volumes of poems, classifications of rhymes by type, rhyme, and semantic congruity or disparity. This is a valuable study replete with interesting tabulations that permit the author not merely to analyze the phonetic function of rhyme but to comment upon the semantic relationship of rhyme and meaning; it does not answer the call for that ideal study of Yeats's prosody first issued by Delmore Schwartz in 1942.

There is room also for a detailed study of the relationship between music and poetry in the works of Yeats. Edward Malins's brief monograph for the Dolmen Centenary Papers, *Yeats and Music* (1968),[91] does provide a starting point with its discussion of the poet's association with contemporary musicians and his attempts to find fitting instrumental accompaniment for the plays. But attention should also be given to the rhythms of Yeats's English verse as affected by Gaelic speech patterns that Yeats had "by ear." As Arnold Dolmetsch was the first to note, Yeats was probably tone-deaf, but he had an acute ear for the intonations of the spoken word. Much of the raw material out of which Yeats mined his Irish subject matter, for example, the translations of Douglas Hyde and the Ossianic Society tracts, themselves bore the traces of Gaelic rhythms and assonance. Thomas MacDonagh remarked very early in his influential *Literature of Ireland* (1916) that the attempt to retain the rhythms of Irish and its characteristic assonance was an important feature of the nationalistic literature of the Irish Renaissance. MacDonagh was also the first to cite Yeats's musician's song from *Deirdre* as an example of the unconscious use of the seven-syllable Debhidhe poetry by contemporary Irishmen affected by the rhythms of spoken Irish though they were often ignorant of the rules governing such usage.

New areas of research have been opened by studies of the Yeats manuscripts by Hone, Jeffares, Ellmann, Stallworthy, Parkinson, and others. But by far the most extensive study to date has been that of Curtis Bradford in his *Yeats at Work* (1965),[92] which was intended only as an introduction to more extensive manuscript work in the plays, prose, and poems. Based on a study of representative pieces from the early, middle, and later periods (except for the early plays, omitted from consideration because of their complicated textual development and printing history), his study revealed the high quality of the entire corpus of Yeats copies; it still supplies a wealth of information concerning Yeats as a craftsman who achieved technical mastery of his art early in his career as a dramatist, although writing remained for him always an "unnatural labor." Bradford showed the compositional method of Yeats to be essentially additive, his works like coral reefs accumulating their greatness slowly. His bibliography on the Yeats manuscript collections still tells scholars where to begin.

Jon Stallworthy's *Between the Lines: Yeats's Poetry in the Making* (1963)[93] discusses manuscripts and typescripts of nine major poems, including "Second Coming," "Sailing to Byzantium," and "A Prayer for My Daughter," and seven shorter poems. In a sequel, *Vision and Revision in Yeats's Last Poems* (1969),[94] Stallworthy documents the growth from drafts to final printed form of 13 of the 54 poems in *Last Poems and Plays,* emphasizing the visionary aspects of the last two years of composition. These manuscript studies might serve future scholars as models of the kind of painstaking study yet to be done.

Keeping pace with the expanding popular interest in all things occult, the Yeats industry is rapidly producing a body of "Wisdom literature" and hermeneutics that may in future rival those of its nearest competitors—biblical studies and the Blake industry. One work often overlooked in American bibliographies is Harbans Rai Bach-

---

89. New York: Frederick Ungar.
90. The Hague: Mouton.
91. Dublin: Dolmen Press.

92. Carbondale and Edwardsville, Ill.: Southern Illinois Press.
93. Oxford: Clarendon Press.
94. Ibid.

chan's *W. B. Yeats and Occultism: a Study of his Works in Relation to Indian Lore, the Cabbala, Swedenborg, Boehme and Theosophy* (1965) ,[95] which in its original form was one of the distinguished Cambridge dissertations by Indian scholars. Bachchan attempts to steer a middle course between two views he considers representative extremes, Ellmann's emphasis on Yeats as magician and Auden and Colum's embarrassment at the hocus-pocus aspects of Yeats's occultism. He provides facts concerning Yeats's readings in Eastern mysticism and explores the poet's relationships with Tagore, Mohini Chatterji, and Purohit Swami, among others named in his title. His glossary of Sanskrit words and names should prove to be of continuing help. Allen R. Grossman's *Poetic Knowledge in the Early Yeats: a Study of The Wind Among the Reeds* (1969) [96] is essentially a study of the cabalistic sources of the early poetry. Veering away from discernible literary influences, Grossman finds the roots of Yeats's 1899 volume in the tradition of hidden or secret knowledge and nineteenth-century Celticism and Aestheticism. Grossman's study falls into that category of literary hermeneutics which treats Yeats as an adept, emphasizing the hieratic nature of the poems as almost revelation. Kathleen Raine's monograph for the Dolmen series of New Yeats Papers, *Yeats, The Tarot and the Golden Dawn* (1971) [97] is a good brief survey of the Hermetic scene and of Yeats's involvement with it. A more detailed and historical approach can be expected from George Mills Harper's forthcoming book, *Yeats's Golden Dawn*,[98] which will document the dispute within the Order in which Yeats was leader of one faction during the period February 1900 to April 1901, a time to which Yeats referred as "the worst part of life." Some of the documents relating to this period have already been published by Professor Harper in the first issue of *Yeats Studies: an International Journal.*[99]

Another formerly neglected area, the plays, has been the object of several important studies since 1960. One of the earliest and perhaps the best of these, Helen Hennessy Vendler's *Yeats's Vision and the Later Plays* (1963) ,[100] offers a common-sense reading of *A Vision* not as a mystical hieroglyph for which scholars alone hold the Rosetta Stone but as a "symbolic statement, somewhat cluttered with psychic paraphernalia," against which background the plays may be read with greater understanding. Her assertion that *A Vision* is accessible to "reasonable interpretation" and the close readings she provides to prove her assertion have made life much easier for teachers of Yeats and *A Vision*. Mrs. Vendler's book is proof of the fact that demythologizing may be accomplished successfully without demolishing the object and that scholarly and objective surgery can be performed on such delicate areas as Yeats's sacred book and the later plays even when she considers these much inferior to the lyrics.

Peter Ure's *Yeats the Playwright: a Commentary on Character and Design in the Major Plays* (1963) [101] is a useful critical handbook for study of *The Collected Plays*. It avoids a strictly chronological approach and treats the major plays in thematic groups, except for single essays on *The Countess Cathleen*, *The King's Threshold*, and *Deirdre*. Ure supplies a chronology and critical assessments of plot, characterization, and the "handling of morals and ideas" for each of the fourteen plays treated. S. B. Bushrui's *Yeats's Verse-Plays: the Revisions 1900–1910* (1965) [102] gives an account of revisions of five early plays (*The Shadowy Waters*, *On Baile's Strand*, *The King's Threshold*, *Deirdre*, and *The Green Helmet*) during the formative years of the Irish National Theatre movement and the founding of the Abbey Theatre. The author sees the plays, composed during a gap in productivity of nondramatic poems, as a bridge between Yeats's early and later lyrics; he concludes with an instructive discussion of the change in the poetry after 1910, Yeats's new theory of style, and the influence upon Yeats of Synge's "clay and worms" outlook.

David Clark's *W. B. Yeats and the Theatre of*

95. Delhi: Motilal Banarsidass.
96. Charlottesville, Va.: University of Virginia Press.
97. Dublin: Dolmen Press. Miss Raine's *Life in Death and Death in Life* (Dublin: Dolmen, 1973) studies *Cuchulain Comforted* and *News For the Delphic Oracle* in the light of the influence of Plotinus and Blake on Yeats's idea of the soul.
98. New York: Macmillan, 1974.
99. "'Meditations upon Unknown Thought': Yeats's Break With MacGregor Mathers," *Yeats Studies* 1 (1971) : 175-202. Prof. Harper is guest editor of *Yeats Studies* 4 (1975) , devoted to Yeats and the Occult.

100. Cambridge, Mass.: Harvard University Press.
101. New York: Barnes and Noble, 1963; London: Routledge and Kegan Paul, 1969.
102. Oxford: Clarendon Press.

Desolate Reality (1965)[103] attempts only a brief treatment of four plays (*Deirdre, The Dreaming of the Bones, The Words Upon the Windowpane,* and *Purgatory*) as representative of the early, middle, and later stages of Yeats's development of the "drama of perception" in what Kenneth Burke has called "tragic rhythm," the movement from purpose through passion to awareness similar to the Noh drama's "recognition." Clark sees these plays as sharing a common Dantesque subject matter, the Paolo-Francesca situation, with *Deirdre* as the "cocoon which will release the middle and later dramas of perception." For Clark, the "perception" in all but *Deirdre* concerns supernatural events, while in the early play it is a personal awareness of tragedy. Leonard E. Nathan, in *The Tragic Drama of William Butler Yeats: Figures in a Dance* (1965)[104] provides yet another gloss on Yeats's special uses of the term and concept *tragedy*. In a chronological approach to the plays he traces Yeats's search for a dramatic form and subject matter suited to his view of human existence as essentially tragic, a view that incidentally conditioned Yeats's preoccupation with the heroic ideal of acceptance of tragic destiny. Nathan concludes that the last plays are best because in them Yeats finally satisfied his own requirement of a drama in which the supernatural was a viable reality not open to interpretations that would explain away their supernaturalness as symbol for sociological or psychological realities. John Rees Moore's *Masks of Love and Death: Yeats as Dramatist* (1971)[105] is an interpretive reading of a dozen or so plays which, from early to late, embody what Moore sees as Yeats's concept of the "culture hero," the product of interaction between Yeats's patriotism and poetic practice. Moore focuses on Yeats's early hesitancy to allow full expression to the "rougher" aspects of human nature and shows how this attitude changed to the emotional sophistication of the later plays in which savagery is coupled with intellectual subtlety. He devotes much attention to the poet's strong affinity to ritual and adds another chapter to the growing body of materials on the early Irish sagas and Yeats's Cuchulain as a combination primitive-aristocratic culture hero. Among projects yet to appear on the

subject of Yeats and the drama are George Mills Harper's monograph for the Dolmen New Yeats papers, tentatively entitled *The Mingling of Heaven and Earth: Yeats's Theory of the Theatre,* and the third issue of *Yeats Studies: an International Journal* devoted entirely to Yeats and the theater.

If sheer volume is any indication of corporate health, the Yeats industry is flourishing. But a closer look at the published volumes themselves and at the areas they treat reveals a canker at the heart of the rose. There is little direction or organization in the multifoliation of Yeats studies. In addition to the obvious overlapping of critical commentaries, it is evident that doublespeak and academese have infected the Yeats industry as they have almost every other area of human communication. Yet this situation should not be tolerable in human intercourse on a scholarly plane where, presumably, "only words are certain good."

There is good reason for the recent warnings of Hazard Adams, Helen Vendler, Harold Bloom, and others concerning the unreadability of certain writings about Yeats and the over-enthusiastic or uncritical treatments of his works that have produced not hagiography (a respectable genre, after all) but hagiolotry (always heretical). The malaise in academic circles will probably continue to affect all areas of research and publication as budgetary exigencies cause greater emphasis to be placed upon "competency-based" evaluation of scholars and teachers not only for promotion and tenure but for retention and dismissal—one proof of competency in research-oriented institutions of higher learning being publication of almost anything. To let such considerations erode the quality of scholarship would be self-defeating. Co-authorship and greater collaboration among Yeatsians through some kind of dependable clearinghouse of information about works in progress might be one solution.

There is certainly room for more good scholarly work on Yeats, especially the neglected middle period, and of single important movements and influences as they have affected the poems, plays, and prose. Perhaps there should be a moratorium declared upon use of the adjectives *Paterian* and *Pateresque* until someone has produced that ideal study defining both the term and the influence of Pater's aesthetic upon Yeats. And some common agreement might be hoped for as to the

103. Dublin: Dolmen Press.
104. New York: Columbia University Press.
105. Ithaca, N.Y.: Cornell University Press.

exact meaning of the terms *icon* and *iconography* as these apply to Yeats.[106]

On the germane matter of book production, university presses—allies in the battle of the scholar and the dollar—might be alerted to the embarrassing ease of the typo *antimony* for *antinomy*.[107] In an industry in which gold and silver imagery and value judgments are sometimes related, the difference could be crucial.

---

106. The term *icon,* derived originally from C. S. Pierce by way of Wimsatt and Beardsley, is used by Snukal to mean "the stories that poets tell us" and by Parkinson to mean either symbol or image or both; perhaps Wallace Stevens has had the last word in the section of "The Rock" entitled "The Poem as Icon."

107. Cf., for example, Levine (p. 104). Eddins (p. 38).

Bibliography of Works Mentioned

Adams, Hazard. *Blake and Yeats: the Contrary Vision*. Ithaca: Cornell University Press, 1955.

_____. "Criticism, Politics and History: the Matter of Yeats." *Georgia Review* 24 (1970): 158–82.

_____. "Scholarship and the Idea of Criticism: Recent Writing on Yeats." *Georgia Review* 26 (1972): 249–78.

_____. "Yeats Scholarship and Criticism: a Review of Research." *Texas Studies in Literature and Language* 3 (1962): 439–51.

Adkinson, R. V. "Criticizing Yeats." *Revue des langues vivantes* (Brussels) 33 (1967): 423–30.

Albright, Daniel. *Myth Against Myth: a Study of Yeats's Imagination in Old Age*. New York: Oxford University Press, 1972.

Bachchan, Harbans Rai. *W. B. Yeats and Occultism: a Study of His Works in Relation to Indian Lore, the Cabbala, Swedenborg, Boehme, and Theosophy*. Delhi: Motilal Banarsidass, 1965.

Beum, Robert Lawrence. *The Poetic Art of William Butler Yeats*. New York: Frederick Ungar, 1969.

Bloom, Harold. *Yeats*. New York: Oxford University Press, 1970.

Bradford, Curtis Baker. *Yeats at Work*. Carbondale and Edwardsville, Ill.: Southern Illinois University Press, 1965.

_____, ed. *W. B. Yeats: The Writing of "The Player Queen."* De Kalb, Ill.: Northern Illinois University Press, 1974. (Vol. 2, *Manuscripts of W. B. Yeats*, ed. David R. Clark.)

Brian, John. "Hurt into Poetry: Some Recent Yeats Studies." *Journal of General Education* 18 (1967): 299–306.

Bornstein, George. *Yeats and Shelley*. Chicago: University of Chicago Press, 1970.

Bushrui, Ṣ. B. *Yeats's Verse-Plays: the Revisions 1900–1910*. Oxford: Clarendon Press, 1965.

Clark, David R. *W. B. Yeats and the Theatre of Desolate Reality*. Dublin: Dolmen Press, 1965.

Clark, David R., Mayhew, George P. and Sidnell, Michael J., eds. *Druid Craft: the Writing of "The Shadowy Waters."* Amherst: University of Massachusetts Press, 1971; Dublin: Dolemen Press, 1971. (Vol. 1, *The Manuscripts of W. B. Yeats*, ed. David R. Clark.)

Connor, Lester Irvin. *A Yeats Dictionary: Names of the Persons and Places in the Poetry of W. B. Yeats.* (Thesis, Columbia University, 1967.)

Cross, K. G. W., and Dunlop, R. T. *A Bibliography of Yeats Criticism 1887–1965*. London: Macmillan, 1971.

_____, and Jeffares, A. N., eds. *In Excited Reverie: a Centenary Tribute to W. B. Yeats, 1865–1939*. New York: Macmillan, 1965.

Domville, Eric. *A Concordance to the Plays of W. B. Yeats.* (In progress.)

Donoghue, Denis. *William Butler Yeats*. New York: Viking, 1971.

_____ and Mulryne, J. R., eds. *An Honoured Guest: New Essays on W. B. Yeats*. London: Edward Arnold, Ltd., 1965; New York: St. Martin's Press, 1965.

Eddins, Dwight. *Yeats: the Nineteenth Century Matrix*. University, Ala.: University of Alabama Press, 1971.

Ellman, Richard. *The Identity of Yeats*. New York: Oxford University Press, 1954; 2nd ed., 1964.

_____. *Yeats: the Man and the Masks*. New York: Macmillan, 1948.

Engleberg, Edward. *The Vast Design: Patterns in W. B. Yeats's Aesthetic*. Toronto: University of Toronto Press, 1964.

Finneran, Richard J. *The Prose Fiction of W. B. Yeats: the Search for "Those Simple Forms."* Dublin: Dolmen Press, 1974. (No. 4, New Yeats Papers.)

_____, ed. *William Butler Yeats, the Byzantium Poems*. Columbus, Ohio: Charles E. Merrill Publishing Co., 1970. (Merrill Literary Casebook series.)

Fletcher, Ian. "History and Vision in the Work of W. B. Yeats." *Southern Review* 4 (1968): 105–26.

Garab, Arra M. *Beyond Byzantium: the Last Phase of Yeats's Career*. De Kalb, Ill.: Northern Illinois University Press, 1969.

Gordon, D. J., ed. *W. B. Yeats, Images of a Poet*. New York: Barnes and Noble, 1961.

Grossman, Allen R. *Poetic Knowledge in the Early Yeats: a Study of the Wind Among the Reeds*. Charlottesville, Va.: University Press of Virginia, 1969.

Gwynn, Stephen L. *William Butler Yeats: Essays in Tribute*. Port Washington, N.Y.: Kennikat Press, 1965.

Hall, James and Steinmann, Martin, eds. *The Permanence of Yeats*. New York: Macmillan, 1950; rpt., 1961.

Harper, George Mills. "'All the Instruments Agree': Some Observations on Recent Yeats Criticism." *Sewanee Review* 74 (1966) : 739–54.

_____. *"Go Back to Where You Belong": Yeats's Return from Exile*. Dublin: Dolmen Press, 1974. (No. 6, New Yeats Papers.)

_____. "'Meditations Upon Unknown Thought': Yeats's Break with MacGregor Mathers." *Yeats Studies* 1 (1971) : 175–208.

_____. *The Mingling of Heaven and Earth: Yeats's Theory of the Theatre*. Dublin: Dolmen Press (In progress) .

_____. "'Sing Whatever Is Well Made': Recent Books About Yeats." *CEA Critic 33* (1971) : 29–35.

_____. *Yeats's Golden Dawn*. London: Macmillan, 1974.

_____. Richard J. Finneran, William Murphy, eds. *Letters to Yeats*. London: Macmillan (In progress) .

Henn, Thomas R. *The Lonely Tower: Studies in the Poetry of W. B. Yeats*. London: Methuen, 1950; New York: Barnes and Noble, 1965.

Hone, Joseph. *W. B. Yeats*. London: Macmillan, 1942; New York: St. Martin's Press, 1962; rpt. 1965.

Jeffares, A. Norman. "An Account of Recent Yeatsiana." *Hermathena* 72 (1948) : 21–43.

_____. *The Circus Animals: Essays on W. B. Yeats*. London: Macmillan, 1970; Stanford: Stanford University Press, 1970.

_____. *A Commentary on the Collected Poems of W. B. Yeats*. Stanford, Calif.: Stanford University Press, 1968.

_____. *The Poetry of W. B. Yeats*. London: Edward Arnold, Ltd., 1961.

_____. *W. B. Yeats*. London: Routledge and Kegan Paul, 1971. (Profiles in Literature series.)

_____. *W. B. Yeats, Man and Poet*. New York: Barnes and Noble, 1949, 1966.

Jochum, Klaus Peter S. "Additions to the Yeats Bibliography." *Bulletin of Bibliography* 28 (1971) : 129–35.

_____. *W. B. Yeats's Plays: an Annotated Checklist of Criticism*. Saarbrücken: Anglistisches Institut der Universität des Saarlandes, 1966.

Keane, Patrick J., ed. *William Butler Yeats: a Collection of Criticism*. New York: McGraw-Hill, 1973. (Contemporary Studies in Literature.)

Koch, Vivienne. *W. B. Yeats: the Tragic Phase, a Study of the last Poems*. London: Routledge and Kegan Paul, 1951; Baltimore, Md.: Johns Hopkins, 1952.

Levine, Bernard. *The Dissolving Image: the Spiritual-Aesthetic Development of W. B. Yeats*. Detroit, Mich.: Wayne State University Press, 1970.

MacNeice, Louis. *The Poetry of W. B. Yeats*. London: Oxford University Press, 1941, 1967.

MacKenzie, Norman. "The Yeats Canon and Recent Scholarship." *Queens Quarterly* 78 (1971) : 462–64.

Malins, Edward Greenaway. *Yeats and Music*. Dublin: Dolmen Press, 1968. (No. 12, Yeats Centenary Papers.)

Marcus, Phillip L. *Yeats and the Beginning of the Irish Renaissance*. Ithaca, N.Y.: Cornell University Press, 1970.

Maxwell, D. E. S. and Bushrui, S. B., eds. *W. B. Yeats, 1865–1965: Centenary Essays on the Art of W. B. Yeats*. Ibadan, Nigeria: Ibadan University Press, 1965.

Miller, Liam. *The Dun Emer Press, Later the Cuala Press*. Dublin: Dolmen Press, 1975. (No. 7, New Yeats Papers.)

Moore, John Rees. *Masks of Love and Death: Yeats as Dramatist*. Ithaca, N.Y.: Cornell University Press, 1971.

Murphy, William M. *Prodigal Father: the Life of John Butler Yeats*. London: Oxford University Press, 1975.

_____. *The Yeats Family and the Pollexfens of Sligo*. Drawings by J. B. Yeats. Dublin: Dolmen Press, 1971. (No. 1, New Yeats Papers.)

Nathan, Leonard E. *The Tragic Drama of William Butler Yeats: Figures in a Dance*. New York: Columbia University Press, 1965.

O'Driscoll, Robert, ed. *"The Tables of the Law: a Critical Text."* *Yeats Studies* 1 (1971) : 87–118.

Orel, Harold. *The Development of William Butler Yeats: 1885–1900*. Lawrence, Kan.: University of Kansas Press, 1968. (No. 39, Humanistic Studies.)

Parkinson, Thomas F. *W. B. Yeats: the Later Poetry*. Berkeley and Los Angeles, Calif.: University of California Press, 1964.

_____. *W. B. Yeats: Self-Critic*. Berkeley and Los Angeles, Calif.: University of California Press, 1951.

_____. *W. B. Yeats: Self-Critic and the Later Poetry*. Berkeley and Los Angeles, Calif.: University of California Press, 1971.

Parrish, Stephen Maxfield. *A Concordance to the Poems of W. B. Yeats*. Programmed by James Allan Painter, Ithaca, N.Y.: Cornell University Press, 1963.

Perloff, Marjorie. *Rhyme and Meaning in the Poetry of Yeats*. The Hague: Mouton, 1970.

Raine, Kathleen. *Life in Death and Death in Life: Cuchulain Comforted and News for the Delphic Oracle.* Dublin: Dolmen Press, 1973. (No. 8, New Yeats Papers.)

_____. *Yeats, the Tarot, and the Golden Dawn.* Dublin: Dolmen Press, 1971. (No. 2, New Yeats Papers.)

Rajan, Balachandra. *W. B. Yeats: a Critical Introduction.* London: Hutchinson University Library, 1969.

Reid, Benjamin L. *W. B. Yeats: the Lyric of Tragedy.* Norman, Okla.: University of Oklahoma Press, 1961.

Ronsley, Joseph. *Yeats's Autobiography: Life as Symbolic Pattern.* Cambridge, Mass.: Harvard University Press, 1968.

Saul, George Brandon. *Prolegomena to the Study of Yeats's Plays.* Philadelphia: University of Pennsylvania Press, 1957.

_____. *Prolegomena to the Study of Yeats's Poems.* Philadelphia: University of Pennsylvania Press, 1957.

Seiden, Morton Irving. *William Butler Yeats: the Poet as a Mythmaker, 1865–1939.* East Lansing, Mich.: Michigan State University Press, 1962.

Sidnell, Michael J. "Versions of *The Stories of Red Hanrahan.*" *Yeats Studies* 1 (1971): 119–74.

Skelton, Robin and Saddlemyer, Anne, eds. *The World of W. B. Yeats: Essays in Perspective.* Victoria, British Columbia: University of Victoria, 1965.

Snukal, Robert, *High Talk: the Philosophical Poetry of W. B. Yeats.* Cambridge: Cambridge University Press, 1973.

Stallworthy, Jon. *Between the Lines: Yeats's Poetry in the Making.* Oxford: Clarendon Press, 1963.

_____. *Vision and Revision in Yeats's Last Poems.* Oxford: Clarendon Press, 1969.

_____. *Yeats's Last Poems: a Casebook.* London: Macmillan, 1968.

Stauffer, Donald A. *The Golden Nightingale: Essays on Some Principles of Poetry in the Lyrics of William Butler Yeats.* New York: Macmillan, 1946.

Stock, A. G. *W. B. Yeats: His Poetry and Thought.* Cambridge: Cambridge University Press, 1961.

Stoll, John E. *The Great Deluge: a Yeats Bibliography.* Troy, N.Y.: Whitston, 1971.

Tindall, William Y. *W. B. Yeats.* New York: Columbia University Press, 1966. (No. 15, Columbia Essays on Modern Writers.)

Torchiana, Donald. *W. B. Yeats and Georgian Ireland.* Evanston, Ill.: Northwestern University Press, 1966.

Unterecker, John E. *A Reader's Guide to William Butler Yeats.* New York: Noonday Press, 1959.

_____. *Yeats: a Collection of Critical Essays.* Englewood Cliffs, N.J.: Prentice-Hall, 1963. (Twentieth Century Views.)

Ure, Peter. *Towards a Mythology: Studies in the Poetry of W. B. Yeats.* Liverpool: University Press of Liverpool, 1946; New York: Russell and Russell, 1967.

_____. *Yeats the Playwright: a Commentary on Character and Design in the Major Plays.* New York: Barnes and Noble, 1963; London: Routledge and Kegan Paul, 1969.

Vendler, Helen. "Assimilating Yeats." *Massachusetts Review* 7 (1966): 590–97.

_____. *Yeats's Vision and the Later Plays.* Cambridge, Mass.: Harvard University Press, 1963; rpt. 1969.

Wade, Allan, ed. *A Bibliography of the Writings of W. B. Yeats.* 3rd ed., revised and edited by Russell K. Alspach. London: Rupert-Hart-Davis, 1968.

Whitaker, Thomas R. *Swan and Shadow: Yeats's Dialogue with History.* Chapel Hill, N.C.: University of North Carolina Press, 1964.

White, James. *John Butler Yeats and the Irish Renaissance.* Dublin: Dolmen Press, 1973. (No. 5, New Yeats Papers.)

Yeats, John B. *Letters from Bedford Park: A Selection from the Correspondence (1890–1901) of John Butler Yeats.* Selected and edited by William M. Murphy. Dublin: Cuala Press, 1974).

Yeats, William Butler. *Ah, Sweet Dancer: W. B. Yeats, Margot Ruddock, a Correspondence.* Edited by Roger McHugh. London: Macmillan, 1970.

_____. *The Autobiography of William Butler Yeats.* Garden City, N.Y.: Anchor Doubleday, 1958.

_____. *The Collected Plays of W. B. Yeats.* "New Edition." New York: Macmillan, 1953.

_____. *The Collected Poems of W. B. Yeats.* "Definitive Edition." New York: Macmillan, 1956.

_____. *John Sherman and Dhoya.* Edited, with an introduction, collation of texts and notes by Richard J. Finneran. Detroit, Mich.: Wayne State University Press, 1969.

_____. *The Letters of W. B. Yeats.* Edited by Allan Wade. New York: Macmillan, 1954.

_____. *Yeats Letters.* Edited by John Kelly and Eric Domville. (In progress.)

_____. *Letters on Poetry from W. B. Yeats to Dorothy Wellesley.* Edited by Kathleen Raine. New York: Oxford University Press, 1940; London: Oxford University Press, 1964.

_____. *Letters to Katharine Tynan.* Edited by Roger McHugh. New York: McMullen Books, 1953.

_____. *Manuscripts of W. B. Yeats.* Transcribed, edited and with a commentary by David R. Clark,

George P. Mayhew, Michael J. Sidnell. (In progress: *Yeats's Versions of Sophocles*, ed. David R. Clark and James Maguire; *W. B. Yeats: The Death of Cuchulain*, ed. Phillip L. Marcus; *W. B. Yeats: Deirdre*, ed. Virginia Rohan; *W. B. Yeats: The Countess Cathleen*, ed. Michael J. Sidnell.)

_____. *Memoirs.* Translated and edited by Denis Donoghue. New York: Macmillan, 1972.

_____. *Reflections.* Transcribed and edited by Curtis Bradford from the Journals. Dublin: Cuala Press, 1970.

_____. *Selected Poems and Two Plays of William Butler Yeats.* Edited by M. L. Rosenthal. New York: Collier Books, 1970 (8th printing).

_____. *The Senate Speeches of W. B. Yeats.* Edited by Donald R. Pearce. Bloomington, Ind.: Indiana University Press, 1960.

_____. *Some Letters from W. B. Yeats to John O'Leary and His Sister, from Originals in the Berg Collection.* Edited by Allan Wade. Folcroft, Pa.: Folcroft Press, 1953, 1969.

_____. *The Speckled Bird.* Edited by William O'Donnell. Dublin: Cuala Press (In progress).

_____. *A Tower of Polished Black Stones.* (Early versions of "The Shadowy Waters.") Dublin: Dolmen Press, 1971.

_____. *Uncollected Prose by W. B. Yeats.* Volume 1: *First Reviews and Articles, 1886–1896.* Collected and edited by John Frayne. New York: Columbia University Press, 1970. Volume 2: collected and edited by Colton Johnson, in collaboration with John P. Frayne (In Progress).

_____. *The Variorum Edition of the Plays of W. B. Yeats.* Edited by Russell K. Alspach, assisted by Catherine Alspach. New York: Macmillan, 1966.

_____. *The Variorum Edition of the Poems of W. B. Yeats.* Edited by Peter Allt and Russell K. Alspach. New York: Macmillan, 1957.

_____. *A Vision* (1925). Edited, with a commentary by George Mills Harper. (In progress.)

_____. *W. B. Yeats and T. Sturge Moore: Their Correspondence 1901–1937.* Edited by Ursula Bridge. London: Routledge and Kegan Paul, 1953.

_____. *W. B. Yeats, Selected Plays.* Edited by A. Norman Jeffares. London: Macmillan, 1964. New York: Collier Books, 1971 (U.S. title: *Eleven Plays of W. B. Yeats*).

_____. *Yeats and Patrick McCartan, a Fenian Friendship: Letters with a Commentary by John Unterecker and an Address on Yeats, the Fenian, by Patrick McCartan.* Edited by John Unterecker. Dublin: Dolmen Press, 1967. (No. 10, Yeats Centenary Papers.)

Yeats Studies: an International Journal. Edited by Robert O'Driscoll and Lorna Reynolds. Shannon: Irish University Press. vol. 1 (1971), Yeats and the 1890s; vol. 2 (1972), Theatre and the Visual Arts; vol. 3 (1974), Yeats and the Theatre; vol. 4 (1975), Yeats and the Occult; vol. 5 (1976), John Butler Yeats.

Zwerdling, Alex. *Yeats and the Heroic Ideal.* New York: New York University Press, 1965.

Part II

JAMES JOYCE

Photographs by William York Tindall

James Joyce, Platzspitz, Zurich 1938. *Photo by C. Giedion-Welcker. Courtesy of Mrs. Giedion.*

James Joyce after eye operation, Zurich, May 1930.
Photo by Georges Borach. Courtesy of Mrs. Giedion.

Martello Tower, parapet and gun rest. *Photo by Tindall.*

"He pointed his finger in friendly jest and went over to the parapet, laughing to himself. Stephen Dedalus stepped up, followed him wearily halfway and sat down on the edge of the gunrest, watching him still as he propped his mirror on the parapet, dipped the brush in the bowl and lathered cheeks and neck." (*Ulysses*, pp. 3–4)

"He turned seaward from the road at Dollymount and as he passed on to the thin wooden bridge he felt the planks shaking with the tramp of heavily shod feet. A squad of Christian Brothers was on its way back from the Bull . . ." (*Portrait of the Artist as a Young Man,* p. 165)

The Bull Wall. *Photo by Tindall.*

No. 7 Eccles Street. (Note: Bloom's door is on the left.) *Photo by Tindall.*

"What action did Bloom make on their arrival at their destination? At the housesteps of the 4th of the equidifferent uneven numbers, number 7 Eccles street, he inserted his hand mechanically into the back pocket of his trousers to obtain his latchkey." (*Ulysses*, p. 668)

"He told Cranly that the clock of the Ballast Office was capable of an epiphany. . . . Imagine my glimpses of that clock as the gropings of a spiritual eye which seeks to adjust its vision to an exact focus. The moment the focus is reached the object is epiphanised." (*Stephen Hero,* p. 211)

Clock on Ballast Office, Westmoreland Street. *Photo by Tindall.*

Bust of Sir Philip Crampton, founder Botanical Museum, Phoenix Park. *Photo by Tindall.*

"After you with our incorporated drinkingcup. Like sir Philip Crampton's fountain. Rub off the microbes with your handkerchief. Next chap rubs on a new batch with his." (*Ulysses*, p. 170)

"He put on his glasses and gazed towards the metal bridge an instant. —There he is, by God, he said, arse and pockets. Ben Dollard's loose blue cutaway and square hat above large slops crossed the quay in full gait from the metal bridge." (*Ulysses*, p. 244)

Metal Bridge. *Photo by Tindall.*

Merchant's Arch. *Photo by Tindall.*

"A darkbacked figure under Merchants' arch scanned books on the hawker's car . . .—*Sweets of Sin,* he said, tapping on it. That's a good one." (*Ulysses,* pp. 227, 237)

". . . and, now standing full erect, above the ambi-jacent floodplain, scene of its happening, with one Berlin gauntlet chopstuck in the hough of his ell-boge . . . pointed at an angle of thirty-two degrees towards his *duc de Fer*'s overgrown milestone as fellow to his gage. . . . I am woo-woo willing to take my stand, sir, upon the monument, that sign of our ruru redemption. . . ." (*Finnegans Wake*, p. 36)

Wellington Monument. *Photo by Tindall.*

Sandymount strand. *Photo by Tindall.*

"Didn't look back when she was going down the strand. Wouldn't give that satisfaction. Those girls, those girls, those lovely seaside girls." (*Ulysses*, p. 371)

5

The Cracked Lookingglass

Raymond J. Porter

WHAT RELATIONSHIP EXISTS between the fiction of James Joyce, Ireland at the turn of the twentieth century, and Irish writers of the second half of the twentieth century? Do Joyce's works—particularly *Dubliners, A Portrait of the Artist as a Young Man,* and *Ulysses*—embody a vision of Irish life that only an Irishman could contrive, and are they part of a native literary tradition for both Irish reader and writer? These questions all ask the same thing: Is Joyce an Irish writer?

The puzzle of what constitutes Irish literature in the English language as opposed to English literature written by an Irishman and the related puzzle of what constitutes an Irish writer have a fascination and interest difficult to resist. But a thorough investigation of these matters in relation to Joyce and his literary efforts would require more space than is available here, and must be postponed for another time. So, rather than begin at the beginning with consideration of Swift and Sheridan, Edgeworth and Carleton, Lover and Lever, Wilde and Shaw, and with references to Daniel Corkery on "Anglo-Irish Literature"[1] and Thomas Flanagan on "The Nature of the Irish Novel,"[2] I will start with some quotations from a number of contemporary Irish critics and writers on Joyce's fictional presentation of Irish life and his place in the Irish literary tradition. Then on to the principal matter: the treatment accorded the Irish cultural revival of the turn of the century in Joyce's fiction. I have restricted my consideration of this matter to two stories from *Dubliners* and to selected portions from *Portrait* and *Ulysses.*

Irish poet and critic John Jordan has written of the impact that *Dubliners* had upon him as a fifteen-year-old schoolboy: "surely no normal boy could fail to be electrified at finding his own city, the setting of his works and days, enshrined in a book peopled by familiar persons speaking in a familiar idiom." *Dubliners* reflected, he said, "the fabric of my life."[3] For Irish short-story writer and novelist Aidan Higgins, *Portrait* and *Ulysses* have been "the great discoveries in my own literature," and demonstrate that Joyce knew the Irish people "better than they knew themselves."[4] Niall Montgomery, Dublin architect and commentator on the works of Joyce, has concluded that Joyce's "was the exposition, the true expression of the life of the Irish in the early twentieth century and his work is very much part of our cultural heritage, very much part of our richness and our treasures."[5]

A cultural heritage and, as part of it, a literary tradition are crucial for a writer. Thomas Kinsella—in the opinion of many the leading Irish poet of the present day—has written eloquently and in-

1. Daniel Corkery, *Synge and Anglo-Irish Literature* (Cork: Mercier Press, 1966), pp. 1-27.
2. Thomas Flanagan, *The Irish Novelists, 1800-1850* (New York and London: Columbia University Press, 1958), pp. 35-50.
3. John Jordan, "Joyce Without Fears: A Personal Journey," *A Bash in the Tunnel: James Joyce by the Irish,* ed. John Ryan (London: Clifton Books, 1970), pp. 136-37.
4. Aidan Higgins, "Tired Lines, or Tales My Mother Told Me," *A Bash in the Tunnel,* p. 59.
5. Niall Montgomery, "A Context for Mr. Joyce's Work," *The Celtic Master,* ed. Maurice Harmon (Dublin: Dolmen Press, 1969), p 11.

cisively of the modern Irish writer's difficulty when he seeks to identify and connect with his native roots. The Gaelic literary tradition, a long and rich vein, lies on the other side of a great rift.

> Why can I not make living contact with that inheritance, my own past? Others have. It's because I believe I would have to make a commitment to the Irish language; to write in Irish instead of English. And that would mean loss of contact with my own present—abandoning the language I was born in for one which I believe to be dying. It would also mean forfeiting a certain possible scope of language: English has a greater scope, if I can make use of it, than an Irish which is not able to handle all the affairs of my life.[6]

Joyce must have experienced similar feelings during his apprentice days; his fiction seems to indicate so. Certainly the rift that Kinsella refers to, the end result of several centuries of English efforts to Anglicize Ireland, is clearly present. A striking example of de-Gaelicized Ireland, whether Joyce intended it so or not, appears early in *Portrait*. The scene is Stephen's mathematics class at Clongowes Wood College, and the Jesuit instructor has divided the boys into two groups to compete in the working out of sums. What is instructive here are the names given to the opposing sides: "Now then, who will win? Go ahead, York! Go ahead, Lancaster!"[7] Nothing very Irish here, as P. H. Pearse noted in 1912 when he attacked educational practices in Ireland: "The English thing that is called education in Ireland is founded on a denial of the Irish nation."[8] Sports had its part in the denial too, and *Portrait* indicates that the Clongowes boys played cricket and rugby, not hurling and Irish football.

During his university days, Stephen is consciously aware of the break in Ireland's cultural tradition. His thoughts, as he discusses aesthetics and the word *tundish* with the dean, explicitly dwell on Ireland's loss of her native language in previous centuries and her gradual adoption of English.

> The language in which we are speaking is his before it is mine. How different are the words *home*,

Christ, ale, master, on his lips and on mine! I cannot speak or write these words without unrest of spirit. His language, so familiar and so foreign, will always be for me an acquired speech. I have not made or accepted its words. My voice holds them at bay. My soul frets in the shadow of his language. (p. 189)

Gabriel Conroy in "The Dead," less sure of himself than Dedalus, would prefer not to have the Irish language brought to his attention. To him, it is a mark of social and cultural inferiority. And so, when Molly Ivors needles him for vacationing on the Continent rather than in the west of Ireland and for keeping in touch with European languages rather than Gaelic, Gabriel retorts, "Irish is not my language."[9]

A more humorous, but none the less serious, presentation of the language situation occurs in the first chapter of *Ulysses*. Using the old milk woman as an allegorical figure for Ireland, itself an adaptation of a long-established practice in Irish literature (both Gaelic and English), Joyce has Haines, the visiting Englishman, address the woman in Irish. Her response: "Is it French you are talking, sir? . . . I'm ashamed I don't speak the language myself. I'm told it's a grand language by them that knows."[10]

It was to remedy this situation, to put the Irish people back into contact with their Irish heritage —their language, literature, history, music, folklore, legends, myths, and sports—that organizations like the Gaelic League and the Gaelic Athletic Association came into being during the last two decades of the nineteenth century. In addition to these two well-known groups, there were countless others doing similar work at this time and after the turn of the century: the Young Ireland Society, the Contemporary Club, the Pan-Celtic Society, the Celtic Literary Society, and, of course, the Irish National Literary Society, which had ties with the Irish Literary Society in London. Add to this the many amateur dramatic groups that sprang into existence, including what later became the Abbey Theatre company; numberless text books, translations, journals, and newspapers; and the work of writers like Yeats, Lady Gregory, and George Russell to produce a

---

6. Thomas Kinsella, "Irish Literature — Continuity of the Tradition," *Poetry Ireland* 7, 8 (Spring 1968) : 110-11.

7. James Joyce, *A Portrait of the Artist as a Young Man* (New York: Viking Press, 1964), p. 12. All references to *Portrait* are from this edition and are cited in parentheses in the text.

8. P. H. Pearse, "The Murder Machine," *Political Writings and Speeches* (Dublin: Talbot Press Ltd., 1952), p. 16.

9. James Joyce, "The Dead," *Dubliners*, ed. Robert Scholes and A. Walton Litz (New York: Viking Press, 1969), p. 189. All references to *Dubliners* are from this edition and are cited in parentheses in the text.

10. James Joyce, *Ulysses* (New York: Modern Library, 1961), p. 14. All references to *Ulysses* are from this edition and are cited in parentheses in the text.

distinctively Irish literature in English, and one can see some justification for Edward Martyn's alleged message to George Moore that the "sceptre of intelligence" was passing from London to Dublin.[11]

However, these activities failed to capture and hold the imagination of James Joyce and his fictional creation, Stephen Dedalus. While Joyce devoted considerably more time to Gaelic than Stephen's one lesson and while there is some cause to believe that he attained "a modest competence"[12] in the language, the fact remains that, with some exceptions, the Gaelic that appears in his works is "elementary and commonplace" and often faulty in grammar.[13] Joyce used whatever knowledge he had of the Irish language in the same manner that he used hundreds of other bits and pieces of information that he had gleaned from myriad sources: all was woven into the pattern of his fabric. By no stretch of the imagination was he a language-revival enthusiast. As he wrote to his brother, Stanislaus, on November 6, 1906, "If the Irish programme did not insist on the Irish language I suppose I could call myself a nationalist."[14]

Portrait mentions that while Stephen is at Belvedere College the "movement towards national revival had begun to be felt" and "yet another voice had bidden him to be true to his country and help to raise up her fallen language and tradition" (p. 84). But the voice is "hollowsounding" and Stephen holds himself aloof from engagement. Later, at the university, Davin, a committed nationalist and language revival enthusiast, urges Stephen to join the movement, but Stephen declines: "My ancestors threw off their language and took another. . . . Do you fancy I am going to pay in my own life and person debts they made? . . . nationality, language, religion. I shall try to fly by those nets" (p. 203).

Although neither Joyce nor Stephen committed himself to the language and cultural revival, the revival and characters associated with it are not invariably presented in a negative manner in the fiction. There is no scarcity of examples on the

negative side, of course. The chauvinistic "Citizen" in *Ulysses*, and Mulligan's witty quip, "That's folk. . . . Five lines of text and ten pages of notes about the folk and fishgods of Dundrum. Printed by the weird sisters in the year of the big wind" (pp. 12–13) come to mind immediately. As do the grasping and social-climbing Mrs. Kearney of "A Mother" and the catcalls and hisses of Stephen's fellow students at the performance of Yeats's *Countess Cathleen* in *Portrait* (p. 226). But Molly Ivors and the west of Ireland, associated with the Irish language, are positive forces in "The Dead," and Davin of *Portrait* is an attractive and engaging figure, the only character able to melt Stephen's icy reserve.

Some readers have cast Miss Ivors in the role of a heavy, taking her to be an overly intense, narrow-minded, and humorless advocate of the Irish-Ireland movement. Such an interpretation is a misreading of the text; it ignores a good deal of evidence that points in quite a different direction. Actually, after the bitterness of Lily, the serving girl, the inanities of Mr. Browne, the testiness of Aunt Kate, and the piano playing and blushes of Mary Jane, Miss Ivors is a breath of fresh air in the story. Involved, alert, challenging, and playfully teasing, she is a vital and likable individual.

Molly Ivors's direct and frank challenges disconcert Gabriel Conroy, who is accustomed to presiding patronizingly at the Misses Morkan's annual dance. First he murmurs "lamely" (p. 188), then responds "awkwardly" (p. 189); the exchange between them is an "ordeal which was making a blush invade his forehead." Such a response would be justified if Gabriel were being verbally attacked by an insensitive bore determined to inflict her views upon her listeners and intent on bringing embarrassment to the "nonbeliever." But Molly Ivors is not such a person. The text reveals that although she teases Gabriel at being a "West Briton" because of his book reviews in the pro-English *Daily Express* (Joyce also did some reviewing for this paper), she answers his lame response to this accusation in a "soft friendly tone" and comments that she liked his recent review of Browning's poetry "immensely" (p. 188). Dedication to the revival movement has not made a stone of Molly's heart, has not robbed her of human warmth. While dancing, she takes Gabriel's hand "in a warm grasp" (p. 188); and when she asks Gabriel to join a summer excursion to the Aran Islands, she lays "her warm hand ea-

11. George Moore, *Hail and Farewell: Ave* (London: William Heinemann Ltd., 1947), p. 72.
12. Brendan O Hehir, *A Gaelic Lexicon for "Finnegans Wake"* (Berkeley and Los Angeles, Calif.: University of California Press, 1967), p. vii.
13. *Ibid.*, p. ix.
14. *Letters of James Joyce*, vol. 2, ed. Richard Ellmann (New York: Viking Press, 1966): 187.

gerly on his arm" (p. 189). It is only when Gabriel petulantly asserts, "I'm sick of my country, sick of it!" that Miss Ivors displays some annoyance: "Why? . . . Of course, you've no answer" (p. 190). Whereas Gabriel's reaction to this last assertion is "agitation," Molly quickly recaptures her good spirits; and Gabriel, when the two of them come together again in the quadrille they are dancing, is "surprised to feel his hand firmly pressed."

Molly Ivors, then, as I read the story, is a figure of vitality, a life-giving force. And so is the west of Ireland, with its Gaeltacht, or Irish-speaking areas. "The Lass of Aughrim," Michael Furey, Gabriel's wife, Gretta—in short, passion—are associated with the west, and passion is the missing ingredient in Gabriel's life. He comes to realize this lack and concedes that "the time had come for him to set out on his journey westward" (p. 223). As Richard Ellmann has written, this sentence affirms "the west, the primitive, untutored, impulsive country from which Gabriel had felt himself alienated before."[15]

Davin in *Portrait* is also associated with the revival movement and with the country districts of Ireland, though not the west. Stephen is drawn to the "peasant student," though not to the movement he espouses. Of all the university students, only Davin calls Stephen "Stevie"—the rest employ the more formal "Dedalus"—and this "homely version of his christian name on the lips of his friend had touched Stephen pleasantly . . ." (p. 180). But, although he is attracted by Davin's "quiet inbred courtesy of attention or by a quaint turn of old English speech or by the force of its delight in rude bodily skill," Stephen is at the same time repelled by a "grossness of intelligence or by a bluntness of feeling or by a dull stare of terror in the eyes, the terror of soul of a starving Irish village in which the curfew was still a nightly fear" (pp. 180–81).

Davin ultimately stands for a part of Irish life whose "hidden ways" (p. 181) Stephen cannot penetrate. And Davin's worship of the "sorrowful legend of Ireland," his attitude toward Irish myth and the Roman Catholic religion—that of a "dull-witted loyal serf"—are completely foreign to Stephen. "Eager of speculation," young Dedalus is put off by a certain "reluctance of speech and deed" in his country friend, this reluctance signifying restriction, fear, and subservience to the as-

piring artist. Perhaps Stephen is right in his conclusion, for later, in a discussion between the two friends as to why Stephen will not join the national movement, Davin quietly but firmly states, "But a man's country comes first. Ireland first, Stevie. You can be a poet or mystic after" (p. 203). Stephen cannot subscribe to this, and neither could James Joyce, although he loved his country.

"A Mother" presents some other aspects of the revival movement that Joyce couldn't subscribe to either. Written in the second half of 1905, before both "The Dead" and *Portrait,* this story is much harder on the revival than the later two works. In it, Joyce exposes with great irony the social climbing and self-seeking motives of some of the revivalists, the lack of competence and professionalism among performers and organizers of artistic events, the culturally impoverished state of Dublin audiences, and the willingness of the Irish people to accept mediocrity and failure. The picture he paints is somewhat exaggerated, somewhat unfair, but it is not without its share of truth.

Mrs. Kearney, the mother of the title, bears the brunt of Joyce's attack on social climbing and insincere espousal of revival principles. Convinced of her cultural and social superiority and determined to enhance her family's position in the Dublin community, she avails herself of an opportunity that the Irish revival has put in her way. As luck would have it, her daughter, like the daughter of Houlihan, carries the name Kathleen; and so a teacher of Irish is employed for lessons and the Kearneys join the language movement. Joyce inserts an effective detail in his brief account of the family's use of the Irish language after he notes that on "special Sundays" the Kearneys attend Mass at the pro-cathedral and then gather on a nearby corner with nationalist friends to share gossip: the only Irish spoken by these enthusiasts is a brief goodbye (p. 138). This practice was, and still is today, a common one in Ireland. Irishmen have read and heard many a political speech that opens and closes with a Gaelic phrase but is otherwise innocent of Irish.

Mrs. Kearney's efforts bear fruit when Kathleen becomes recognized as a "believer in the language movement" and is granted a contract to be the accompanist at four concerts sponsored by the Eire Abu Society. The fruit, of course, turns out to be sour, and at the end of the story it is clear to all that Mrs. Kearney is not really interested in nurturing the growth of things Irish. But *en route*

15. Richard Ellmann, *James Joyce* (New York: Oxford University Press, 1959), p. 258.

to this exposure, the organizers of the concerts, the performers, and the audiences are subjected to Joyce's irony.

The first mistake the planning committee made was to arrange for four concerts. This becomes evident when the first one is sparsely attended. The quality of the performances is so "mediocre" that the "few people in the hall grew fewer and fewer" (p. 140), and the concert "expired shortly before ten and everyone went home quickly." A death apparently painless—for the committee, at any rate, if not for Mrs. Kearney—for the secretary of the Society, Mr. Fitzpatrick, "seemed to bear disappointments lightly" (p. 139).

The second concert takes place amid the discarded paper debris of the night before; and, although a larger crowd turns out, the audience "behaved indecorously" (p. 140). So does Mr. Fitzpatrick, the esteemed secretary, who entertains himself by standing at the edge of the screen and "from time to time jutting out his head and exchanging a laugh" with some friends in the balcony. During the evening, the committee announces its belated decision to cancel the third concert and make an all-out effort to fill the hall for the Saturday performance.

Saturday brings rain, however, and Miss Beirne, one of the committee, demonstrates a disconcerting willingness to accept failure:

> The little woman hoped they would have a good house. She looked out at the rain until the melancholy of the wet street effaced all the trustfulness and enthusiasm from her twisted features. Then she gave a little sigh and said:
> —Ah, well! We did our best, the dear knows. (p. 142)

But a sizable audience shows up, and begins to clap and stamp and whistle at the delay of curtain caused by Mrs. Kearney's insistence on payment to her daughter for the canceled concert of the night before. Among the performers presented for its listening enjoyment are a young man named Duggan, who had marred his operatic début "by wiping his nose in his gloved hand once or twice" (p. 142), and Madam Glynn of London, who "sang *Killarney* in a bodiless gasping voice" (p. 147). Although some of the audience "made fun of her high wailing notes," the crowd responds warmly to the more gifted vocalists who follow and applauds a "stirring patriotic recitation delivered by a young lady who arranged amateur the-

atricals." The implication is that, on the whole, the concert is a success according to revival Dublin standards; and this success constitutes a condemnation of those standards.

"A Mother" is a damning indictment of Irish life, as are many of the other stories of *Dubliners*. Joyce himself, before he completed the collection, commented on this to Stanislaus in a letter of September 25, 1906: "Sometimes thinking of Ireland it seems to me that I have been unnecessarily harsh. I have reproduced (in *Dubliners* at least) none of the attraction of the city. . . . I have not reproduced its ingenuous insularity and its hospitality."[16] Joyce put some of this "attraction" in "The Dead," which he started writing in the spring of 1907. However, although he mentions Dublin's "ingenuous insularity" as an "attraction," it is the very quality that convinced him to leave Ireland and live and write on the Continent.

To Joyce, the Irish revival was a manifestation of Ireland's insularity, and he could not become part of a literary movement that looked to the past. He was not ignorant of his country's past, and he had no wish to deny his Irish heritage: " 'Ireland is what she is . . . and therefore I am what I am because of the relations that have existed between England and Ireland,' "[17] he remarked to Frank Budgen in 1919. But he refused to turn to the past. As Thomas Kinsella has written, Joyce "was able to reject (that is, accept) the whole tradition as he found it—as it lay in stunned silence, still recovering from the death of the Irish language."[18]

From the Continent, Joyce devoted himself to writing of Ireland. In his "nicely polished lookingglass,"[19] the "cracked lookingglass of a servant" (U, p. 6), he presented a vision of *modern* Ireland, a vision in which the local is universalized. This vision, this accomplishment, has proved to be a valuable contribution to world literature—and to Irish literature. For the Irish writer today, "Joyce is the true father. . . . Joyce stands for it [the Irish tradition] as healed—or healing—from its mutilation."[20]

16. *Letters*, 2: 166.
17. Frank Budgen, *James Joyce and the Making of "Ulysses"* (Bloomington, Ind.: Indiana University Press, 1960), p. 152.
18. Kinsella, p. 114.
19. Letter to Grant Richards, 23 June 1906, *Letters of James Joyce*, vol. 1, ed. Stuart Gilbert (New York: Viking Press, 1957): 64.
20. Kinsella, p. 115.

6

Striking the Lost Chord: The Motif of "Waiting" in the Sirens Episode of *Ulysses*

Margaret C. Solomon

THE SIRENS CHAPTER in *Ulysses* stands out so prominently in the novel as an achievement of painstaking craftsmanship that it has understandably attracted scholars whose knowledge of the artful structurings of music exceeds that of the rest of us Joyceans. Studies have called attention to the many ingenious ways Joyce was able to approximate music through the medium of words: for example, in orchestral or operatic organization, in onomatopoeia, in the inclusion of songs and song-fragments, names of instruments and suggestions of their sound-distinctions.[1] The delightful irony of the episode is that such assertions as that it resembles a grand, Wagnerian composition[2] can be made about a production that depends largely upon the input of bits and pieces from popular opera, popular songs and ditties, and melodies that have none of the complexity of either a splendid opera or a magnificent symphony. The words intoning lost love and celebrating heroic martyrdom are mawkishly nostalgic or else sentimentally patriotic. The tunes alluded to employ conventional musical phraseology; the lyrics, for the most part, are those of prosaic verse forced into uncomplicated rhyme schemes. Moreover, the narrative that incorporates the melodies and lyrics presents no high-minded heroes or great lovers. Yet there is no other section of the novel in which the formal manipulation of language is more skillful; in fact, the Sirens chapter has often been denigrated as a mere *tour de force*. Nor is there any other chapter serving better as a demonstration of how Joyce manages the metamorphosis of the mundane into "music of the spheres." Any sensitive student of *Ulysses* knows, by the time he has reread the book, that ironic debasement of the mythological archetypes has somehow resulted in at least a momentary return to generic identification. The trivial events, played as parodic notes in the lives of comparatively insignificant Dubliners during an ordinary day, have produced an orchestration that not only transcends every single unit of its composition but also precludes a paraphrase of the "score" in terms of meaningful denouement. In other words, through words a wordless metempsychosis has been accomplished, an *effect* resembling which the octaval re-

---

1. Of most help in this study have been Zack Bowen, "The Bronzegold Sirensong: A Musical Analysis of the Sirens Episode in Joyce's *Ulysses*," *Literary Monographs I*, eds. Eric Rothstein and Thomas K. Dunseath (Madison, Milwaukee, and London, 1967), 247-298; and Don Noel Smith, "Musical Form and Principles in the Scheme of *Ulysses*," *Twentieth Century Literature*, XVIII, 2 (April, 1972), 79-92. Zack Bowen is the source for the information on song titles and lyrics alluded to in the text.
2. Joyce's remarks to Georges Borach and Ottocaro Weiss suggest that he was apparently trying to outdo Wagner (Richard Ellmann, *James Joyce* [New York, 1965], p. 473). Moreover, the development of the chapter may be called Wagnerian in some respects; i. e., formal frustrations, relating to the resolution of countering motifs are abnormally prolonged. Of course, the same could be said of the entire novel.

turn feels as much like a beginning as it does a resolution—more like a transitional linguistic vacuum than a triumphant consonance of language.

The Sirens chapter seems to me to be a representation in microcosm of the entire production of *Ulysses,* the deliberate craftsmanship of the chapter serving to provoke a three-way relationship among (1) the singing of and listening to a song, within the total context of music; (2) the outward and inward manifestations of discourse, within the total context of language; and (3) the active and passive roles of individual relationships, within the total context of human history. Structural codes underlying music, spoken or written language, and human life do set limits on each unique creation. One waits for the development of the song, the novel, the human personality to "die" according to the pattern set up by the initial, predetermining "key." What Joyce insists upon, however, in both his historical overview and his aesthetics, is that *all* resolutions are open-ended in that they become input for a larger continuity. Songs are remembered and sung again and again; fragments, motifs, and "chords," in language, music, and former lives, are used over and over in new combinations. So the fiction that touches universality in its imprint of formal aesthetic satisfaction is "remembered" long after it is finished, just as an individual's personality continues in the memories of his successors because the events of his life, through his development in time, have ousted other possibilities in history and have created a variation on the theme of acting-and-waiting in the period between birth and death.

The point to be made is that *Ulysses* has for its *subject* the correspondence between the work of art and the life that is lived within the context of language. Joyce's formal craft is devoted to such an identification. The productions of both *Ulysses* and *Finnegans Wake* demonstrate the fallacy of any perception that treats plot and character as if they were contents to be enhanced, elucidated, or hidden by form. Structure pushed to its outermost limits by developmental variations *is* the content. "Numbers it is," says Bloom in the Ormond Hotel. "All music when you come to think. . . . Vibrations. . . . Do anything you like with figures juggling. . . . Musemathematics. And you think you're listening to the ethereal. But suppose you said it like: Martha, seven times nine minus X is thirtyfive thousand. Fall quite flat. It's on account of the sounds it is. . . . Time makes

the tune" (p. 278). Well, the statement may not be terribly profound as a description of the aesthetics of music, but Bloom's confused struggle to explain in words the seductive power of music deserves examination for what Joyce is suggesting concerning the mysterious affective quality of the working of formal devices upon themselves. Resonances make the connections and the differences; in *Ulysses,* memory, unconscious desire, and hope are put into vibration through the interaction of utterances and silent spaces. Let us examine some of the components of the word-machine that turns out the special product of the Sirens episode.

In characterization, Bloom is the major input. On the realistic-plot level, we already know that he has some problems in his present relationship with his wife; indeed, the fragments and variations of "love's old sweet song" point up the contrast, in the first long movement, between the time of his courtship of and early years with Molly and the tense anxiety of the present. On the one hand, his siren's call is from the past, seducing Bloom with memories far more pleasing than the contemplation of what is going to happen this afternoon; on the other hand, there is a counterlure, a call to move out and prevent the adultery. One lure is a longing to go back to the beginning (*da capo*); the other is a desire to end this waiting by acting, no matter what happens. Obviously, the first is humanly impossible, except in memory; the other is a risk that Bloom considers but does not take. The strongest enticement turns out to be delay. As Ulysses bound himself to the mast in order to hear the sirens' song without having to move to his own destruction, Bloom waits at the Ormond Bar, binding his "four fork-fingers" and then his "troubled double, fourfold, in octave" with a rubber band.

The motif of "waiting" occurs and recurs throughout the chapter. Its insistent repetition strikes vibrations, stirs the reader's recollection that the word *wait* has punctuated Bloom's interior monologue many times earlier in the novel. It has functioned as a hesitation, an attempt to stop for a moment the flow of his thinking, to recall something, to correct an impression, to create a shift in his mental processes. The concept of *waiting,* to my mind, is the most important component in the linguistic input of the Sirens episode. It forces the relationships between music, language, and human history and acts as a catalyst for both an *evocation* of the Homerian *Odyssey* as structural key and the *return* to a mythological point of view produced by the episode. Joyce plays all possible variations on the waiting motif. In the first two movements of the chapter, waiting, as applicable to time, is given every shade of meaning: lurking, lying in wait; holding on, holding off, suspending; hesitating, lingering, postponing, allowing oneself to be detained, meandering, idly dreaming; expecting, anticipating, hoping, listening for an answer; resting, pausing. A less subtle distinction in the denotations of waiting, still having to do with time, is personified in Pat, the waiter: waiting upon, serving. And finally, in the third movement of the chapter, Joyce plays upon the sound of the word in an emphasis on "weight," at the same time shifting the auditory attention from tenor keys to a heavier bass register.

The "opening" (I don't know what else to call the series of fragments) serves as a conditioning in suspense, warning us of the necessity for holding in tension the unresolved fragments of the narrative in much the same way as a listener holds the unfinished statements of a musical composition, waiting for a blending that promises resolution. It is true that the image of approaching death is announced at once: light-and-bright bronze and gold hear the hoofbeats of darker-and-heavier iron and steel. Aging "blue bloom" shadows "Gold pinnacled hair." And the "rose of Castille" already has a double meaning for the reader remembering Lenehan's riddle in the Aeolus chapter; it evokes the heavier, more sinister phrase, "rows of cast steel." Other fragments hint that a "soft word" can be a "decoy." Even the more cheerful phrases, "The bright stars fade. . . . The morn is breaking," are deceptive, for they are excerpts from a song about the too-brief bliss of lovers and their trying to accept the fact that the night of ecstasy is over and it is time for them to part ("Goodbye, Sweetheart, Goodbye").

At the end of the introduction of linguistic and musical fragments ("Done. Begin!"), the two young bargirls play the roles of sirens, "Waiting for their teas [tease] to draw" (p. 258). Immediately, Joyce extends his analogies beyond the Sirens myth; looking and seeing are as seductive as calling and listening. "Look at the fellow in the tall silk. . . . He's looking. Mind till I see. . . . He's killed looking back" (p. 257). Like Lot's wife, anyone who turns toward the past is in danger. "It's them [men] has the fine times," Miss Kennedy says sadly (p. 258). Sirens, like Molly

who never stirs from her home shore, must lie in wait for the "sweets of sin," for Raoul. Men are a counterlure. A mention of the "old fogey in Boyd's" provokes Miss Kennedy to protest, "O, don't remind me of him for mercy'sake!" "But wait till I tell you, Miss Douce entreated," whereupon Miss Kennedy plugs her ears so as not to hear. "I won't listen, she cried. . . . Don't let me think of him or I'll expire. . . . Will you ever forget his goggle eye?" At this moment, "Bloom's dark eyes" go by "Bassi's blessed virgins," thinking of goddesses who bring "rakes of fellows in" (p. 259).

The first male to enter the scene is the young "boots," *serving* the barmaids their teas. Curiously, they do not heed him as a potential victim, taking no notice, dismissing him with a complaint about his impertinent insolence (p. 258). Well, he is too young to be enticed to look back. In one interpretation, the sirens' call in this episode is to those who are living only in memory, those who enter the bar to drink the same old drinks again, to sing or listen to the same old songs, to repeat in their thoughts and emotions an initial experience, which comes only once; everything after is echo, a vain hope for "return." Waiting, in this sense, is the process of resinging the anticipation, mourning the lost love or the martyr, listening and waiting for the echo. Every time one sings an old song of love or heroism he repeats something in his memory, goes back to the beginning to an event that nothing thereafter has been able to approximate. This kind of "harking back in a retrospective sort of arrangement" (p. 277) by singing or listening to a nostalgic song is a way of forgetting the present, holding off the future, delaying any new acting for oneself. Simon Dedalus is the first likely candidate for this kind of destructive passivity. He is not only a victim, however ("Tempting poor simple males," he mocks), but will play a singing role in the enticement of "dumb" listeners (p. 261).

Mr. Bloom crosses the bridge of "Yessex" (pp. 261–62). It is close to 4:00 o'clock, when Boylan is supposed to keep his assignation with Molly. For Blazes, four is half-octave, midway between the opening key and the return. He is younger than Bloom, has had a call from a siren of some substance, and, although he "waits" for a short period at the bar, postponing his doom, perhaps teasing his siren—at least drawing out the anticipation—he will soon jog away, "atrot in heat," impatient to experience his consummation. Bloom is older. "Four" for him means midafternoon, two-thirds of his day done. He has crossed the bridge, putting "Yes, sex" into "yesterday," and in the narrative, is about to enter the dining room of Ormond's to listen to love's old sweet song. From the counter in Daly's he has seen Boylan's jauntingcar "afar," the coincidence of which gives him pause (p. 263). In the moment of indecision, Bloom "hears" two opposing calls. One is from Molly, or rather from the Molly that Bloom remembers from happier days: "Follow. Risk it. Go quick. At four. Near now. Out" (p. 264). But it isn't the real person of the present that one wants; it's the repetition of the feeling that one got at the high point of his own experience. The other call, the sound of a tuning fork left behind in the bar by a blind piano tuner, may not be stronger, but it is "long in dying." It sounds again, a "longer in dying call" (p. 264). Immediate risk or postponement? For blue Bloom on the rye, the choice is really not at all hard to make.

This presentation of "waiting" as a holding off of the end, a drawing out of one's personal time, may be the most cynical of all the shades of meaning Joyce gives to the term. That the first real note of music in the narrative is sounded by the tuning fork provides a key to a symbolical paraphrase. For it is a fixed tone that governs the pitch of all other keys, if the player is to play in tune. It is wordless, generating the music and constituting the first call, in this episode, to "play." (That the tuning instrument is "forked," and that it belongs to an absent, blind tuner is surely a significance that will have to be explored.) The first lure of all, then, is the call to *begin*. "Players" respond to the call, obeying the pitch of the fork, the one pure note; each performer plays in his own key and creates his own variations. Woman plays on man as a harp; man plays on woman as a flute. The first tone is wordless; the first "playing" needs no words. Indeed, Bloom recalls his first "true" love in terms of sense stimulations rather than of word-exchange. The language of love is the looking and the feeling. One does not "sing" of love unless he has already experienced it. (Ironically, on their first meeting, Molly was singing a song called "Waiting," the call of a siren longing to be rescued by a lover from her dull bondage [p. 275]). Bloom is *not* Molly's "first," with whom she confuses, in her monologue, all her subsequent lovers.) Therefore, when a song

is sung it is already a reminiscence, a longing for a repetition of something one already knows: "When first I saw that form endearing" . . . or, "Come back. Return." If the first music is all, and every song thereafter is only an echo, does it matter how much time is consumed in living out the repeating echoes of one's life? Why stave off the final "return"—death? Unquenchable desire and hope, however vain, deny that choice. Even death-in-life means longer-in-dying, a holding off of deafness in order to hear the echoes and also to share vicariously the high notes of other lives.

The stressing of this theme continues throughout the first movement, but it is necessary to follow rather closely, in linear fashion, the complications by means of which an effect of much wider significance evolves. Even before the tuning fork sounds the first tone, we are introduced to a kind of waiter who is personally deficient in musical appreciation; Lenehan, who has no personal music to remember, apparently, is tone-deaf, and arouses no interest in the waitress-sirens. Miss Kennedy will not "see" him, even though he "[winds] his round body round" to "peep" and to make "overtures." His "droning" is a vain attempt. No wonder: the "no-song" is flat, has no rhythm and absolutely no variety, consisting of one-syllable repetitions of a single note. "Ah fox met ah stork. Said thee fox too thee stork: Will you put your bill down inn my troath and pull upp ah bone?" (p. 262). Lenehan is waiting for Boylan, who does at least have an ear for music and can be counted on to provide Lenehan with some second-hand thrills. (Lenehan, it will be recalled, was a specialist in vicarious experience in the *Dubliners* story "Two Gallants.") In fact, Lenehan waits *on* Boylan as a servant, recognizing and hailing him as "conquering hero." Boylan raises his glass with a toast. "Here's fortune, Blazes said." "Hold on, said Lenehan, till I . . ." (p. 265). Boylan's presence is the factor persuading Miss Douce to sound the only note that excites Lenehan: the smack of a garter against her thigh. "Sonnez la cloche!" Like a gleeful chimp, Lenehan has learned to recognize the sound indicating the passage of time. "Trained by owner. No sawdust there" (p. 266). And he senses that there are experiences he is missing: the climax of sex, for instance.

—I'm off, said Boylan with impatience.
He slid his chalice brisk away, grasped his change.

—Wait a shake, begged Lenehan, drinking quickly. I wanted to tell you, Tom Rochford . . .

—Come on to blazes, said Blazes Boylan, going. Lenehan gulped to go.

—Got the horn or what? he said. Wait. I'm coming.

He followed the hasty creaking shoes but stood by nimbly by the threshold, saluting forms . . . (p. 267)

The passage just quoted is a good example of the density of innuendo in any single selection from this chapter. Boylan's metamorphosis ("change") is stressed: from postponement to impatience; from the sipping of a "chalice" to the going to "blazes." Boylan's drink has been "slow-syrupy sloe"; Lenehan drinks his cup of "bitters" "quickly," to catch up. Boylan's invitation to Lenehan, "Come on to blazes," is an invitation to Hell's fire, but also suggests a homosexual come-on resonating with the last words of the climactical song of the chapter: "Come to me." Blazes has "got the horn," all right, but we know that Lenehan's "Wait. I'm coming" is a wishful dream for this server who stands aside for his betters. He is the perfect example of a life that is lived in unawareness; he can hear the stroke of the hour, but is only dimly conscious of either the music of firsthand human experience or the loss and anxiety, the diminution of hope and expectation, that come with the aging process.

Pat, another waiter-server, is a puzzle harder to solve at this point in the narrative. From his baldness and his deafness, we might guess that he is a finished waiter, no longer participating in the past and no longer hoping for the future, simply serving others who pause to remember and wish. But Pat is "bothered"—both-eared; later, we learn that he "seehears lipspeech."[3] Is he doubly sensitive? Or absolutely nonsensitive, just an instrument to be played upon by others? Bloom ponders this (farther on in the narrative, p. 283), wondering if Pat has a wife and family waiting for him at home, questioning whether Pat has a life of his own. The hard-of-hearing waiter remains a mysterious motif in the orchestration of the chapter until the second movement is in progress.

After the first long-in-dying call of the tuning fork, the next lure comes in instrumental form, the keys of the piano tempting "a voice to sing the strain of dewy morn, of youth, of love's leave-taking, life's, love's morn." Word-fragments from the lyrics are inserted into the narrative—for the song is a familiar one—but it is a "voiceless song," sung from "within" (p. 264). Allusions to and bits of words from other songs have already appeared in the barroom conversations, for each person has internalized songs that insinuate themselves into discourse, reverberating with his presently live existence. Nevertheless, in presenting the music actually audible in the bar, Joyce sets up a very precise progression. Ben Dollard and Father Cowley have been lured into the saloon by the sound of Simon Dedalus's playing ("We heard the piano": p. 267). Simon says he was only "vamping," holding off, delaying the full rendition of the song. In fact, we have been told that his hands have been "faltering" on the keys; that chords have "strayed," been "lost," and then been "found" again (p. 266). Ben coaxes Simon to sing ("Come on . . . give us a ditty": p. 267); Simon tries to entice Ben to sing ("Love and war, Ben. . . . God be with old times"). But before the marriage of words and music, the trio of cronies celebrate old times with talk alone. This coming marriage is anticipated in the language preceding the actual sound of Ben's singing voice: in the discussion of Ben Dollard's "wedding garment," of Bloom's and Molly's marriage, and of their old home on Holles street where they lived in "Merrion square style." Molly is referred to as "Mrs Marion"; Bloom and Goulding, eating, are said to be "married in silence" (pp. 268–69).

The first wedding of voice and accompaniment is in a song meant for a duet between tenor and bass; moreover, it is a song with a double subject, love and war. The only difference between the words of the first two verses of the song is an exchange of the tenor's words "Love" and "Lovers" with the bass's words "War" and "Soldiers." Then the two parts are "married" in the last verse:

> Since Mars lov'd Venus, Venus Mars,
> Let's blend love's wounds with battle's scars,
> And call in Bacchus all divine,
> To cure both pains with rosy wine . . .

The rendition gets off to a false, a faltering start. Ben Dollard, bass, starts the Lover's lines, booming heavily and inappropriately, according to Fa-

---

3. P. 283. Fritz Senn has pointed out, in a note to be published in *James Joyce Quarterly* ("Trivia Ulysseana"), that the word "bothered" would be recognized by any Irishman as the English spelling of the Gaelic word for "deaf": *botair*. For a confirmation of the further ambiguity supplied by "both-eared," see FW 156. 20, 23, where the Mookse predicts that the Gripes will go blind ("belined") and the Gripes counters that the Mookse will be deaf ("botheared").

ther Cowley, who stops him at once, saying that he should be singing the warrior's part, that the lover's part should be rendered in "half time," with a more "loving" delivery. In his position of stage manager behind the scenes, Joyce is also insisting on "half time": high notes are to be prolonged, drawn out, in this longest movement of the episode's construction, belonging to love and to the tenor register. Bloom's stream-of-consciousness unwittingly confirms, however, the marriage of these two themes in the episode and also their blending in the composition of an individual's life: "Love and war someone is." His stopping short of the word "singing" leaves intact a statement of existence. We know, too, that the right chord that will make these two themes harmonize in the chapter has not yet been struck. Ben Dollard stops singing; Father Cowley stops playing (p. 270). The theme of lost love needs more time for development. And we do not yet know what the addition of words to music is going to mean in the total production of the episode.

Bloom, in the dining room, unseen (as he thinks) by the performers, has his ear open to listening from "afar." And his first silent comments on the subject of music concern the relation of player to instrument. Cowley, he muses, "sits in to" the piano "like one together, mutual understanding," whereas musicians tuning up—waiting "between the acts"—are at war with one another and with their instruments. Except for a girl and a harp. That plucking never sounds like tiresome scraping. "We [Boylan and I] are their harps," thinks Bloom. "I. He. Old. Young." When one is young enough to be "played upon," it doesn't matter whether he can sing or not, for, as Bloom sneers later, Boylan "can't sing for tall hats." The implication is reinforced that the wordless music of original love precedes any kind of song. When love is done and war is over—whether won or lost makes little difference—one's "dancing days are done" (the line is from "Johnny I Hardly Knew Ye," about a soldier who comes home from war with his legs shot off); this is Simon's protest when he is urged to sing even if he has to "get it out in bits." Father Cowley presents one alternative in the first complete rendition of a song, "A Last Farewell," which voices a determination to leave forever the "base world" and all its distresses (p. 271). Still, that is not what most people do; rather, they suspend their sentences of doom (all men, from birth, are condemned to die), waiting for a

repetition of the remembered joy, while ironically emphasizing, in their nostalgic songs, the *loss*, the emptiness that marks both the end of love and the beginning of death-in-life.

Bloom says to himself that his eating-companion, Richie Goulding, is probably closer to death, with Bright's disease, than the latter realizes. It is appropriate, says Bloom, for Richie to sing "Down Among the Dead Men" (dead men = empty bottles), a song that calls men to drink up "while we have breath,/ For there's no drinking after death." Richie is typical of all these drinking singers in his wanting to "stave it off a while" (p. 272). And Richie's fumbling attempts to describe in language his own remembrances of the high notes in his life are doubly revealing. In the first place, his bad memory has warped his discrimination. It is no longer possible for him to recall the beauty in terms of his personal loss; he only remembers how much better the singers of the past were, and he utters the very same superlatives about the boy-tenor Joe Maas as he does later about the voice of the young Simon Dedalus. In the second place, he can find no meaningfully descriptive words to re-create even those secondhand experiences, and his sentences trail off into silences that emphasize this linguistic inadequacy. "Never would Richie forget that night. As long as he lived, never. . . . And when the first note. . . . Never in all his life had Richie Goulding." The time spent in "waiting" can dull the recollection of the original note until a listener like Richie, as Bloom puts it, "rhapsodies about damn all." The staving off of the end becomes a habit, becomes all there is to living. Bloom is Richie's companion in this kind of waiting; still, he does remember the sweetness of love that was answered by the loved one. The song alluded to in his stream-of-consciousness, however, again stresses loss—"How Sweet the Answer *Echo* Makes" (italics mine)—and is called to mind by Richie's whistling of the aria *Tutto è Sciolto* (pp. 272–73).

> All is lost now,
> By all hope and joy am I forsaken.
> Nevermore can love awaken
> Past enchantment, no nevermore.

The theme of vicarious experience is thus reinstated. Boylan is experiencing his love with Molly for the first time, and Bloom will be "living" it with him. There may be no future for the person who waits in this sense, listening to the echoes, except a participation in others' experiences from a distance. When Bloom considers that he might "still hold her back," and then despairs, "Too late. She longed to go. That's why. Woman. As easy stop the sea. Yes: all is lost," he is not considering the danger to Molly, but is anticipating in his empathic imagination the inevitability of loss to all those who have not yet experienced the "climax" of love. He refers especially to Milly: "Innocence in the moon. . . . Brave, don't know their danger. Call name. Touch water. . . . Wise child that knows her father, Dedalus said. Me?" (p. 273). The reference to both "naming" and the recognition of "father" anticipates the development in the third movement of the chapter.

All of the songs sung so far, as well as those alluded to in the interior monologue and inserted as fragments into the conversations in the bar, have jointly constituted a prelude to *"M'appari,"* the climactical song-symbol uniting the motifs of this first long section of the chapter. That Simon Dedalus's rendition, recorded throughout three pages, is meant to be a word-representation of the progression toward sexual orgasm—the seduction ("A chord longdrawn, expectant drew a voice away"), the increasing heat of desire, the swelling, throbbing, flooding and gushing, the outcry of passion—has been noted by many commentators on the Sirens episode. There should be a reminder, however, in this study of the concept of "waiting," that the exposition fastens on the "coming," the suspense and tension. Like the "coming" of sex, and like the high note to which the tenor clings, the high point of one's life is a *held* note—not the last note, but the climax before the end of the song. Bloom, in listening to Simon's sustained "Come!", thinks about the note in terms of a soaring bird *holding* its flight; paradoxically, he says it is "leaping," "swift," "speeding," and he also suggests, in an involuntary plea, that the joy of a moment "of the ethereal bosom" is almost unbearable: "don't spin it out too long long breath he breath long life." Don't make life too long-in-dying? The high note is waiting, hoping, anticipating, "all soaring all around about the all, the endlessnessness." But then, once a climax is achieved, it is gone. The long-in-dying suspension is all there is. The ending words, "To me!", mean consummation, corresponding to the end in store for the sailor who leaps into the sea to respond to the sirens' call (pp. 273–76). Except that the "com-

ing" in a sexual act ironically initiates the longing for a repetition. The paradox of the octaval return is implicitly stated. Beginning calls for an inescapable ending; ending means *da capo,* return to the beginning. When Cowley stops playing, the chords die, but the text says that "the air is made richer" (p. 276), an ambiguous phrase suggesting lingering echoes and also positing the enrichment of an "air" each time it is sung. In the latter reading, we are forced into doubt about the earlier impression that waiting for second, third, and fourthhand repetitions means only a useless perpetuation of death-in-life.

The end of the song, like the end of sexual tension, is a release for both singers and listeners. "But Bloom sang dumb" (p. 276). He does not participate in the aftermath of laughter, play, applause (his hands are crisscrossed and bound), talk, and the activities of drinking, serving, and paying. Of course he has been empathically involved. He alone continues singing without words. A partial release is indicated in his slackening the tension of the rubberband, uncrossing his hands, and absentmindedly stretching and plucking the "catgut thong" to produce a buzzing, twanging "music." There is, for Bloom, a prolongation of that instant of "difference" between the anticipation and the passing of climax, the exact instant when all possibility of *talking* about sexual gratification disappears, when some truth, inexpressible through language, is perceived. Bloom's consciousness, during the singing of that high note, has been submerged in some unfathomable sea. One part of him now listens to Richie's chattering again about climaxes that do not even closely approximate subjective reality; another part listens to the silence: "It's in the silence you feel you hear. . . . Now silent air" (p. 277).

In this mood, Bloom gets "near" to an understanding of the Sirens myth. An unnameable someone or something "Let[s] people get fond of each other; lure[s] them on. Then tear[s] asunder. Death. Explos. Knock on the head. Outtohellout-ofthat. Human life. Dignam" (p. 277). It seems "cruel" to reduce the meaning of life to those bare facts of existence. Dignam is dead; already he is forgotten, and those who are left sing and listen to their own personal desires. I, too, muses Bloom, will be forgotten; I *am* forgotten already in Molly's call to Blazes Boylan. But when Bloom continues to ponder the cruel fatefulness of it all, he realizes that one day Boylan will leave Molly and then she, too, will suffer. Bloom charges Richie, as well, with self-preoccupation. "He doesn't see my mourning. Callous: all for his own gut." The hard, realistic thinking that has pulled Bloom out of the sea onto very dry land has at least snapped his bonds with a "Twang." He may have been listening to the "Grandest number in the whole opera," but if life can be reduced to a mere counting of time through predestined events, then the singing of a musical number that can make you "think you're listening to the ethereal" must be flatly analyzable as a lie covering up the bald fixing of a tune by time (p. 278).

Bloom's consideration of music as numbers is closely associated, in the text, with the theme of the deceptive quality of words. Lidwell and the "first gentleman" try to convince Misses Kennedy and Douce that something is so: "really and truly." The bargirls do not "believe." At the same time, Bloom decides to write Martha a deceptive little letter: "You must believe. . . . It. Is. True." Such protestation is unnecessary when one believes his own words and trusts that the response elicited will be true. Bald deaf Pat brings Bloom a "quite flat pad" on which he will write a few provocative lines in order to "keep it up," even though he has no intention of ever *seeing* Martha. Deceptive language is necessary; a letter written in the abstract language of mathematics would "fall quite flat." Bloom also justifies his deceiving Molly in this teasing exchange of words between himself and Martha. Telling all would be "Useless pain. If they don't *see*" (italics mine). Moreover, he goes to some pains to keep Richie from *seeing* the actual words he is writing, trying to fool Richie into thinking he is answering an ad (pp. 277–79). Bloom's thoughts and actions have implied, then, that if one were really honest he would know that all music and all life is numbers and a tune in time, but one needs to fool himself in words and to think that he is listening to the music of the ethereal in an experience of love.

What Bloom is doing, moreover, is pretending one thing, doing another, and at the same time fooling himself with his own pretenses. Writing words to Martha, he admits, is boring, but he is going to keep it up anyway—stalling, waiting around, "vamping," fooling around, fooling Martha, fooling himself as to what he really wants. Every person in the episode (every person in the

world?) is doing the same sort of thing. Bloom doesn't want Martha. But one has to keep "believing" that he is interested in the person to whom he addresses himself, when, as a matter of fact, he is interested in his own gut, his own desire for something it is impossible for him to get. Certainly Bloom is in this situation. Satisfaction even with Molly would be impossible, although he, like the others, fools himself with the memory of his "first-love" with her. He remembers what he thinks was the "beginning," when Molly seemed to be everything to him. In fact, she is only the chief surrogate for the object of his real desire, which has nothing to do with any available person. That's why a true "return" would only mean death. And the premise leads to the inference that personages to whom one addresses his words of love will not believe. Why should they? Each person knows that his own demand is never satisfied, somehow knows that he is telling himself lies and hearing lies as answers from other persons. Put baldly, a letter or a song that attempts to serve both sides of the gap between desire and one's self-in-the-world-of-others falls quite flat.

In this connection, Bloom, waiting for Pat to return with the quite flat pad and ink, muses about how one gets "lost" in language. He is listening to Cowley's improvising on the piano, a "fooling around" that continues through Bloom's writing of the note to Martha. Bloom says the improvisation "Might be what you like till you hear the words." From then on, it is going to be necessary to "listen sharp" to counteract the "flat" tendency in discourse. Bloom says the *beginning* is all right, but sooner or later the chords are going to sound "a bit off," so that a person feels lost in the "obstacle race" that is the song of his life in time (p. 278). An "improvising intermezzo" allows for a dallying between repeated songs. In this dallying, of which the writing of the letter to Martha is a part, Bloom thinks of Hamlet, through the recollection of Shakespearean clichés: "Music hath charms. . . . To be or not to be." Does one just continue the singing, the listening, the waiting? Or does one choose not to be—choose to speed the striking of the ending chord, the return to the octave? Or would *that* mean Being? In Shakespeare's play, Hamlet hears the Word of his ghost-father—which he may or may not accept—is given a command to act—which he determines to obey if the Word is "true"—and the whole production is constructed upon the variety of ways in which he post-pones action.[4] "Wisdom while you wait," comments Bloom to himself, but in his life that cliché is an irony. For "One life is all. One body. Do. But do." Bloom's "Done anyhow," in all of its meanings, is a bathetic descent from such an existential statement (p. 280) ; he has at least completed the writing of a letter repeating the old, old song of empty words; he is also excusing himself from any responsibility to act because his "dancing days are over," like those of Simon Dedalus; and, finally, he is saying that, while he has been killing time by listening to the intermezzo and writing the letter, it has become too late to prevent the act between Boylan and Molly. The first movement of the episode is over. Time inches along, whether one's mind is on or off the subject. And what is the subject? Who is it? Where is it?

The densest cluster of the word-variations of "waiting" occurs in a paragraph following Bloom's statement of resignation ("Done anyhow"), and is presented in a context that focuses on Pat, the waiter. The section quoted below opens the short transitional movement between the opposing "lures" presented in the first and third movements. The interlude is a dance movement (no songs-with-words are sung), turning our attention from "talk" to "walk."

> Walk now. Enough. . . . Walk. Pat! Doesn't hear. Deaf beetle he is.
> Car near there now. Talk. Talk. Pat! Doesn't. . . . Lot of ground he must cover in the day. Paint face behind on him then he'd be two. Wish they'd sing more. Keep my mind off.
> Bald Pat who is bothered mitred the napkins. Pat is a waiter hard of his hearing. Pat is a waiter who waits while you wait. Hee hee hee hee. He waits while you wait. Hee hee. A waiter is he. Hee hee hee hee. He waits while you wait. While you wait if you wait he will wait while you wait. Hee hee hee hee. Hoh. Wait while you wait. (p. 280)

Significant in this latter paragraph is the repetition of the second- and third-person pronouns, "you" and "he," and the absence of the first-person "subject," "I." In spite of what Bloom says, the songs have not kept his mind off himself; he

has thought of the duet of Boylan and Molly in terms of himself as subject. He has been waiting while Boylan waited in the bar and kept Molly waiting at home. Here again he insists, deceiving himself, that when you're interested in someone else's waiting it "keeps your mind off."

Pat's function in the chapter can now be more closely examined. The transitional passage just quoted says that he neither hears nor talks (nor will he "walk" in response to Bloom's call until the end of this dance movement), and also suggests that he faces two ways, backward and forward. Since the first "Tap" ("Pat" backwards) in the chapter appears on the very next page (p. 281), we can assume that "Pat" is about to present the other face; the contrast between the two commands in the quoted passage—"Walk. Pat! . . . Talk. Pat!"—confirms our expectation of some kind of reversal. ("Tap," of course, is associated with blindness, rather than deafness. The phonic affinities of "sea" and "see"—the latter pertaining to both vision and understanding—are emphasized in this movement.) Now, Pat *does* actually hear; he is only "hard of his hearing," and he can read lips. And he is certainly able to communicate drink- and food-orders. Nevertheless, in this center movement, he stands as a blank—unseeing, unhearing, nonmoving—just folding the napkins between "calls." (Mitering, of course, is in another sense a joining process.)

The language in this entire section trips lightly backward and forward over an emptiness, an absence, an inexplicable gap of which Bloom has already become dimly aware in the aftermath of Simon Dedalus's "Come to me" call. Yet time is not stopped. The minuet that Cowley plays is a hesitating dance—forward, backward—but it is movement in time (p. 282). Lydia is bringing back, in an *empty shell*, an echo from "a gorgeous, simply gorgeous time," and George Lidwell is permitted to listen secondhand to her time; in the shell he too can hear the sea (see). And Bloom, *seeing* the shell at their ears, hears more faintly and from a greater distance what they hear: "the plash of waves, loudly, a *silent* roar" (italics mine). Bloom is, as usual, practical-minded. He says, "The sea [see] they think they hear," but sound and see are in the blood. The blood *is* a sea in a way—"Corpuscle islands"—so that what one hears is within, an unconscious thing that has nothing to do with words or man-made music (p. 281).

The three single taps that help to mark time

---

4. "Word" as Logos, and "ghost-father" as God in spirit form, are intentionally implied here: "In the beginning was the Word, and the Word was with God, and the Word was God. The same was in the beginning with God" (John 1:1, 2). Analogously, *speaking* as given by—indeed, demanded by—the parent language, is the beginning of the acting Self-in-the-world, as opposed to the lost Being of unconscious silence.

in this movement (pp. 281–82) are those of the "seeing" stick belonging to the approaching piano tuner. Bloom, wondering what is music in the non-human world and what is noise, unwittingly contrasts himself with Stephen, for whom the blind tuner is a surrogate. "Never have written it," he says. "My joy is other joy." He can listen, feel, look—like the peasants he imagines looking in on the court dancers of the minuet: "both are joys." "Chamber music" can be made in "empty vessels." Women can't "manage men's intervals," but there is a "gap in their voices too," which calls silently to be filled. One may not be a creator of great music, but one can contribute to the music by being "filled," and, although Bloom may be the empty-vessel character in this novel, he does "play" his part and his "noises" are an important component in the total composition. There is more than one way, then, to "play" and be played upon. Three notes, apparently to be apprehended as struck simultaneously, end this short movement: (1) Bloom decides to *move,* on the slight chance that he can get home "Before"—can "Do. But do"; (2) at this very time, Boylan is presumed to be rapping on the door-of-Molly "with a loud proud knocker, with a cock"; (3) in the same instant, the "tap" of the tuner reminds us that an absent artist ("chamber music" has certainly evoked the ghost-artist, Joyce) can play on empty vessels too (p. 282). He may not *see* them in the way first-lovers claim to see each other; the kind of separation suggested by blindness may aid his perception. He can make music by playing upon the separate keys of each of his characters—and *upon his own words.* If he is skillful, he may even chance upon the lost chord, which for an instant fills with harmonious presence the mysterious absence.

The third movement begins with the call for another song, and with Pat's "returning" to Bloom, without further delay. "He came, he came, he did not stay. To me" (p. 283). The lines resonate with Bloom's querulous comments to himself as the notes of *"M'appari"* died: "She ought to. Come. To me, to him, to her, you too, me, us." The longed-for *absence* Bloom has wanted to personify is here, in the person of Pat, the Janus-faced waiter, presence of an absence. But it is a "he" who came, not the "she" of Bloom's demand. Metempsychosis. A waiter turning two ways.

The purpose of Bloom's signal to Pat was to ask for an accounting: "How much?" The motif of numbers has returned, but with a difference; whereas Simon's tenor voice sang of love in the key of F, one flat, Ben Dollard's bass barreltone will sing of "unlove" in the key of F sharp major, six sharps. From high to low; from light bronze-and-gold to dark "Lumpmusic." "Bob Cowley's outstretched talons gripped the black deepsounding chords," and Bloom, who has said, "I'll go," is gripped by a new fascination. "But wait. But hear." Even in this introduction to darker, heavier imagery, we are reminded that the blind tuner strikes the pitch for both love and war, both tenor and bass; his single tap (a drumbeat, this time, instead of the pure tone of a tuning fork) is inserted in the narrative immediately following a parphrase of lines from the first stanza of the "grave" and "painful" song, "The Croppy Boy": "The priest he sought, with him would he speak a word." Again, the motif of the struggle with language appears in the score. Dollard is "doing his level best to say it," to sing something that is impossible to express in words, which are substituting signifiers for the real subject. It comes out as a "croak of vast manless moonless womoonless marsh" and is doomed to "other *comedown*" (italics mine). In his personal comedown, Ben Dollard, with the "fat of death" on him, is said to have "failed to the tune of ten thousand pounds." So an increase in both numbers and weight gives us the clue to a changed meaning for "waiting." The balance has shifted; indeed, Pat is now weightier, because he's been tipped (by Bloom), and, if he stands for the colon or the blank between the two "life sentences" dealt with in the chapter, his tipping gives weight to a third movement about one-quarter as long as the first (p. 283). The weight of nostalgia has also shifted, from listening man to listening woman. Bloom, watching bronze Lydia, "hypnotised, listening," comments to himself on the "thrill" that "pity" gives women. The deceptive hope that Lydia's *looks* are for him is destined for a "comedown" (p. 284).

"The Croppy Boy" song is a tale with a war setting, but it is about betrayal through a false Father. The seduction to "step in," to "enter a lonely hall," destroys youth in a different way (p. 283). The croppy boy's separation from his mother has imposed upon him a heavy guilt; he "forgot to pray for his mother's rest." (Again, the ghost of Stephen Dedalus enters the chapter.) The ritual of confession takes on symbolic value of a particular sort, for through the medium of words a penitent trusts the Father to remove the anguish of the compulsion to look back. Ironically, this intermediary, the Father, the only one who can shrive, is symbolic of a force whose "inter-dicting" Word has created the gap in undifferentiated Oneness, has imposed the absence, the space between, that can never be bridged—except in death.

Blanks to be filled in for the correct *Answers* in the "poets' picture puzzle" (cf. "obstacle race" in the first movement) relate to this absence delineated in the second wordless movement. Bloom thinks Ben Dollard, though a "bit addled now," has at least a chance of winning, since he's "no eunuch yet." But Ben has already made mistakes. "Bird sitting hatching in a nest" (surely symbolizing the child coming into the new word-world of the self) Ben thought was the "lay of the last minstrel." "See blank tee" puts the feminine "sea" and the "looking" of love on one side of the gap and the T-phallus of the domesticated male on the other. (Culture begins with the acquisition of language.) "Tee dash ar" makes a sailor like Ulysses a "most courageous mariner," for once one sets sail upon the sea of Selfhood, there are a long wait and many harrowing experiences before the Return (p. 283).

And Bloom? It is time for him "to be shoving" (p. 285). There is discomfort, which Bloom unconsciously recognizes, in the song. "I hold this house" (p. 286) is the Word of the Father determining separation and selfhood, and there must be a chordal consent to the "inter-diction." *"Bless me, father,* Dollard the croppy cried. *Bless me and let me go."* Bloom is still "looking," "unblessed to go." He still thinks of Woman as the "Goddess I didn't see." If he could ventriloquise, think in his stomach, he wouldn't need the words that he cannot say: "Will? You? I. Want. You. To." He has just congratulated himself that he did not sign the letter to Martha (p. 285). That would have meant an assumption of identity, for naming helps create believable identities in the word-world. (The refusal of the barmaids, in the first movement, to believe the tankards' seductive words regarding an unnamed phantom of "love" is reversed, in this movement, to the tankards' acceptance of and belief in the *naming* of Ben Dollard by Misses Kennedy and Douce: pp. 287–88.) Martha has admired the name *Henry Flower,* but this is not his own name. Does Leopold Bloom have an identity? He has wilily avoided signing either name, doubly skirting the issue of selfhood.

Bloom will "get out before the end." He thought he could make things come together—for instance, in the ad he was going to get depicting crossed keys—but he now decides that such a quest will have to wait. We are back to the theme of Bloom's avoidance, of keeping unconscious whatever it is that has almost surfaced. So Bloom stands up and passes by the both-eared, two-faced Pat in the doorway (p. 286). He wants to get outside of the bar, partly to get "shut of" the things that have accumulated internally. The wind that he must let escape is wound round now inside, a counterpart to the rubber band that was earlier wound round his fingers. The ambiguity of his near-perception is expressed in a split sentence with two subjects: "Her hand that rocks the cradle rules the. Ben Howth. That rules the world" (p. 288). Whether it's the Mother-sea or the Father-mountain that rules the world is still a problem for Bloom.

Our wanderer has already been far removed, in one respect, in the dining room of the bar, but now, from an even farther vantage point, he can look with more skepticism upon the music that has held him and from which he has barely escaped. His farther and farther removal from the bar is countered, in the text, by the tuner's approaching closer and closer. The single tap struck at intervals during the second movement has increased to two and then three by the time Bloom passes out the door (p. 286). The number of taps will increase in this coda from four to five (a musical fifth) and then to eight (the octave), before their reduction to silence (p. 289). As each of these two character-components proceeds in opposing directions, Bloom's "Far. Far. Far. Far" is immediately followed by the tuner's "Tap. Tap. Tap. Tap" (p. 288). Analogously, as Joyce's character, Bloom, avoids the "truth," the artist, Joyce, gets closer and closer to it, *through* Bloom's experience, even through Bloom's noise-music, a kind of travesty of the sentimental songs, which are themselves parodies of something the artist struggles to say through empty vessels like Bloom; signifiers substitute for signifiers in an attempt to "get it out in bits."

At this significant point, Bloom talks to himself about an organist he once knew who wasted time all day at the organ, talking to himself (or to his "server" waiting on him at the bellows). The allusion, in Bloom's silent mutterings, to another song, "The Lost Chord," is of some consequence in the final blending of all the elements of the episode (p. 288). The words are important.

> Seated one day at the organ,
> I was weary and ill at ease,
> And my fingers wandered idly
> Over the noisy keys.
> I knew not what I was playing
> Or what I was dreaming then;
> But I struck one chord of music,
> Like the sound of a great Amen,
> Like the sound of a great Amen.

Hands "maundering" over the "noisy" keys, the artist-improviser strikes by chance a "lost" chord, *like* a "great Amen," the absent Word. (Cf. Stephen's cry: "Tell me the word, mother. . . . The word known to all men": p. 581.) This is how Joyce's craft is transcended, how the mythological level is evoked through familiar songs sung by ordinary people engaged in trivial pursuits, people depicted by the artist as unable to apprehend any universal meaning in their song-lives and doomed to search forever for the lost chord. It is up to the artist to blend all of these notes which, by chance, cross each other, until, by chance, the lost chord is struck. Joyce's craft depends upon the same thing language depends upon: a structure, a code that precedes him, into which he is born; and an opportunity for unlimited creativity within the structure. All a writer has to work with is language, but fortunately, as every sentence is open-ended, every utterance a new creation, so is a work of art a "sentence" that is never the last word. One of the titles given to the "letter" in *Finnegans Wake* is *The Suspended Sentence;* it encompasses the idea of tension, waiting, open-endedness, but it also suggests that the time of one's life is a suspension of the death sentence pronounced at birth. There is an octaval return in every person's death, but human life is historically open-ended; therefore, the *da capo* sign stands for cyclical return— in music, in artistic creativity, in human desire, in the struggle for selfhood, and in historical perpetuity. Joyce *relies* upon formal improvisation to hit upon the archetypal chord, which may then be found again in another improvisation by striking other notes and chords. Resolution is only temporary. There is other music to come, for *time* continues; it is not used up in any single composition. Thus history may be repeated, but always with a difference.

Bloom's last act in The Sirens is to demonstrate *his* open-endedness in a fart. His octaval "epitaph" matches the *eight* last words of Robert Emmet— "Let my epitaph be written; I have done"—and follows his thoughts about Meyerbeer's oratorio commemorating the *seven* last words of Christ. (penultimate "seventh"). The word "coming" is reiterated; what is coming now is Bloom's fart. The life of this particular composition is done, and Bloom has done all he is going to do: wait and "blow," set himself free from the whole damn business. At any rate, there is a temporary end of tension in the "Done" (p. 291). Certainly it is important that Bloom has been the agent for our hearing most of the music in this chapter, for he is the promoter, the ad man. He is not the person who writes either the ad or the score; he is rather the diaphane or diaphone (the played-upon organ) through which the crossed keys or the music is given. He passes on unscathed, because there is no finish for Bloom. If his final epitaph is to come only "When my country takes her place among. . . . Nations of the earth," it will never be written, for Jews have no nation. He is the Wandering Jew, the one who typifies the over-and-over-again return, with no final resolution. If Bloom and Stephen do resonate in a single-key empty octave, Joyce reminds us through The Sirens, and through the entire novel as well, that such an emptiness constitutes neither a grand denouement in a novel nor a great chord; it only means the announcement of a new variation on an old theme: "Done. Begin." For it takes other notes between, alternating with "gaps," to make a chord. A perfect octave is two open notes, sounding as one, waiting to be filled. The "lost chord" requires more than two octaval notes sounded simultaneously; it must strike the harmony of a humanity that includes both notes and gaps, presence and absence.

Analysis of this chapter in terms of structural production-in-time makes lengthy summarization unnecessary. All indicators point to Mother, in the broadest sense, as the siren of the first long movement; and to Fatherhood, in the sense of full acquisition of the Word, as the opposing lure in the third, heavier movement. The dance movement in the center, with its backward-forward hesitation, emphasizes the "subject" of the episode as the lost One in conflict with constituted selfhood. The Coda presents the open-endedness, the nonresolution of Desire. Simon Dedalus, contemplating the "last sardine of summer" (male image) on a "bier of bread," has apparently given up Fatherhood, but still will go on singing songs recall-

ing the "last rose of summer" (female image).
Bloom escapes final confrontation. His two desires
—"I feel I want . . ." and "wish I could"—are separated in the text by the eight taps of the octave.
If he just had a "wonderworker" that would work
a miracle for him! Another possibility is litigation
—some legal way to make people "love one another" (p. 289). His only alternative is to "wait,"
to keep the matter unresolved.

Sirens are fictional characters; *real* mother and
real father in this reading are also phantoms, not
to be confused with the dilemma of the true "subject." Each surrogate is a substitution for a truth
that cannot be made conscious. The "hoofirons"
ring from a *vice-regal* cavalcade, not from the original Royal Family. Martha is a phantom-substitute
for Molly. Her mermaid-address is "Dolphin's
Barn Lane"; she can be reached through the post-
office, through a "letter," but she is not apprehended in real life. "Looking" comes closer than a letter; still, Molly's eyes are all Bloom can see over
the sheet; it seems impossible to "find the way in."
But Molly is a surrogate too. Sex is a phantom of
primal union; one finds his way in momentarily,
perhaps, for the phallus is another "letter" (im-
printed forever), symbolizing the impossible consummation of Desire. One is always "coming" or
going; one never arrives, except to "die" and then

to return. For Truth disappears in language, and
the speech of demand is always the broken Word
of unfulfilled Desire. What remains, then, is the
"letter" (with the fart-expulsion, the one other
thing that is "done" in this episode). The image
prefigures the letter of *Finnegans Wake,* the putting into language and its gaps all the things that
one can enumerate yet cannot say about himself;
it is a letter expressing the inability ever to fully
bridge the gap in discourse, the Word that means
the constitution of self-in-the-world.

If someone wants to ask me whether or not
Joyce was "consciously" aware of this subject underlying the structure of *Ulysses* and *Finnegans
Wake,* I will have to state frankly that I don't
know. Certainly Joyce seems to know what he is
doing in drawing the associations between sea-see
and Mother, Word-hear and Father, in Stephen's
stream-of-consciousness in the Proteus episode. But
even there I believe his craft is transcended. Structural analysis shows that "the search for the father" in *Ulysses* is more than just a plot-theme.
For the writer-artist, full establishment in the fa-
ther-word-world of language is a weighty aspira-
tion, and, although we may say that Joyce has attained it in the writing of *Ulysses,* it is evident
that he still knows the meaning of suspension in
all lived experience.

7

The Aesthetics of Joyce: James Joyce and His Fingernails

Nathan Halper

"THE ARTIST, like the God of creation, remains within or behind or beyond or above his handiwork, invisible, refined out of existence, indifferent, paring his fingernails." Taken out of context, these words are misinterpreted. This leads to misunderstanding the Stephen who speaks and the Joyce who writes them.

A Portrait is a novel. Autobiographical—nonetheless a novel. What Stephen says in his lecture on aesthetics does not correspond to his words in *Stephen Hero*. And what he says in that early version is not a literal transcription of what young Joyce actually said to his companions. The writer of *A Portrait* has not only improved on life. He has improved on the improvement.

One may think that, in its final version, the talk is a Platonic form: that it is a realization of what a younger Joyce was awkwardly trying to express; that it is nothing less than a definitive statement of his aesthetic creed.

But is it also the belief of the writer of *A Portrait?* Or is he writing of a phase he has outgrown? of opinions that have been discarded? As he said to Budgen, this is a portrait of the artist as a *young man;* he had not let the young man off lightly.

His view of Stephen is ambiguous. To the writer of *The Dead,* the young man in Dublin can only seem inferior. Yet he must see in him the seed of what Stephen's model, he himself, has become. The more his self-esteem tells Joyce how much he's grown, the more gifted potentially the young man must be.

What happens is presented as it appears to Stephen. It is shaped by his feeling for self-dramatization. There is no explicit comment on the part of an omniscient writer. But he chooses and arranges the events. An account is qualified by some passage or passages that he has quietly inserted elsewhere.

Take the end of the fourth chapter: the scene on the beach when Stephen realizes that he's going to become an artist. The reader is moved by Stephen's exaltation, by his sense of moving into a new world. It is only later that a reader may notice that this scene is only one in a series and that a part of its meaning lies in the series as a whole.

In an early chapter, the boy is "angry with himself for being young and the prey of restless foolish impulses." He wants "to meet in the real world the unsubstantial image which his soul so constantly beheld." "They would be alone . . . he would be transfigured. Weakness and timidity and inexperience would fall . . . in that magic moment."

In the arms of his first whore, he finds such a "moment." ("He had suddenly become strong and fearless and sure of himself.") However, it does not solve his problems; the introduction to sex only brings some new ones.

The scene on the beach is another of these meetings. His dedication to art—whatever else it is—is an attempt by Stephen to get the importance, the fulfillment, that he lacks.

Up to this point, he is acted on. (He is affected by a whore, a sermon about hell, a quarrel of grown-ups at a Christmas dinner.) Now that Stephen knows he will be an artist, a new element is added. In the last chapter he becomes the leading performer. He is trying to create an image. The phrases he composes are the material he uses.

The show-piece of the chapter is the lecture on aesthetics. It is part of a pattern of three conversations, Davin, Lynch, and Cranly. Davin: nationality. Cranly: religion. Between them, at length—like the center-panel of a triptych—they talk about aesthetics.

In the first and last of these conversations, the others take a side to which Stephen is attracted. He is debating with himself. This is what he is doing in his talk to Lynch. But where the others are proponents of what he is trying to reject, here it is Stephen who proposes what he is trying to accept. He is trying to convince himself.

Joyce makes the talk especially persuasive. He gives Stephen a serenity he does not have elsewhere. He gives him memorable phrases. When Lynch interrupts, his remarks are coarse and trivial. That Stephen is heckled by a man of lower sensibility makes what Stephen says the more radiant by contrast.

While Stephen speaks of art removed from loathing or desire, of an artist who, ideally, is not involved in the problems and demands of the human condition, his immediate environment, or his own personality, Lynch is saying that the words have a "scholastic stink"; that Ireland is no place in which to talk of "beauty"; that he needs a "job of five hundred a year." He is saying in effect that, for all his talk, Stephen still is bound. He has not escaped the problems or demands.

These are thoughts that have occurred to Stephen. They are thoughts he is trying to ignore.

At the end of the lecture, when they pass E. C., Lynch addresses Stephen: "Your beloved is here." Stephen's mind is "emptied of theory and courage." A few pages later, there is another comment. Stephen writes a poem, a *Villanelle of the Temptress*. He is not yet ready. With all his talk of art

that is timeless, this example is in the fashion of that moment. With its weary sinfulness, allusion to ritual, hints of adoration and blasphemy, it sounds like a parody of the "esthetic" poets who were considered "modern" near the end of the last century.

His words in the lecture are also inconsistent with the thoughts that he expresses—with an equal fervor—both before and after. "To live, to err. . . ." "I will try to express myself in some mode of life or art as freely as I can and as wholly as I can." "Welcome, O life! I go to encounter for the millionth time the reality of experience."

There are also comments in the pattern itself. There is a correspondence between the forms of art, lyric, epic, and dramatic, which Stephen mentions in his lecture and the sequence of his conversations.

The talk with Davin occurs in the morning. It is full of words like "first." It alludes to youth and birth. Davin is youthful—"simple." His way of speech is "innocent." He believes in "heart." The individual should listen to his heart. Yet all hearts are similar. The individuals should join in a common cause.

He may feel that Stephen is too much in the "mind." However, by and large, Stephen is emotional too. (He speaks "with cold violence." "A tide began to surge beneath the calm surface of his friendliness.") When he says, "You sold him to the enemy," or that Ireland is the "sow that eats her farrow," his reply to Davin's passion is equally impassioned.

The scene with Davin reflects the lyrical form. It anticipates the words Stephen will use in describing this form. "The simplest verbal vesture of an instant of emotion," a "cry such as ages ago cheered on the man who pulled at the oar." (The word *man* is singular. He is an individual. Yet—as Davin would desire—the *man* is engaged in communal activity.)

The talk with Cranly is at night. It turns to age and death—"the day of judgement."

Cranly speaks of what is owed to a social group or institution. There is no warmth for humanity as such. He scorns the individual—his ambition or ideas. ("Idiot." "Pothead." "Every jackass going the roads thinks he has ideas." "Pascal was a pig." Jesus, a "blackguard.") His world narrows down to himself and Stephen.

As in his talk with Davin, there is underlying emotion. But the emphasis is different. Stephen speaks "hotly." ("A bloody excitable man.") But, after awhile he begins to speak with "assumed carelessness." He prepares "words neatly in his mind." His remarks become like Cranly's. They are indirect, cerebral, and casuistical. There is talk about a conscious hypocrisy. Stephen mentions "cunning."

At the end of their dialogue, we learn of Cranly's emotion. He assumes a role, behavior that does not show this. Detached, solitary, he is a parody of Stephen's "God of creation." He often uses phrases "as if he wished his hearer to understand they were used by him without conviction." Stephen listens to "the unspoken speech behind the words." He "began to clean the crevice between two teeth." (Instead of paring his nails.) He has a "loneliness" he fears.

He has "a raw smile which some force of will strove to make finely significant." This is a parody of the artistic process itself. It's what happens when the artist moves into the dramatic form.

The talk with Cranly is about the future. The talk with Davin is about the past. The talk to Lynch—about the eternal present. Symbolically, it is held near the middle of the day.

It is full of the first person. ("I say." "I speak." "I use." "I dislike.") This while expounding a theory that explicitly rejects intrusion of the personality.

Stephen speaks of what "is grave and constant in human sufferings." Of pity and terror: how they unite the mind with the sufferer or cause. Then he rejects the unity, the cause, the suffering—the "human sufferer." He seeks a principle of beauty that will satisfy the Greek, the Turk, the Chinese, as well as the Hottentot and Copt. He comes to an elitist God, "indifferent, paring his fingernails," who has no relationship to the Greek—or Hottentot—with whom the quest for a theory began.

The talk to Lynch—the second member of a triad: between Davin and Cranly, between morning and night, between the past and future—is between the lyric and dramatic.

The talk to Lynch—the lecture on aesthetics—

reflects the epical form. Is this a way of saying that it is the form most suitable for art? that it is the highest of the forms? It is commonly believed that the book is saying that the highest form is the dramatic.

It does not say it. Joyce is like a stage magician. He puts his cards on the table, but uses misdirection so that we do not see them. He builds an illusion. He induces us to see what is not physically there.

He has Stephen say that art "divides into three forms progressing from one to the next." The word "progressing" may or may not mean that there is an improvement. But when Stephen uses the similar "progress" and "progresses" and continues with such words as "refines" and "purified," this helps to give the impression that, in Stephen's mind, the progression of the forms is a ladder of perfection—rising till it takes the artist up to its topmost rung: to "the God of creation." This impression is confirmed by the last few words, the much-quoted image about his fingernails.

The image is gratuitous. The point it is making has already been made. This is a flourish, a theatrical effect, used to sway the listener by means extraneous to the argument *per se*.

One may think that the image is appropriate: a dramatic image used in describing the dramatic form. But this image is dramatic in the sense of melodramatic, not in the sense Stephen uses in the lecture.

Instead of being limited to the logic of his words, instead of depending on the denotation of his words, he exploits the overtones. He has evoked an atmosphere of impersonal aloofness. But to do this he has turned to personal statement. To paint the dramatic—to make the form vivid—he turns to the lyrical.

> I, a God of creation,
> Indifferent, paring my fingernails . . .

It could well be the beginning of a poem.

"Progress," I have noted, is no more than "moving." A rise, a fall, or a combination of both. The pattern of "progress" may be that of an arch: the high point is in the middle. Thus, youth "progresses" to old age, morning to night; high noon is between them.

Such a pattern is used for the sequence of conversations. The second—the conversation about art—is the most important of the triad. Its subject is the important subject.

Indeed, such a pattern is consistent with what is stated or implied about art itself in other portions of *A Portrait*. The artist is the central figure. He is a priest who transmutes. He mediates. He re-creates one kind of life into another.

"The image . . . must be set between the mind or senses of the artist himself and the mind or senses of others." In the lyrical form, "the artist presents his image in immediate relation to himself"; in the dramatic, "in immediate relation to others." The epical is the form in which "he presents his image in mediate relation to himself and to others."

That is, the epical is described by Stephen in terms that correspond to those which he uses for the process as a whole. By analogy (by all of the above analogies) this says the epical form is the one that is characteristic. It is the paradigm of art.

It has not lost the force of the original material. It is gathering the skills that may direct this force. It is the area of fullness. The dramatic, like the lyrical, is only an attenuation. Each is the negation of a quality that is an element of art.

Stephen wishes "to discover the mode of life or of art whereby his spirit could express itself in unfettered freedom." The lecture makes it appear that Stephen has found it. This is not the case. One or two days later, he is still looking—"I will try to express myself in some mode of life or art as freely as I can and as wholly as I can."

The dramatic form—as defined by Stephen—lends itself to the belief that it is the highest of the forms. If Stephen seems to promise he will be a worker in this form, the promise is enough to put him at the pinnacle of art. Further, this form rejects all personal involvement. If Stephen is afraid that he is not able to cope with the problems he encounters (he is too small: they are too big) this enlarges the one and diminishes the others.

He is seeing himself as a writer in that form. His lecture, *inter alia*, is a way of cheering himself on. When he builds his theory, it is equally a matter of building his own courage. (This is in the future. He is draping himself in a mantle that is not yet his; for his present purpose, the anticipation is enough.)

But the reason why this choice is attractive is the very reason why Stephen cannot take it. This role loses sight of why a role is needed. He forgets the wholeness, freeness, of his self-expression.

In his fealty to art, he scants its consort, life. It becomes irrelevant. (It will wither away before the primacy of art.) He fences art itself into an exiguous corner. It is hemmed in with taboos. It's allowed to touch only what is worthy of it.

If, as Stephen knows, he is hampered by "weakness and timidity and inexperience," it is not by evasion. It is by facing these and the mistakes they bring him that he will come to self-realization. "I am not afraid to make a mistake," he says.

He does not say it in the lecture. (He knows his vulnerability; he does not underestimate the pain that he will feel when growing.) The lecture is a daydream. It dwells on future triumph, blocking out the precondition of his having to earn it.

When in the lecture he says that the aesthetic process moves into the dramatic form, it follows from the definitions. But on this occasion he gives it an implication that is not intrinsically there.

The book is so constructed that this implication is what a reader will remember. (The dramatic form. The enthroning of that form. The exaltation—indeed, *apotheosis*—of the writer in that form!)

This is contradicted. The importance of that form is continually undercut. But—the implication is overt. ("Indifferent, paring his fingernails.") The contradictions are presented in a more covert fashion.

Why the misdirection?

Why is a theory of art (whatever it is worth) inserted, like a roadblock, into the flow of the narration? If the theory is not authentic, what—*a fortiori*—is it doing in the novel?

The young man has decided that he will be an artist. He tells his thoughts about aesthetics. This has a biographical aspect. The James Joyce of approximately 1902 had some similar notions. (We are able to trace back a number of the phrases.) However, this is not enough to justify their presence. *A Portrait* is a novel. The lecture has a purpose that is novelistic. The thoughts are proper to the character, the speaker. The lecture about art is an objective correlative of Stephen's personal condition. It is a manifestation of his energy and fervor: of a desire to dedicate himself to something, a desire to make use of the new forces in himself; to adapt these forces to the outside world; to bend this world to the forces in himself; to be portentous; to be serious about himself.

The James Joyce of approximately 1912—living in Trieste, father of a family, a breadwinning employee, a man engaged in writing instead of talking about writing—has a different perspective. He has second thoughts about what Stephen has been saying. He gets them into the novel.

They are not only a comment on the young man's notions. They have a function in the novel. They are a putting into words (into covert words) of Stephen's own suspicions, his own reservations.

It is like a dream. (Early Joyce—beginning with *Dubliners*—looks forward to *Finnegans Wake*.) The manifest level is what Stephen wants to see, what he tries to project. On the latent there is insecurity, a knowledge that he is not ready. There is the feeling that his role is inadequate. The goal he has adopted is not what he really wants.

There is also the reader. At first, he sees by means of Stephen's sensibility. Stephen is trying to persuade himself. The reader is persuaded. He takes Stephen at what is, apparently, Stephen's own valuation.

In time, he sees a different Stephen. He becomes aware of weakness that was always there. As in *The Good Soldier* or the *Alexandria Quartet*, he faces an amended version. But, in *A Portrait*, it is not a case of the reader getting a new pair of glasses from the author. It is rather that his eyes have become accustomed to the conditions of the novel. New shapes come out of the background. It is rather that the reader is older, more experienced. He knows more about the world, about young people, about would-be writers.

The changes in the reader are a functional part of the novel. The meaning of the novel consists of all the changes.

The reader begins to feel even more at home in *A Portrait*. He has a newer perspective. (The reader grows with Stephen.)

The Stephen of the lecture is pretentious. The lecture is specious. "The young Emperor is naked." But he is eloquent. The lecture *is* impressive. "O what beautiful new clothes the Emperor will have tomorrow!"

Stephen (Joyce?) may become an artist. He may be the writer of *A Portrait*.

8

Interview with Carola Giedion-Welcker
June 15, 1973
Burlington Hotel, Dublin

The following interview was taped during dinner at the Burlington Hotel, Dublin. Those present were Mrs. Giedion, Fritz Senn, Mabel Worthington, Robert Boyle, S.J., Mary Power, and Kathleen McGrory, all of whom were in Dublin to participate in the Fourth International James Joyce Symposium. Edited by Kathleen McGrory.

KM Did Joyce ever speak Irish or any words in Irish when he was with you and your husband in Zurich?

G-W Only in songs. He did sing Irish songs, for example, "The Girl in the Red Petticoat." I can't find that song. I bought a book of songs, looking for the "Red Petticoat," but I cannot find it.

KM Only the chorus of that song, "Shule Agra," is in Gaelic. Did Joyce sing the whole song in Gaelic, or only the chorus?

G-W No, he didn't sing it in Gaelic. He sang in English. It was on Christmas evening. First James and Giorgio Joyce sang a very solemn song—a Church song—and then at the end "The Red Petticoat" came, sung by Joyce alone.

KM Did they ever go to a Midnight Mass at Christmastime?

G-W Oh, Nora went to church always. Nora did.

KM Someone has said that Joyce, with his enormous love of music, did not have the same appreciation for visual art.

G-W No, not the modern things.

KM But of painting in general—did he ever speak of specific paintings?

G-W I used to go with him to galleries, looking at things—exhibitions in Zurich, at the Kunsthaus—

where we went through and looked at the pictures. But he didn't have the modern taste.

KM But he did like Renoir, you mentioned earlier.

G-W Yes. His favorite was the little girl with the ball. He liked to see Renoir—soft things, soft landscapes. But not Cubism or Picasso. Although he regretted afterwards that Picasso had not illustrated his book, *Ulysses;* Matisse illustrated it. And I asked him, "Why did you take Matisse?" I love Matisse, but I don't think his illustrations are so impressive. And he said, "If I had to do it again, I would like Picasso. I took Matisse because he is a Mediterranean." But Picasso is also a Mediterranean. But more aggressive, of course.

KM You sometimes hear it said that the Irish have little appreciation of visual art, that they are more attuned to music and verbal arts rather than painting and sculpture. But I wonder whether Joyce's poor eyesight might not explain why he preferred "soft landscapes" rather than works requiring much visual concentration?

G-W No, he didn't like the *mentality* of certain modern painters and their "abstract methods." Once I had him together with Arp, Jean Arp, and they didn't speak a word. But when Max Ernst, the Surrealist, came, Joyce was thrilled. I had bought a big picture of Max's, which Joyce liked very much. It was called, "Europe après la pluie." It was only a land-card,* which was crazy—it becomes crazy, you know? First you look at it and say, "Ah, it's the Mediterranean. No, it's the Caucasus—no,

---

* I.e., a relief.

no, it's this or that!" Max wanted to show, as early as 1933, what was coming when Hitler would come to power. The whole world, "Europe après la pluie." Hitler will have changed the whole world when he gets at it, "after the rain." And Joyce was thrilled. Those two men got along marvelously. Max Ernst played word games and all sorts of things with him—not optically, no visual problems —but word problems. Hassan* was the first one I have heard make a relationship between visual art—the collage he spoke about—and Joyce. He was absolutely right. Do you know the work of Schwitters? We have one of the greatest Schwitters collages that exists. He is for me a parallel to Joyce in what he does with the rubbish of everyday life and transforms it in composition. Perhaps today the young people want to see more of the psychological elements in literary art. They don't want comparisons with visual art. Is this true of your students?

KM No, I find our students equally interested in the visual arts and the psychological elements in Joyce. Last year, for example, one Master's candidate wrote her thesis on Joyce and Picasso. By the way, is your new book available in America?

G-W My scripta?** It is published by Dumont in Cologne. It's a selection of my articles on Joyce, Arp, Picasso, Brancusi, Ernst, Schwitters, and others, written from 1926 to 1971.

KM Did Joyce know Schwitters?

G-W No, he was dead then.

KM But Joyce did know the Ernst relief, "Europe après la Pluie"?

G-W Oh yes. He spoke about it with Max, the painter, when I brought them together at my home for tea. "Europe après la pluie" was what they spoke about, and Joyce made a puzzle out of it—a word puzzle. Max was terribly happy. I have the puzzle. I'll send it to you. It was a wordplay made out of "Europe après la pluie"—he turned it over another way and made a pun.***

KM But he liked the painting itself?

G-W Oh, he adored that. He loved it, because it was for him a stimulant to make a wordplay, of course.

KM Did it seem to you that Joyce, looking at some-thing like the Max Ernst relief, liked best those paintings that gave him an inspiration for word-play?

G-W Yes. He never asked about the Schwitters. He sat under his collage and played the piano, but do you think he would ever look at Schwitters? But he looked at this thing of Max Ernst and made a wordplay. This he liked. He made a puzzle out of it. No, he never asked about Schwitters. There was an Arp there, too. And Arp himself was there once. Those two sat more or less silent next to each other.

KM They never talked?

G-W One word, two words, then no more.

KM What was Joyce looking for in a person when he met him? Why would it be that Max Ernst appealed to him immediately but Arp did not? Was it personality?

G-W Yes, a sense for the ironic, lightness. Not too much involved in their own problems. He had enough of those in his own life. Arp, too, was like that—deep in his own problems. He was a poet and was once a Dadaist.

KM Your new book contains the articles you wrote on Joyce?

G-W Yes, only articles, a selection of articles since 1926. I had enough time to write. But not the biographies on Brancusi or Arp, Klee and modern sculpture: these were the works with which America helped me, to publish them in English. Wittenborn—he's marvelous. One of the most charming editors I ever had. And then Abrams. You know Abrams? He did the Arp monograph in English. It exists in English and German. In the *Schriften,* instead of that silly photograph of me on the back cover, I wanted the portrait Schwitters did of me. You can imagine how he makes a portrait of a woman! But only my head and shoulders—then he put a lot of papers on my head. You don't see my eyes. It's a very funny picture, a collage. And he wrote under it, "To Carola Giedion-Welcker, a readymade poet 1947." I have a quill pen in my hand and appear to be writing. It's so funny. I wanted that instead of the photograph. But I was told that on the *réclame* part, the advertisement, I can't interfere. Today we are in *Naturalisme* again, I have been told, in photo-reproductions. You, too, in America. That is why they put a photograph on the bookjacket. Those on the cover are very nice, introducing all the artists who are treated in the volume. But not my photo. It looks so arrogant.

---

* Ihab Hassan (University of Wisconsin, Milwaukee).

** *Schriften. Stationem zu einem Zietbild 1926–1971* von Carola Giedion-Welcker. ("Scripta. Stages of an Epoque," trans. supplied by C. Giedion-Welcker.)

*** "Europe — Purée — Pyorrhée" (Letter from Mrs. Giedion-Welcker, 27 September 1973).

KM In the future, possibly you could have the Schwitters collage as a frontispiece in another book. That would be nice. What did you think of recent discussions of the word *post-modern?*

G-W Yes, that word has been so attacked. *Post-modern,* that is a dangerous word.

KM It seems to be a nonconcept word, or as Fritz Senn says, a nonword, a copping out. Do you happen to have any of the portraits of Joyce done by his contemporaries?

G-W No. He liked Augustus John very much. We saw it at the National Gallery. His painting of Joyce's father was always hanging in the sitting room in Paris over the desk. If his suicide occurred in the 30s then Joyce must have heard about it.

KM Joyce seems to have been very much affected by the deaths of people he felt close to.

G-W Oh yes. Nora told me about the effect of her mother's death on him. [Thomas] McGreevy told me that he was so terribly shaken when his father died. But also when the mother of Nora in Galway passed away—she was nearly 90—and they heard about it when they were in France, down in Saint-Gérand-le-Puy. And Nora told me, "I was sad and cried, but Jim—Jim was broken down for three days."

KM He must have been a deep-hearted man as regards people he really liked.

G-W Yes. He didn't show it.

KM He didn't show it? Was he very reserved and cool?

G-W Madame Jolas says the same thing. We both knew him, she since 1927, I since 1928. All the time—with my husband, with me, with the children, he would never use the Christian name. Madame Jolas said no one would ever dare say "Jim" to him. In America you very quickly use the Christian name. But he was reserved.

KM Some of the Irish have a certain reserve, a great need for privacy. You see it in the fences around their homes, the gates they put up. They are outspoken in company, but once they retreat to their homes they become very private people. Bob Boyle likes to quote Joyce's line, "Every Irishman's home is his coffin."

G-W But they are so nice in the street, they are like clowns. I think that is so marvelous. In Switzerland we are so strict. Here they help you and they laugh. I came in a taxi and the driver said, "What a marvelous hat you have! Can't I marry you?" I said, "You can marry the hat." "No," he said, "you and the hat—that is one thing." Never in Switzerland would somebody make such a joke. I think

it's marvelous. In Switzerland and Germany on *Fastnacht,* (the carnival before Lent), that's a different thing. Then they are all *dénoués.* They kiss on the streets. In Cologne, too. But once a year only.

KM Did Joyce show real affection? Did he hug and kiss friends?

G-W Not that, but he was full of empathy—you know: my child was once sick with an illness of the glands. But nobody knew that it was glands. They thought perhaps she had a tumor. Joyce immediately gave me books about glands and said, "Oh that's another thing entirely, that's another affair." Then he went to Paris and didn't tell me that he was working for me. He went and visited *the* doctor for glands, La Fagulière was the great man at that time. And then suddenly I received a card saying, "I've arranged everything for you. You can come with your daughter to Fagulière. He will accept you." Then another card came a day later: "You don't need to come. I spoke with him and have a man in Zurich"—he mentioned a doctor in Zurich who was just in the same line as he. He should treat my daughter. Professor W. Löffler. He did all that very quickly and accurately. But of course he thought perhaps Lucia and my daughter were alike. But it was nothing mental with my daughter; it was purely a gland affair; puberty was for Joyce an illness. He always wrote, "How is she doing? Is she better?" He had time and interest for that.

KM He seems to have been an extraordinarily good father.

G-W To his children, always. Enormously. In regard to others, I used to hear him speak of Pound. He excused Pound always. He said, "Pound was a great, great help to me all my life." Practical help, I think; Pound helped him with money and everything, and put him in the *Little Review.* He was terribly grateful to Pound. Once he had a Saint Patrick's evening in Paris, and there was Pound. I was invited—I was alone in Paris. And we danced! You know Joyce danced only solo dances. You couldn't dance with him. Afterwards, Joyce asked me, "How did you like dancing with him?" —with Pound. And I said, "As a man, he's not so terribly attractive, and the dancing didn't go so well." Joyce said, "Now don't you underestimate that man!"—and he had a sermon—a sermon on Pound and his *qentillezza.*

KM He was afraid you didn't think enough of him. You must have been a good dancer yourself.

G-W Yes, I was a good dancer. And Joyce danced

marvelously. But not with another person. He drove the partner crazy. He jumped kicking his legs in the air one evening in our house. He had an old-fashioned straw hat, trimmed, with a crown on it, in the style of the 90s, I think. We all went home to my place; Mr. Jolas was there, too,—and we began to dance. Joyce had a solo dance. He took off his hat and danced with his feet against it until it was full of holes. And the *équilibre!* He was like a—clown, and his *équilibre* was enormous! And all this with his bad sight!

KM Perhaps his equilibrium was good because of his bad sight. I once tutored a blind child who liked to turn in circles to Handel's *Water Music* without ever losing her balance—semicircular canals and balance control.

G-W Is that so? That's very interesting. I always admired that especially because he didn't see so well, but it may be because he didn't see so well. He was not a man who posed as a poet. He was just for fun.

KM Was he graceful?

G-W Enormously. Look at that picture, how he stands there. Isn't that a graceful man? I took his photo. Isn't it elegant? Here is another, taken when we were making a trip to Luzerne—Nora, myself, Joyce, and a friend of ours. My husband took that picture. I still have his walking stick at my house.

KM Would you consider Nora a beautiful woman?

G-W Her complexion was beautiful. She was a ripe woman when I knew her, you know—about 50—but she had a complexion and hair a little gray already, but so fluffy. And she told me how to brush my hair—she had a woman's trick for everything.

KM She was a *real* woman?

G-W Yes, she was. There Joyce looks more like a blind person. How he holds himself there—that is a tragic photo.

KM He certainly suffered.

G-W Yes. Never said a word. In that photograph he looks very elegant, with his coat over his shoulders. Once in Paris we went to the opera. He took me to a Verdi because his friend Sullivan was singing.

KM Oh yes, Mr. Sullivan came to one of the Joyce Society meetings in New York, where I met him.

G-W Did you? *Did* you? Is he still alive? Oh, Joyce adored Sullivan.

KM I believe he is, but I'm really not sure. He told about going with Joyce, after the opera, into a little café and singing there. Joyce would ask Sullivan to sing certain arias, and then would join in and sing with him.

G-W Yes. Wonderful! He took me to that Verdi in Paris just to hear Sullivan. And then he said, "You can't imagine how chic the men were twenty years ago when they went to the opera with a woman. They had a cape over their shoulders . . ." Oh, he adored that.

KM He seemed to like elegance in everything. He had an innate elegance himself.

G-W Natural elegance, yes.

KM Did he have a favorite opera?

G-W Oh, all of Verdi he liked. You know we took them out once to a little bistro, the "Seerose," in the Seefeld. There was a Professor Fehr, an *Englandist,* who had written in 1925 a first article on Joyce in Switzerland. My husband and I thought we would invite Mr. Fehr and that Joyce would be interested in him because he had written about him. Then we would go to this bistro and perhaps the two would speak about poetry or something like that. Not at all. They began, after the first dish, to sing Verdi! And the whole place was looking toward our table because they were singing. The professor was also a Verdian—he loved Verdi. And they sang all the bel cantos from *The Huguenots* to *The Force of Destiny*—the two of them. They thought we had gone crazy at our table.

KM What did he like best, *Il Trovatore?*

G-W Yes, very much, but also the later ones like— *Die Macht des Schicksals—The Force of Destiny.*

KM You know, Mrs. Giedion, people like you give us something to work on. You make Joyce come alive as a person for us.

G-W But you have a feeling for him—you tell me things that are absolutely right. I had a great chance to live in a time—a great chance—when those people who lived and later became great figures were writing and fighting for their new methods of thinking and expressing. My husband and I, we had a feeling of their quality. We had a great chance. And those people became *copains.*

KM But that calls for an innate sense of person and of greatness. Some people live with others and never recognize their greatness or appreciate them as persons.

G-W But Joyce was never adored like a great person in our house. Just a *copain*—but with respect and *distance.* When I took those pictures, Joyce was even flattered. I told Nora, "Now, can I photograph Mr. Joyce tomorrow afternoon? I want to photograph him." She said, "Yes, all right. I'll tell

Jim." And then I took the photos. Afterwards, she came and said, "Mrs. Giedion, I must tell you how the man fixed up! He was washing, and combing, and tidying—I got sick of it!" she said. Do you think I could tell a story about Beckett?

KM Please do.

G-W One evening I was with Joyce and Beckett—he had invited me to a very chic restaurant in the Champs Elysées, "Fouquet." Beckett was rather silent, but Joyce told jokes. And at the end, after Beckett had left, he said to me, "What did you think of Beckett?" Well, I saw how Beckett imitated Joyce—I was very unjust to Beckett—and that took me away from the real impression of that strong emanation he had. He used a walking stick—he didn't need to go with a stick, but he was imitating Joyce. That made me a little impatient and I said, "I don't like the way he imitates you." Joyce said, "He is a poet," and later, "He's a sexy man." I said, "You have *much* more sex!"

KM I'll bet Joyce loved that.

G-W That he liked *very* much to hear.

KM Did he use the word "sex" very much?

G-W Yes, yes, he used it—but he did *not* use the word "sex appeal."

KM If he was such a sexy person as a writer and so concerned with sex, did he talk much about it?

G-W No. No.

KM That's interesting. Someone has suggested that he was puritanical. That's a funny word to use of Joyce.

G-W No. His jokes were not puritanical. They were not dirty jokes. He was clownish, not dignified. But *distance* he liked.

KM Quite a few Irishmen have two sets of jokes—their parlor stories, which they will tell when the ladies are present, and their other stories. I can remember my father telling his first set of stories when the children were present, but after we had left we could hear gales of laughter coming from the room and we would know . . .

G-W That was cruel!

KM And perhaps not very good educationally! Did Joyce ever do this?

G-W No, no.

KM But he was careful of the children?

G-W He was rather careful. He adored his children. For my feeling, he exaggerated a little. But he was very worried because of Lucia's illness. But concerning sex, I remember once Lucia stayed at our house for three weeks. He wanted her to have a little rest, and I invited her. My husband was not

there and I had a servant with me. I said, "Well, we three women are together." Joyce said, "That's not good for Lucia. Now you take her out with men—you have men friends. She has to have young men who take her swimming. Go to the *plage* in Zurich. She needs that. But not you three women, you and the servant and Lucia—that will make the girl wild."

G-W What Joyce told me of the Jesuits was so marvelous.

KM It's nice that he preserved a gratitude for them as educators.

G-W He spoke about their great knowledge. Once I was traveling alone and went to Machu Picchu. It was raining and we had to wait in a little *cabine* until we could go on the mountain. There was an Irish Jesuit priest there and far, far away in Peru we began to speak about Joyce. And he said to me, "I'm so worried—can you tell me if Joyce always speaks with hatred about religion and the Jesuits?" I said, "Never. Never. Very naturally, very quietly and very gratefully about the Jesuits." But to go to Machu Picchu to have a conversation like that with a person—it is the same as with Finnegan, "Here Comes Everybody." Strange people, strange geography—and here comes Joyce again!

KM And he's still bringing people together. He seems to have had a passion for reconciling opposites. For example, his attitude toward the Jewish people was so good.

G-W Very good, very good. In the Hitler time and in the beginning of the war (then he was still alive)—he ran about helping the Jewish people, trying to get money for them and relations with those who could help them. He was absolutely involved, fantastic.

KM Yeats, too, seemed obsessed with the idea of reconciling opposites. Perhaps because Ireland as a country has always been in opposition within itself. There are extremes—warriors and peacemakers. I think someone like Joyce who loved music might normally carry over that desire for harmony into art and human relationships. Was he the kind of person for whom internal family discord was aesthetically disruptive—did he seem to need a peaceful atmosphere for work?

G-W Throughout the illness of Lucia, his daughter, it was very difficult, of course. She sometimes became wild, you know. She threw bottles in the hotel rooms fighting with her mother. And that was difficult because he was—how do you say, *placide*—quiet, and the explosions made him suffer, but without excitement, in a deeper way.

KM Many of Joyce's male characters, in *Dubliners* for example, seem to be passive, almost helpless, while the women are portrayed as the backbone of the family, holding it together. The women seem to be stronger—

G-W Aggressive, almost aggressive.

KM That's true of Synge and O'Casey, too.

G-W Yes—"The Playboy of the Western World." That's Irish, then. The Mollys are all strong. There is a different situation in Switzerland, just the contrary. There the man rules. He goes into a restaurant in the evening—he did, perhaps fifty years ago—leaving the woman alone, to have a drink with his friends.

KM Well, that's Irish, too—perhaps universal. In American literature there are many dominant male characters.

G-W But in America the women are strong, too—in my opinion.

KM But in literature, at least, the strong male characters predominate.

G-W But in reality the women are strong. They rule. In galleries and museums, women have a lot to say—in foundations, too—all those women over 50.

KM It's true that women have more opportunities in America to hold executive positions. Certainly in Ireland that's not the case.

G-W That's it. They are in the real world, working in the world. My husband* was an art historian, especially interested in architecture, you know, *Space, Time and Architecture*. He spent half the year teaching at Harvard and half in Switzerland. I was often there, too, with him at Harvard. And all our friends there were working in architectural branches. You can't get them so interested in literary things.

KM Now in America there is much interest in cross-disciplinary studies. In Connecticut the State Colleges employ an architect whose other field is aesthetics and logic.

G-W My husband was enlarging architecture in a new sphere. There you are.

KM How long has your husband been dead?

G-W Since 1968. There is a marvelous thing about him in *Finnegan*. When the children write the night letter**—they were our children.

KM Really?

G-W Yes. They called him "Pep." The father, my husband, they used to call "Pep." And in the night letter, the children write to me and my husband, to Pep and Memmy, who are in Harvard. Now the queer thing is that this was written by Joyce before the war. Then the war broke out, I came home to stay with the children, my husband stayed for a term longer at Harvard. And the only way we had of communicating was by night letter.

KM Why the night letter as the only form of correspondence?

G-W It was the only reliable one in wartime. Joyce wrote the night letter as a joke in his book, the night letter, the dream letter. But afterwards it became a reality for us, the only way of communication for the family. It was prophetic how Joyce had put it.

KM It is interesting how prophetic he was in so many ways. He intuited much that happened later on. Do you think it is true that Joyce had an apocalyptic vision?

G-W Yes. He was sometimes distressed about the future, what would happen to us all, like an apocalyptic vision. But I have been thinking about that—whether a man who is so much for "fun for all" could have primarily an apocalyptic view? Fun is so important—you recall my story about how Nora couldn't sleep because he read and laughed and laughed the whole night, about his own writing—fun was an enormous factor in that book. Would that same man have a disastrous view of the world's future, could he?

KM I don't know. But many of the great American humorists—Mark Twain, James Thurber, Emmet Kelly—people who have made a career out of making others laugh—have had tragic personal lives, the idea of under the mask a breaking heart . . .

G-W The tragedy of the clown. But it isn't always the *humour noir*, as they say in France—as Jarry* had it. Joyce has another humor, a lighter humor.

KM Did Joyce particularly like *Pagliacci*? Did he ever go to see that opera? I wonder whether the figure of the clown there interested him, too.

G-W Yes, but not especially. He went to all those operas of Verdi because the human voice was for him the greatest miracle, as he often said. Because he liked very much the *bel canto*. He did not care for Wagner. The *Meistersinger* he liked— that was the only one he liked. I never saw him go to a Wagner—not even to the *Meistersinger*, when it was given.

* Sigfried Giedion.
** *Finnegans Wake*, p. 308.

* Alfred Jarry.

KM Did you ever see Joyce laugh uproariously at anything? Or was he reserved in his laughter, too?

G-W When he had drunk a little, he spoke a lot. But I never saw him drink so much that he fell down or anything, or lost his way, or became disagreeable. But he became very animated in speaking. But with that white wine he drank, I think he killed himself. A sour white wine, Neuchâtel, that he loved most. Yes, he used to say, "Neuchâtel ist ein Sommernachtstraum."

KM A summer night's dream?

G-W Yes. And somebody once asked me if Joyce began drinking early in the daytime. Joyce always said, "I never drink a glass of wine before the sun has gone down."

KM Miss Frances Stelloff serves Joyce's favorite wines after the Joyce Society meetings in the Gotham Book Mart in New York. Once, I recall, it was a Fendant de Sion.

G-W Yes, yes, that's right. In the earlier times it was a Fendant, and later Neuchâtel. I remember I brought it once to Paris to give him pleasure. But wine is so sensitive that it was quite another wine. I had put it in my hatbox—but it wasn't the same at all. Wines are so like very delicate people, sensitive. I don't know what happened, whether it was the train or the new climate.

KM Was Joyce careful about wine?

G-W Yes, very careful. Choosing a wine was very important for him. Very little eating. I often wondered, how can the man exist? He was so slim already. *Very* little food. I once heard that people who like to drink eat very little.

KM You seem to do little of either.

G-W Well, if I were to drink this glass of wine, I couldn't speak to you—I would fall asleep and be very happy.

KM Maybe you should let yourself go. You've had a very busy week.

G-W No, no, no. When will I see you again in this world? No wine for me, although we learned as children, "Du poisson sans boisson c'est poison." ("Fish without wine is poison.")

G-W I think sometimes about art today. Art has become more or less an intellectual manifestation—I see this in the visual arts. To get something spiritual out of the artistic world is very difficult. Art is no longer an emotional affair—I don't want an intellectual affair only. The mechanization and "syphillisation" as Joyce called it is going on and on. Intellectualized art is a dangerous thing. Kan-

dinsky is not an aesthetic affair primarily—his art is an emotional affair. He wants to awaken the innermost emotions of the human being, through his spiritual "vibrations"—he wants to express them visually.

KM Kandinsky tried very hard, didn't he, to transmute music into painting?

G-W Yes, yes. Through music he got the courage to be an abstract painter, in the beginning when it was very difficult to do so.

KM Kandinsky influenced Pound very much in his Vorticist phase. Pound tried to write poems as Kandinsky painted music.

G-W Is that so? I didn't know this.

KM The whole Vorticist movement from around 1913 or 1914 had as its aim to express the arts in terms of other arts. Poets were trying to make poetry that was hard, like sculpture, poetry like painting—

G-W A universal language for all.

KM Like Marinetti and the Futurists they tried to use the harshness of modern life, the machine for example, and to turn it into poetry.

G-W Yes, but Marinetti, Boccioni and the painters in the beginning all wanted a new *dynamisme*. That is why they adored the big cities. The artificial light in the night was emphasized. And the automobile—they wanted to take the Nike of Samothrace out of the Louvre and put an autocar there instead. Think of that! That's more than pop.

KM In poetry, too, the violence of modern life, the war, was so great that it became obvious to the poets too that the machine could also destroy.

G-W But artists later very much needed the Futurists and Marinetti for their new systems. Because Futurism did not want to give a representation of the static world but a deliberation of movement by disintegration of mass and the play of light.

KM Did Futurism influence Joyce at all as it did Pound?

G-W Yes, Futurism did. I believe the only modern movement that influenced Joyce was Futurism.

KM Did he ever talk about Marinetti or Kandinsky?

G-W No, never. But there are passages in *Ulysses* where you feel he has seen those pictures—those pictures he has really seen. And since he loved Italy always in all states, I can imagine his attraction to a movement that came from Italy. But that was before my time. When I came into movement about all those things, they were still alive in the consciousness of the following generations. Kandinsky, whom I knew personally, was much more *idéaliste* than the Futurists.

KM *Uber das Geistige in der Kunst* certainly shows this.

G-W It exists in English—*On the Spiritual in Art.* Speaking of the visual arts—we had a *graphologue* in Switzerland, a very high-level man, Max Pulver. Not only did he see illnesses through handwriting, but character also. He studied man. At first he wanted to become a poet, then wrote a few novels. But he was clever enough to see that he would always be a third-rank poet. He had to have something of his own. And that something was graphology. He often came to our house and liked my husband very much. One day I got a letter from Joyce and showed him only the envelope. I said, "What do you think of that handwriting?" Do you know what he said? "Niveau Goethe." It's fantastic, isn't it? The qualification—not that Joyce was a type like Goethe. But "Niveau Goethe." He didn't say, "He has something the matter with his eyes," but he saw something more important for his qualification. Later on, Joyce sent Lucia's handwriting to him. But he was very disturbed by Lucia's handwriting, Pulver was. He told me, "I can't tell him." I said, "Don't." I introduced Pulver to Joyce—I was always a great "mixer"! Joyce knew by heart passages which Pulver liked very much, of our Swiss poet Gottfried Keller, an end-of-the-century man. So the two men [Pulver and Joyce] recited some of Keller's poems together. Joyce's German accent was good, a clear pronunciation. But he didn't like it so much as Italian, or speak it so well.

KM When was it that Pulver saw Joyce's handwriting?

G-W It was about 1932.

KM Did you ever tell Joyce what Pulver had said about his handwriting?

G-W No. I had restrictions. I only told him, "I think the man is a great graphologue." Then Joyce gave him Lucia's handwriting. Pulver never said, "That must be a woman's handwriting." No, that's a human being. He didn't want any sexual *Begriffe*—how do you say?

KM Concept?

G-W Determination. That came later for him.

KM Thank you, Mrs. Giedion, for joining us tonight and for sharing so many of your reminiscences of James Joyce.

G-W It was a genuine pleasure for me. It reminded me so much of those days and evenings with Joyce—the conversation was so stimulating. I wish we could meet again.

9

The James Joyce Industry: A Reassessment[1]

Bernard Benstock

THE JOYCE INDUSTRY was founded in 1929 by James Joyce. Its initial board of directors, selected by the founder somewhat casually from the international intellectuals then resident in Paris, were twelve in number: Samuel Beckett, Marcel Brion, Frank Budgen, Stuart Gilbert, Eugene Jolas, Victor Llona, Robert McAlmon, Thomas McGreevy, Elliot Paul, John Rodker, Robert Sage, and William Carlos Williams. Their major concern was the Joyce product then in progress, the full impact of which they were not fully aware, for while the patent was still pending Joyce kept the title a personal secret. Yet a full ten years before the completed *Finnegans Wake* was unveiled before the general public, the disciples produced *Our Exagmination Round his Factification for Incamination of Work in Progress*, an exercise in soft sell. Although many of the essays proved oblique and only half-informed, the general thrust was apparent: that concentration on bits and pieces of the overall machinery was essential for any eventual investigation of the final work. Even before these "pioneers" undertook their *Exagmination*, public relations, led by Jolas in *transition*, had been making exaggerated claims, assuming for Joyce a niche in the new "Revolution of the Word." And like any master industrialist, Joyce allowed this semi-misleading publicity to be perpetuated in bringing his image before a widening audience. Image-building had indeed been of importance to Joyce once *Ulysses* was completed:

even before he was forty years old he had commissioned Herbert Gorman to write his biography, purposely planting ideas and even misconceptions that he considered vital to an appreciation of his artistic output.[2]

The 1930s, a period of economic slump throughout Europe, witnessed rapid growth in the packaging and selling of the Joycean product. While *Finnegans Wake* was still in progress, Joyce deployed two of his trustees for work on *Ulysses*, having reversed his previous attitude that only the new book was worthy of concern. Budgen undertook an analysis of *Ulysses* that stressed the process of its creation, while Gilbert was sent to hunt down the Odysseyan elements in Joyce's redaction.[3] With neither was Joyce totally candid, any more than he had been with Gorman and Jolas, allowing each commentator the freedom of making certain mistakes of his own, particularly in overstress and confused emphasis. His faith in his own work —that it could survive critical errors—permitted him these lapses and even encouraged him into believing that the aura surrounding the novel enhances its attractiveness. His own trustees he could successfully oversee, but the Joyce Industry soon expanded outside of his own control, primarily because Anglo-Saxon tariffs made *Ulysses* almost

---

1. In part this essay is an advance on "The James Joyce Industry: An Assessment in the Sixties." *Southern Review*, n.s. 2 (Winter 1966), and I have attempted to avoid duplication with the material there.

2. Herbert S. Gorman, *James Joyce: His First Forty Years* (New York: B. W. Huebsch, 1924); subsequently, *James Joyce* (New York: Rinehart, 1940; revised 1948).

3. Frank Budgen, *James Joyce and the Making of Ulysses* New York: Harrison Smith and Robert Haas, 1934); most recent reprinting includes "other writings," with an introduction by Clive Hart (London: Oxford University Press, 1972); Stuart Gilbert, *James Joyce's Ulysses: A Study* (London: Faber and Faber, 1930).

completely unavailable to readers in the English-speaking world. In England and America, as well as on the Continent, the first rash of books on Joyce by others than those within the corporation began to appear, mostly concerned with the masterpiece that readers were curious about but unable to obtain. By the early thirties slim studies by Paul Jordan Smith, Charles Duff, and Louis Golding[4] were offered as substitutes for the real thing, but on a higher intellectual level the decade (the last one of Joyce's life) is best bracketed by the endeavors of Edmund Wilson: his *Axel's Castle* (1931) analyzed *Ulysses* and introduced aspects of the new work, while his reviews of the completed *Wake* in 1939[5] were welcomed along with the review by Harry Levin as two of the best by Joyce himself.

With Wilson and Levin (particularly the latter's *James Joyce: a Critical Introduction*, 1941)[6] the center of the Joyce Industry shifted significantly to the United States. Already an international cartel by dint of Joyce's exilic relocation on the European continent, the corporation had essentially flourished in Paris while that city remained the center of expatriate activities and a healthy focus of French art and literature. With the devastation of the war years many intellectual concerns suffered dislocation, moving either underground or to safer bases of operation. Joyce's death only weeks after his rearrival in neutral Zurich left 'almost no power base there, nor was his native Ireland conducive for critical work on its still unhonored and almost totally unread prophet. The rapid expansion of the American universities, with financial strength in research grants and manpower development through building graduate programs, has kept the Joyce Industry largely within the hands of American scholars and students for three decades. The first doctoral dissertation on Joyce was written by Joseph Prescott in 1944, setting the trend that has resulted in hundreds. Only within the past decade has the phenomenon spread outside the United States to any important extent.

The war years created a watershed for Joyce criticism. Joyce was dead, having lived long enough after the publication of *Finnegans Wake* to realize that the advent of a European conflict would prove disastrous for the reception of his last work. The *Wake* in 1939 no longer excited the expectations of an increasingly sophisticated reading public; instead it seemed to be a frivolous excursion at a time of serious peril, a luxury outmoded by the reality of current events. As D. H. Lawrence's literary reputation reached rock-bottom in the Marxist thirties, so did Joyce's plummet in the war-conscious forties, although the pattern was significantly altered in America. Still somewhat removed from the full impact of the European conflict, American criticism held out better against the demands of the times: at three-year intervals important works on Joyce emerged during the decade. Levin's "introduction" was the first book to cover the totality of Joyce's output; published just after Joyce's death, it included *Finnegans Wake* within the scope of its investigation. In 1944 the pioneer book on the *Wake* appeared: the *Skeleton Key* produced by Henry Morton Robinson and Joseph Campbell[7] would eventually prove to be a mixed blessing, but at the time it asserted with daring that the *Wake* could be read through as a work of literary fiction, that its difficulties were keyed to a complex set of schematic patterns evolved by the author and not the result of arbitrary hoaxes, and that many roads were available (cultural anthropology for one) into the maze. And if Campbell and Robinson initiated the process of rescuing the *Wake* from obscurity, Richard M. Kain in *Fabulous Voyager* (1947)[8] contributed to rescuing *Ulysses* from pedantry: balancing Gilbert's intensive mining for Homeric parallels, Kain's book treated *Ulysses* as a readable novel about the lives of fictional characters in the real setting of Joyce's Dublin. None of these American commentators seemed at all in awe of either the immediacy of Joyce's presence hovering over them or the momentousness of Joyce's breathtaking impact. Instead, they fulfilled their functions as detached scholars and unhurried readers, establishing the bases for Joyce's literary work to outlive the Joycean legend.

The present state of Joyce's reputation derives

---

4. Paul Jordan Smith, *A Key to the Ulysses of James Joyce* (New York: Covici-Friede, 1927); Charles C. Duff, *James Joyce and the Plain Reader* (London: Harmsworth, 1932); Louis Golding, *James Joyce* (London: Thornton Butterworth, 1933).

5. Edmund Wilson, *Axel's Castle* (New York: Scribner's, 1931); "H. C. Earwicker and Family: Review of *Finnegans Wake*," *New Republic* 94 (28 June and 12 July 1939).

6. Harry Levin, *James Joyce: A Critical Introduction* (Norfolk, Conn.: New Directions, 1941).

7. Joseph Campbell and Henry Morton Robinson, *A Skeleton Key to Finnegans Wake* (New York: Harcourt, Brace, 1944).

8. Richard M. Kain, *Fabulous Voyager: James Joyce's Ulysses* (Chicago: University of Chicago Press, 1947).

essentially from the momentum that became apparent in the 1950s and has been gaining headway ever since. Within these twenty years Joyce has moved from coterie darling and fanciful artificer to a position unequaled for a twentieth-century writer. Whereas Proust is an established titan whose works are acknowledged and unread, Joyce continues to amass a continually growing reading public, *Ulysses* alone having sold in the hundreds of thousands. For most of the other major figures of the early part of the century a period of gradual winding down is apparent, a tightening of their reputations into a position of solid respectability and reserved veneration. Yet posthumous factors that on occasion chip away at their reputations fail to faze Joyce's: publication of his letters[9] reveals that he had almost no belle-lettristic ability in his casual correspondence and *Giacomo Joyce*[10] (for whatever it is) is hardly more than a laundry list compared to Joyce's novels. And when Richard Ellmann's objective biography[11] replaced Gorman's "authorized" effort, even glimpses at the human Joyce with faults and follies augmented rather than diminished the public esteem. Nor have the debunkers had much success: Oliver St. John Gogarty's feeble fusillades, like "They Think They Know Joyce,"[12] could convince only those Irish detractors who were already convinced. What remained essential in establishing Joyce had become permanent fixtures for the present generation: *Dubliners, A Portrait of the Artist as a Young Man, Ulysses,* and *Finnegans Wake.* No matter what else is revealed about Joyce to his detriment, nothing scratches the polish of those four works.

The one constant in Joycean criticism during the past two decades has been *Ulysses.* Regardless of the vagaries of *Wake* scholarship and the uneven quality of speculation regarding the early Joyceana, work on *Ulysses* has persisted along even lines of development and remained a favorite, probably for the same reasons that conditioned Goldilocks's choice of beds: the *Wake* is too hard and the early works presumably lack sufficient depth. *Ulysses* scholars have had the solid underpinning of Budgen's *James Joyce and the Making of Ulysses,* Gilbert's *James Joyce's Ulysses,* and Kain's *Fabulous Voyager,* an excellent trio of basic approaches upon which to build, as well as the early effort in concordance, Miles Hanley's 1937 *Word Index.*[13] (The errors in the *Index* would make any self-respecting computer blush, and the recent multiplicity of editions of *Ulysses* make the page references a source of frustration, but it provided at least a quantitive guide and a map of shortcuts for many years during which *Finnegans Wake* remained a maze to its exegetes.) Not that the earlier works on *Ulysses* were accepted without question: Kain was very specific about Gilbert's cycloptic view, which sought out "esoteric symbolism" at the expense of the "artistic and philosophic values" of Joyce's book, as he also takes Levin to task for missing the humanity and philosophy inherent in *Ulysses.* A decade later William Schutte attempted to bury the disciples altogether in his introductory survey of *Ulysses* criticism in *Joyce and Shakespeare.*[14] The pedantic seriousness of the Gorman-Gilbert discipleship now seems incongruous for a master humorist, especially one who was fond of jokes at the expense of his worshipers (but Schutte is somewhat uncomfortable at having to employ Gogarty and J. F. Byrne against the Gorman-Gilbert contingent). A full generation has evolved; the clique of the twenties is now in disrepute and a new wave of objective examiners has laid claim to James Joyce.

New schisms, however, are quick to replace old ones, and Schutte's critical eye discerned two extreme schools of Joycean criticism in 1957: on the one hand the symbol-hunters, who so often drop the bone in the pond as they plunge in to snare its reflection; on the other hand the Dublin skeptics, either insisting on the literalness of *Ulysses* as a slice of Dublin life or dismissing it with fury as trash or with disdain as a leg-pull. The Dublin position was not so much a school of literary criticism as it was strategic opposition: a vital essence of Irish genius and critic of Irish life was being drained from their midst primarily by the aggrandizement of American professors, but also

9. *Letters of James Joyce,* vol. 1, ed. Stuart Gilbert (New York: Viking, 1957); vols. 2 and 3, ed. Richard Ellmann (New York: Viking, 1968).

10. *Giacomo Joyce,* ed. Richard Ellmann (New York: Viking, 1968).

11. Richard Ellman, *James Joyce* (New York: Oxford University Press, 1959).

12. Oliver St. John Gogarty, "They Think They Know Joyce," *Saturday Review of Literature* 33 (18 March 1950): 8-9, 35-37.

13. Miles L. Hanley, *Word Index to James Joyce's Ulysses* (Madison, Wis.: University of Wisconsin Press, 1937; revised 1965).

14. William M. Schutte, *Joyce and Shakespeare: A Study in the Meaning of Ulysses* (New Haven, Conn.: Yale University Press, 1957).

(rarely admitted) by the apathy and inertia of the Irish. Resistance reached its zenith with the May 1951 special Joyce number of *Envoy,* where Patrick Kavanagh contributed his delightful and absurd piece of doggerel, beginning:

> Who killed James Joyce?
> I, said the commentator,
> I killed James Joyce
> For my graduation.[15]

Despite some fine touches and accurate insights, the collection is generally cranky and out-of-sorts, but how can anyone succeed in explaining to the down-at-the-elbows Dublin intellectuals that professors rarely get rich writing exegeses of James Joyce? In time part of this attitude has mellowed—or died out with its advocates—especially since a handful of the disgruntled have come to America and taught at some of the "prairie universities" that one of them disparaged twenty years ago. It is even more important that national boundaries have broken down, that an internationalization of interest in Joyce scholarship has brought Irish and Americans and others together. The change is reflected in *A Bash in the Tunnel,* a 1969 Irish collection of commentaries on Joyce, edited like the *Envoy* by John Ryan.[16] Some of the old rancor is still there, but most important is an indication that a new generation of Irish writers has emerged aware of Joyce and his influence and devoid of chauvinistic disgruntlement. But one source of that old self-consciousness still remains: Joyce is not nearly so carefully read in his native Ireland as he is in many other parts of the world.

Schutte's case against the exponents of intensive symbol-hunting has not held up well historically. He poses it against two of the earliest pioneers of the search, William York Tindall and Marvin Magalaner, and he does isolate examples of overreaching: asserting the existence of a symbolic value without substantiation. In effect these forerunners and early practitioners should be credited with indicating one of the most important directions in Joyce scholarship, the ultimate reliance on symbolic overtones and understructure to carry the weight of expanded significance in almost all of Joyce's writing. In *Ulysses* in particular this has become essential, especially when we become aware that certain "givens" in this mammoth novel are actually stated only once (or twice at best) and their relevance must be sustained by the ripples caused by the single casting of a pebble: that Rudy was born deformed, that Bloom alone has been responsible for the break in normal marital sex relations with Molly, that Molly's infidelities in the past are probably nonexistent, and so forth. Only the kind of insistence upon detail suggested by the Tindalls and the Magalaners could have alerted readers to the technique of intimating the substance from its shadow, the technique of a literary use of the gnomon. But between the excesses of the literalists and the exaggerated symbol-ferreters, Schutte insists upon a middle course, and singles out Kain, Levin, and Douglas Knight.

The problems of the mid-fifties remain very much the problems of today. By then the ghosts of obscenity and formlessness had been laid to rest, but the tension between naturalistic details and symbolic stress remained, as did the dilemma of Joyce's attitudes toward his characters and the inconclusiveness of the "resolutions" of the plot. When Kain and Magalaner joined their individual efforts together to publish *Joyce: the Man, the Work, the Reputation* in 1956, there was already a potent body of data on *Ulysses* (but still a manageable one), and Kain summarized the dilemma of interpretation:

> If the position of *Ulysses* in modern letters be entrenched, as it now seems to be, the basic problem remains that of interpreting the narrative's resolution. How seriously must the meeting of Stephen and Bloom be considered in theory, when it remains so ineffectual in fact? Is the end result merely that of ineradicable loneliness, or does Molly's final "Yes" indicate acceptance of the life force? To Tindall, Stephen's quest concludes with his discovery of reality, his personal salvation from pride and egocentricity, and his artistic dedication to the theme of humanity. To D. S. Savage, on the other hand, the only outcome is the pagan acceptance of nature, and the basic themes of the work are "Unbelief, Nature and Necessity, Physicality, Promiscuity."[17]

As late as 1972 (the fiftieth anniversary of *Ulysses* and definitely a year of commemoration) the same concerns in similar terms were still being expressed. At a conference at the University of Tulsa these issues were once again reopened when twelve latter-day symposiasts met to discuss *Ulys-*

15. *Envoy* 5 (May 1951), Dublin, Ireland.
16. John Ryan, ed., *A Bash in the Tunnel: James Joyce by the Irish* (Brighton [England]: Clifton Books, 1970).

17. Marvin Magalaner and Richard M. Kain, *Joyce: The Man, the Work, the Reputation* (New York: New York University Press, 1956), pp. 214-15.

ses in the light of fifty years (the essays have now been published in the *James Joyce Quarterly*).[18] One governing factor may have been the impact of Leslie Fiedler's 1969 Symposium lecture, "Bloom as the Humanity of Joyce" (printed in the *Journal of Modern Literature* and *New Light on Joyce*),[19] reaffirming Edmund Wilson's position in 1931, that Stephen had found in Bloom "someone sufficiently sympathetic to himself to give him the clew, to supply him with the subject, which will enable him to enter imaginatively—as an artist—into the common life of the race."[20] This is the attitude that Schutte attacked because of lack of any concrete evidence within the text of *Ulysses* that Stephen has at all been moved in the direction of either Bloom as a person or common humanity in general.

At some time or another all three principals in *Ulysses* have suffered lapses in their reputations. The Bloom who now seems well established as either a good Samaritan or symbol of mankind (or both) has come a long way from such 1922 attitudes as that of Joseph Collins ("a moral monster, a pervert and an invert")[21] and Ezra Pound, who had at first hailed Bloom ("Bloom is a great man, and you have almightily answered the critics who asked me whether having made Stephen, more or less autobiography, you could ever go on and create a second character"),[22] later recanted, "wanting to know whether Bloom . . . could not be relegated to the background and Stephen Telemachus brought forward."[23] Molly has been the constant source of disgust and dismay, from Mary Colum's pronouncement of her as exhibiting the "mind of a female gorilla"[24] (1922) to Erwin R. Steinberg's insistence that she is "completely egocentric . . . snobbish and self-confident . . . sensual . . . ignorant, inconsistent, and superficial"[25] (1958) and J. Mitchell Morse's condemnation that "Molly is not honest, she is not kind, she is

not creative, she is not free, she hasn't enough *élan vital* to get dressed before three P.M., and her fertility is subnormal"[26] (1959). Morse even concludes that "Molly's soliloquy is the bitterest and deadliest thing Joyce ever wrote" and that "he let Molly damn herself as the very center of paralysis."[27]

So too has the tide occasionally turned against Stephen Dedalus, particularly in the mid-fifties when so much reevaluation was taking place. The pioneer against Stephen seems to have been Hugh Kenner in *Dublin's Joyce*,[28] a work that established a tradition of Stephen-hating, although a careful rereading of Kenner's delightful book may indicate very little actual hatred and much more of detached criticism. What needed correction was the long-prevailing association of the author and his character, the Joyce who was a mature man in his thirties and the young Stephen of 16 June 1904, especially if Wilson and others persisted in having the Stephen of *Ulysses* destined to write *Ulysses,* and even return to 7 Eccles Street for further communion with Bloom and possible congress with Molly. Kenner viewed the Stephen of the last chapter of *A Portrait* and of *Ulysses* as far more the fictional creation of Joyce's ironic imagination, characterizing him as "the egocentric rebel become an ultimate. There is no question whatever of his regeneration. . . . The Stephen of the first chapter of *Ulysses* . . . is precisely the priggish, humourless Stephen of the last chapter of the *Portrait*."[29] In less emphatic form this attitude was anticipated by Tindall at the beginning of the decade, when he commented that a careful reading of *A Portrait* "makes it apparent that Joyce is aloof and generally ironic in his treatment of Stephen. . . . His attitude toward Stephen is more obvious in *Ulysses* where the priggish hero is subjected to Mulligan's deflation and permitted to display his humorless egocentricity."[30] Yet far from being a Stephen-hater, Tindall maintains that "the encounter with Bloom has changed Stephen's inhumanity to humanity. The egoist has discovered charity, the greatest of virtues, and compassion for mankind . . . and leaving Bloom,

18. *James Joyce Quarterly* 10 (Fall 1972); other commemorative issues include *Mosaic* 6 (Fall 1972) and a forthcoming volume from *Etudes Anglaises*.
19. Leslie Fiedler, "Bloom on Joyce; or, Jokey for Jacob," *Journal of Modern Literature* 1 (1970); Fritz Senn, ed., *New Light on Joyce from the Dublin Symposium* (Bloomington, Ind.: Indiana University Press, 1972).
20. *Axel's Castle*, p. 202.
21. Robert H. Deming, ed., *James Joyce: The Critical Heritage*, vol. 1 (London: Routledge and Kegan Paul, 1970): 225.
22. *Letters*, 1: 423.
23. *Letters*, 2: 126.
24. *Critical Heritage*, 1: 233.
25. Erwin R. Steinberg, "A Book with a Molly in It," *James Joyce Review* 2 (Spring-Summer 1958): 61.
26. J. Mitchell Morse, "Molly Bloom Revisited," *James Joyce Miscellany* 2 (Carbondale, Ill.: Southern Illinois University Press, 1959): 140.
27. *Ibid.*, p. 149.
28. Hugh Kenner, *Dublin's Joyce* (London: Chatto and Windus, 1955).
29. *Ibid.*, p. 112.
30. William York Tindall, *James Joyce: His Way of Interpreting the Modern World* (New York: Scribner's, 1950).

he goes away to write *Ulysses*."[31] (A common virtue shared by Kenner and Tindall in their work on Joyce is a functional sense of the comic: whereas many commentators decry stuffy pedantry when writing about the comic genius James Joyce, Kenner and Tindall actually practice their preachments.)

Schutte's approach in *Joyce and Shakespeare* establishes a landmark of sorts in *Ulysses* criticism: he is able to funnel a great deal of commentary on Joyce's book through an examination of a single element of source and subject matter, Joyce's "use" of Shakespeare. In effect this posits a *Ulysses* that has been accepted as a classic and as a well-explicated text. No longer does Joyce's "monster" have to prove itself, but is accepted as worthy of scholarly discussion. From the beginning it has seemed essential that *Ulysses* be discussed chapter by chapter (as Budgen and Gilbert had done in pre-Woolseyan days of inaccessibility), a process that treats it as a series of uneven steps exhaustingly mounting toward its final "Yes." This has shaped such disparate works as Stanley Sultan's *The Argument of Ulysses* (1964), the longest climb to date; *The Celtic Bull* (1966), an exercise in unfortunate undergraduate enthusiasm; Harry Blamires's *The Bloomsday Book* (1966), perhaps more of a crutch than a guide; Clive Hart's *James Joyce's Ulysses* (1968), where the succinct run-through is bracketed by well-integrated analysis; and Richard Ellmann's *Ulysses on the Liffey* (1972), which attempts to mask the "guide" with imaginative speculation.[32] This sequential approach invariably runs the risk of treating all readers as students (and sometimes not very bright ones). From *Fabulous Voyager* on, the possibility of book-length studies of *Ulysses* along thematic lines has established itself, and with *Joyce and Shakespeare* the even closer scholarly approach has become desirable.

Ulysses in the sixties[33] was best ushered in by S. L. Goldberg's *The Classical Temper* (1961),[34] which introduces an "English" contender in the field. Goldberg is quite specific on why Joyce has remained so much the property of Americans ("Joyce's sensibility is Roman Catholic and Irish, the literary models to which he looked were Continental rather than English, while his art is more self-conscious, more abstract, more concerned with spiritual and social alienation, than is usual in the English novel. None of these characteristics is a disadvantage in America; on the contrary, American literature has always possessed many of them itself") [35] and makes no bones about his quarrels with *Ulysses* ("the enormous elaboration of the material, the rather pretentious parade of literary machinery, the encumbering and mortifying boredom").[36] With these two hands tied behind his back—he will go on to tie a third and unprecedented one when in his short book, *James Joyce*,[37] he despairs totally of dealing with *Finnegans Wake*—Goldberg nonetheless does a fine job with *Ulysses*. Goldberg is the ideal example of the Goldilocks syndrome, settling for *Ulysses* because *Chamber Music, Exiles, Dubliners*, and *A Portrait* are "not major works," while the *Wake* "opens up possibilities in the use of language; but art has deeper obligations than that, and whether its experiments ever achieve any historical importance is a question we may leave to the scholars of the future."[38] What he does commit himself to is a careful application of Joyce's own comments and theories of aesthetics to the fabric of *Ulysses*. It is not surprising in the light of his thesis and his attitudes that Goldberg places himself in the middle-ground position advocated by Schutte: Dublin inability to take Joyce seriously is immediately dismissed; charges of "moral nihilism" are disallowed; "No Hunting" signs are posted to dissuade those entering the forest with their Symbol-guns half-cocked; the view that *Ulysses* is a negative reaction to the modern world is discouraged as limiting; and the alternate concept of resounding affirmation (Yes in Thunder) is disparaged. *The Classical Temper* attempts to balance these last two interpretations, allowing for a reasonable amount of symbolism as well.

31. *Ibid.*, pp. 26-27.

32. Stanley Sultan, *The Argument of Ulysses* (Columbus, Ohio: Ohio State University Press, 1964); Judy-Lynn Benjamin, ed., *The Celtic Bull: Essays on James Joyce's Ulysses* (Tulsa, Okla.: University of Tulsa Department of English Monograph Series, 1966); Harry Blamires, *The Bloomsday Book: A Guide Through Joyce's Ulysses* (London: Methuen, 1966); Clive Hart, *James Joyce's Ulysses* (Sydney: Sydney University Press, 1968); Richard Ellmann, *Ulysses on the Liffey* (New York: Oxford University Press, 1972).

33. For secondary materials on Joyce through 1961 see Robert H. Deming, *A Bibliography of James Joyce Studies* (Lawrence, Kans.: University of Kansas Libraries, 1964).

34. S. L. Goldberg, *The Classical Temper: A Study of James Joyce's Ulysses* (London: Chatto and Windus, 1963).

35. *Ibid.*, pp. 18-19.

36. *Ibid.*, pp. 21-22.

37. *James Joyce* (Edinburgh: Oliver and Boyd, 1962).

38. *Classical Temper*, p. 16.

No quantity of symbolic overreading, however, has prevented *Ulysses* from being read as a novel about the *real* Dublin, and several early reviewers from that city were actually jostled by the appearance of *real* Dubliners in the book. Shane Leslie and others somehow found the presence of Father Conmee and Arthur Griffith distracting in what was presumably a work of fiction.[39] Yet serious students of the book have taken these people in stride and sought to evaluate the Joycean deployment of the real among the fictional. *Fabulous Voyager* began the trend; its appendixes included "A Biographical Dictionary" and "A Directory of Shops, Offices, Public Buildings, Professional and Civic Personages." This detective work was added to by Robert M. Adams in *Surface and Symbol*,[40] who discovered consistencies and inconsistencies in Joyce's creation and re-creation of characters. Recently a history of Irish Jewry focused on *Ulysses* within its context,[41] and it is now apparent that in surrounding his fictional Bloom with other Dublin Jews, Joyce relied exclusively on reality, that Leopold Bloom is the only Dublin Jew in the book who did not actually walk the streets of that city. And a forthcoming "Gazetteer" by John Van Voorhis may well cap the search for people and places that preexisted Joyce's fictional imagination when he began work on *Ulysses*.

The *Ulysses* boom has been occasioned in part by the growth in student consumption, resulting in a plethora of guidebooks to service the new clientele. The progenitor of the line is Tindall's *A Reader's Guide to James Joyce* (1959)[42] which, although it did not invent them, typifies the weaknesses of the system: insufficient explanation, lack of coherence of the parts, suggestions without substantiation, "directed" readings, arbitrary isolation of particulars, loss of emphasis. With the hope of being a lot more thorough, Harry Blamires devoted three times the space allotted to *Ulysses* by Tindall, but *The Bloomsday Book* errs in the other direction. It is plodding and dull, *Ulysses* writ small and by a pedagogue rather than by a literary genius. Moreover, it runs the danger of replac-

ing Joyce's book, the danger of a paraphrase, and if its intention is to avoid the necessity of rereadings by offering a companion volume, perhaps it in itself is the best available argument for rereading *Ulysses* instead. Abjuring the word *guide* from either title or subtitle, Clive Hart's slim volume, *James Joyce's Ulysses,* is the best-balanced attempt to be of service to student readers. The emphasis is on the totality of the work, offering multiple approaches in short doses, a "simple reading" of the text, and critical apparatuses. It prepares the reader for his travels before he begins, rather than placing an obstacle before him when he wants to be viewing the real thing.

Works of service to the *Ulysses* scholar have not, surprisingly enough, been plentiful. When one realizes the battery of apparatuses that surrounds the *Wake* specialist when he sits down at the typewriter, it comes as a shock that the Ulyssean is not so well aided. The *Word Index* is there for basic use, and scholars like Joseph Prescott and A. Walton Litz have provided analyses of Joyce's methods of composition by examining drafts and worksheets, notes and page proofs,[43] but Litz's comment in 1961 that "Joycean criticism has entered a phase of consolidation distinguished by a number of specific studies"[44] actually applies more to *Finnegans Wake* than to *Ulysses*. In 1968 Weldon Thornton published *Allusions in Ulysses*,[45] identifying thousands of allusions in "the areas of literature, philosophy, theology, history, the fine arts, and popular and folk music." Its five hundred pages more than just dent the surface, yet the thickness of the allusive method in *Ulysses* is of such proportions that hundreds of other allusions still cry out for inclusion. And the most recent effort on behalf of the *Ulysses* exegete comes from Phillip F. Herring, whose *Joyce's Ulysses Notesheets in the British Museum*[46] presents a transcription of manuscript notations used by Joyce for the construction of the last seven chapters of *Ulysses*.

The direction of present *Ulysses* criticism re-

---

39. *"Ulysses* Without Dublin," *James Joyce Quarterly* 10 (Fall 1972).

40. Robert M. Adams, *Surface and Symbol: The Consistency of James Joyce's Ulysses* (New York: Oxford University Press, 1962).

41. Louis Hyman, *The Jews of Ireland: From Earliest Times to the Year 1910* (Dublin: Irish University Press, 1972).

42. William York Tindall, *A Reader's Guide to James Joyce* (New York: Noonday Press, 1959).

43. Joseph Prescott, *Exploring James Joyce* (Carbondale, Ill.: Southern Illinois University Press, 1964); A. Walton Litz, *The Art of James Joyce: Method and Design in Ulysses and Finnegans Wake* (London: Oxford University Press, 1961).

44. Litz, p. vii.

45. Weldon Thornton, *Allusions in Ulysses: An Annotated List* (Chapel Hill, N. C.: University of North Carolina Press, 1968).

46. Phillip F. Herring, ed., *Joyce's Ulysses Notesheets in the British Museum* (Charlottesville, Va.: University Press of Virginia, 1972).

mains as diverse as ever, with general studies still the favorite. Perhaps it is merely the human condition that every Joycean has a *Ulysses* book in him and each insists upon his prerogative to give it form and shape. David Hayman, in attempting a short work on *Ulysses: The Mechanics of Meaning* (1970), comments, "perhaps we have surrounded the monster with a wall that can still be breached by a modest volume designed to serve the general reader as a descriptive introduction,"[47] and his particular involvement with structure and technique in *Ulysses* as they develop the function of the novel raises his 100-page introduction from guide-level. Richard Ellmann, however, makes no pretense to being introductory in *Ulysses on the Liffey* (1972). Instead, he proposes a new mythic interpretation, relying heavily upon the schemas given by Joyce to Carlo Linati and to Gorman and Gilbert, and dividing *Ulysses* with strong emphasis along chapter lines. The eighteen sections of the book are then viewed as trios containing six segments of thesis-antithesis-synthesis, evolving into his theory of the Joycean concept of art-life-love. In the age-old controversy Ellmann comes out on the side of the angels, noting that "having completed his plan, Joyce might well feel that he had succeeded in disengaging what was affirmable in existence, and had affirmed that."[48]

The divergent views expounded through the decades on *Ulysses* led Thomas F. Staley and me to approach a chorus of Joyceans for a compound study of the enigmatic work. Each contributor was offered the freedom of tackling the book from a specific viewpoint along his own lines of thought, and ten essays evolved into *Approaches to Ulysses*.[49] As we had hoped, differences of viewpoint presented themselves in the collection, most particularly when David Hayman and Darcy O'Brien took a close look at Molly Bloom. Without imposing moral value judgments, each critic estimated Molly's extramarital lovers quite differently, O'Brien accepting the literal validity of a sensuous and actively sexual Molly, while Hayman, following suggestions made by Adams and Sultan, exonerated Molly of any affairs before the one with Boylan, although he allows that Stanley Gardner remains an open possibility and might even be a

later Joycean addition. (In *Ulysses on the Liffey* Ellmann also sees Molly as having been a lot less active than was usually assumed, but he accepts Bartell d'Arcy as definitely having been her lover.) And while the controversies continue, the scholarly work continues as well, with such recent books as Herring's edition of the Notesheets and Erwin R. Steinberg's *The Stream of Consciousness and Beyond in Ulysses*.[50]

An overall glance back at the work done on the early Joyce (compared to *Ulysses* and the terra incognita beyond) indicates the degree to which the student has become the major focus of the world of *Dubliners* and *A Portrait,* and the guide and the casebook the traditional media of exchange. The casebooks in effect attest to the preponderance of individual articles and notes in periodicals on the early works, so that when the casebook was in academic vogue less than a decade ago, it was a relatively easy matter to assemble good examples of scholarship and criticism for the college student. Not only are there two extant casebooks on *Dubliners,* but an earlier one on just "The Dead" actually leads the field,[51] containing more items introducing and setting "the story in context" than just the seven articles on the story itself. In 1968 some ten "interpretations" of *Dubliners* appeared, followed in 1969 by a more substantial "critical Handbook,"[52] with but a bare handful of duplications among the three collections. For *A Portrait* the competition began a bit earlier and included heftier volumes and significantly more overlapping, from the two 1962 entries averaging about two dozen items in each to the 1968 "interpretations" with nine articles and eight snippets.[53] The American academic market

47. David Hayman, *Ulysses: The Mechanics of Meaning* (Englewood Cliffs, N.J.: Prentice-Hall, 1970).
48. *Ulysses on the Liffey*, p. 185.
49. Thomas F. Staley and Bernard Benstock, eds., *Approaches to Ulysses: Ten Essays* (Pittsburgh, Pa.: University of Pittsburgh Press, 1970).
50. Erwin R. Steinberg, *The Stream of Consciousness and Beyond in Ulysses* (Pittsburgh, Pa.: University of Pittsburgh Press, 1972).
51. William T. Moynihan, ed., *Joyce's The Dead* (Boston: Allyn and Bacon, 1965).
52. Peter K. Garrett, *Twentieth Century Interpretations of Dubliners* (Englewood Cliffs, N.J.: Prentice-Hall, 1968); James R. Baker and Thomas F. Staley, eds., *James Joyce's Dubliners: A Critical Handbook* (Belmont, Calif.: Wadsworth, 1969).
53. Thomas E. Connolly, ed., *Joyce's Portrait: Criticisms and Critiques* (New York: Appleton-Century-Crofts, 1962); William E. Morris and Clifford A. Nault, Jr., eds., *Portraits of An Artist: A Casebook on James Joyce's A Portrait of the Artist as a Young Man* (New York: Odyssey Press, 1962); William M. Schutte, *Twentieth Century Interpretations of A Portrait of the Artist as a Young Man* (Englewood Cliffs, N.J.: Prentice-Hall, 1968). See also Don Gifford, *Notes for Joyce: Dubliners and A Portrait of the Artist as a Young Man* (New York: Dutton, 1967).

for such collections now having dwindled, these survive as vestigial remains of the format and useful depositories of many basic articles on the subject of *Dubliners* and *A Portrait*.

Large-scaled approaches to *Dubliners* have been rare. In fact until 1969, despite all the periodical literature on the popular subject, no one had published a book-length treatise until Warren Beck's *Joyce's Dubliners: Substance, Vision, and Art*.[54] It is ironic that the first such work on *Dubliners* should be so staid and unimaginative, a mastodon of so prehistoric a mold, abjuring any temptation to investigate symbolic material in the stories. Beck's position is admittedly conservative, and he takes issue with Magalaner and the "Levin-Shattuck prodedure" for their overreadings. Coming as it does a decade after *Time of Apprenticeship*[55] and the even earlier Magalaner articles, Beck's work is a disappointing avoidance of many crucial aspects of the stories and rather cavalier in its ignorance of the efforts of other critics and scholars. Rusty bicycle pumps and corkscrews, rheumatic wheels and chalices, gold coins and yellow-paged books just lie there as literal household items and are never picked up and examined for their greater import. How far removed Warren Beck remains from Tindall's assertion that "Joyce wrote one great work in several books, each of which is connected with the others. *Dubliners*, an early part of this great work, anticipates *Finnegans Wake*, the last, and *Finnegans Wake* returns to the matter of *Dubliners*."[56] By a fortunate coincidence a second book on *Dubliners* appeared the same year, Clive Hart's collection of fifteen essays, *James Joyce's Dubliners*,[57] which serves as a balance and a corrective to Beck. Each story is analyzed by a separate hand, with some of the freshest and most intelligently speculative ideas on the subject in a long time. There are excesses of course, and perhaps once again the pendulum on occasion has swung too far in the other direction (some of the most potent voices on *Finnegans Wake* are heard here *in extremis* on *Dubliners*), but Hart's collection may long remain the best single volume on the subject.

A recent phenomenon worth noticing, and per-haps not too caustically, is a tendency to carve out an area of the canon termed "early Joyce." We have long been familiar with the cleavage between "Wakeans" and the rest of the Joyceans, since the *Wake* has demanded such special attention and concentration that those who profess an expertise there devote much of their energy to it and those inexpert steer clear of it. Now *Ulysses* has also been isolated for special overconcentration or become more forbidding, and a separate militia has banded together to deal primarily with the "early" works. Semblances of this field of specialization have been apparent for some time now, but not so pointedly as with the new books of the 70s: Edward Brandabur's *A Scrupulous Meanness: A Study of Joyce's Early Work* (1971), Edmund L. Epstein's *The Ordeal of Stephen Dedalus: The Conflict of the Generations in James Joyce's A Portrait of the Artist as a Young Man* (1971), and Homer Obed Brown's *James Joyce's Early Fiction: The Biography of a Form* (1972).[58] Brandabur essentially deals with *Dubliners* and *Exiles*, Epstein takes almost all of Joyce for his domain although returning always to his focus on *A Portrait*, while Brown is specific in handling *Dubliners, Stephen Hero,* and *A Portrait*. The coincidence of these books may not indicate the trend for the future (although it is certainly becoming more difficult to juggle *so much* secondary material on *so much* Joycean material within the framework of the normal size of a critical book); instead, it may only be corroborating the adage that doctoral dissertations eventually come home to roost and we are only now receiving the final working out of ideas long in the gestative state.

That *Finnegans Wake* remains a world unto itself, however, is still true, and it may not be overly pessimistic to add that it has become a smaller world with fewer active participants. The élan of early criticism has worn off, that daring which allowed explorers to plunge in and discoverers to make vast claims. A second phase eventually fol-

---

54. Warren Beck, *Joyce's Dubliners: Substance, Vision, and Art* (Durham, N.C.: Duke University Press, 1969).

55. Marvin Magalaner, *Time of Apprenticeship: The Fiction of Young James Joyce* (New York: Abelard-Schuman, 1959).

56. *Reader's Guide*, Preface, opening page.

57. Clive Hart, ed., *James Joyce's Dubliners: Critical Essays* (London: Faber & Faber, 1969).

58. Edward Brandabur, *A Scrupulous Meanness: A Study of Joyce's Early Work* (Urbana, Ill.: University of Illinois Press, 1971); Edmund L. Epstein, *The Ordeal of Stephen Dedalus: The Conflict of the Generations in James Joyce's A Portrait of the Artist as a Young Man* (Carbondale, Ill.: Southern Illinois University Press, 1971); Homer Obed Brown, *James Joyce's Early Fiction: The Biography of a Form* (Cleveland, Ohio: Case Western Reserve University Press, 1972). The indispensable tool for work with *A Portrait* is Robert Scholes and Richard M. Kain, *The Workshop of Daedalus: James Joyce and the Raw Materials for A Portrait of the Artist as a Young Man* (Evanston, Ill.: Northwestern University Press, 1965).

lowed (in the two decades after the *Skeleton Key*) in which specific areas were mined for special lodes and limited corners of scholarship well worked over. It was a period of soberer purposes when one admitted that no real skeleton key actually existed and that the *Wake* would not suddenly reveal all its secrets with the right tap of the right hammer at the right spot. Rather than producing despondency, this realistic attitude permitted Wakeans to work modestly within thousands of small areas of explication, interweaving somewhat larger possibilities as they progressed. Occasionally one heard rumors of "central theories," of a major breakthrough soon to be announced, but as the years wore on the cobwebs settled on such anticipations. From the mid-fifties to the mid-sixties the scholarship amassed, carrying with it a feeling of expectation that major threads could eventually be linked together for cohesive readings of the text. Part of the optimism evolved from group participation, the organization and even internationalization of the Joyce Industry: in 1962 Fritz Senn and Clive Hart began publishing *A Wake Newslitter*, six issues per year mostly devoted to "hard" scholarship in the field; a year later the *James Joyce Quarterly*, edited by Thomas F. Staley, came into being (besides its regular proportion of articles on the *Wake*, the *Quarterly* has also had two all-*Wake* issues—Spring 1965, guest-edited by David Hayman, and Winter 1971). Such industriousness boded well.

Most encouraging was the new availability of the tools of the trade, the reference materials and word lists, which from 1956 began to fall, first by ones and twos, then by threes and fours, at last by fives and sixes of sevens, beginning with Adaline Glasheen's intrepid *A Census of Finnegans Wake*.[59] The personages of the *Wake*, both the fictional characters created by Joyce for his novel and the horde of preexisting people, real and fictional, historic and mythic, are catalogued in the *Census* in alphabetized form, and seven years later the *Second Census*[60] doubled the number of references. In 1959 Hodgart and Worthington added *Song in the Works of James Joyce*,[61] the greatest

portion of which isolated echoes of songs used in the *Wake*, one more avenue of approach to the coagulated masses of materials in Joyce's encyclopedic epic (both a *Third Census* and a second, expanded version of *Song* are well under way). Despite the overwhelming value of both of these volumes, a new and more important salvo was fired by James S. Atherton when *The Books at the Wake* appeared in 1960.[62] Not just a cataloguing of literary allusions and source material used by Joyce, Atherton's book is also an analysis of the *Wake* itself through the allusive method and a reading of *Finnegans Wake* held together by the source material. As such, *The Books at the Wake* is the first book since the *Skeleton Key* to deal coherently with the symbology, though again keyed through a single perspective, but it is better than the *Key* in that the perspective is an aspect of Joyce's book itself.

Textual examination has always loomed as an important consideration in a work that is so complex that possibility of error remains omnipresent, and Joyce himself was the first to examine the printed text critically. His "Corrections of Misprints in *Finnegans Wake*, As Prepared by the Author after Publication of the First Edition" began to be added to later editions and eventually incorporated into the text, and caused new misprints when the type was reset. Sensitive to the creative process involved in the numerous drafts of the *Wake* and to the suggestions available in the notebooks Joyce used while gathering items for his *Wake*, scholars also found themselves working with that which is *not Finnegans Wake*: in 1960 Fred H. Higginson published *Anna Livia Plurabelle: The Making of a Chapter*, an analysis of the drafts of chapter 8; in 1961 Thomas E. Connolly edited *Scribbledehobble: The Ur-Workbook for Finnegans Wake*, one of at least 50 notebooks that Joyce scribbled in while constructing the *Wake*; and in 1963 David Hayman edited *A First-Draft Version of Finnegans Wake*,[63] a piecing-together of the elements of the *Wake* in their earliest stage of composition. Efforts to correct the

59. Adaline Glasheen, *A Census of Finnegans Wake: An Index of the Characters and Their Roles* (Evanston, Ill.: Northwestern University Press, 1956).

60. *A Second Census of Finnegans Wake: An Index of the Characters and Their Roles* (Evanston, Ill.: Northwestern University Press, 1963).

61. Matthew J. C. Hodgart and Mabel P. Worthington, *Song in the Works of James Joyce* (New York: Columbia University Press, 1959).

62. James S. Atherton, *The Books at the Wake: A Study of Literary Allusions in James Joyce's Finnegans Wake* (New York: Viking Press, 1960).

63. Fred H. Higginson, *Anna Livia Plurabelle: The Making of a Chapter* (Minneapolis, Minn.: University of Minnesota Press, 1960); Thomas E. Connolly, *James Joyce's Scribbledehobble: The Ur-Workbook for Finnegans Wake* (Evanston, Ill.: Northwestern University Press, 1961); David Hayman, *A First-Draft Version of Finnegans Wake* (Austin, Texas.: University of Texas Press, 1963).

printed text, however, have so far been unsuccessful, beyond Joyce's hurried list of misprints, publishers proving unwilling to invest in such a resetting of the book when the author himself essentially let it pass as it is. A recent hope for some sort of revision comes from the announcement that James Blish is undertaking the compilation of some 300 suggested corrections to be incorporated into the back of new printings of the *Wake*.

The cache of languages in the *Wake* has often tempted multilingual experts toward the assumption that if one knew all the languages that Joyce knew, *Finnegans Wake* would become readable. Toward this ideal the lexicons flowed. In 1965 Dounia Bunis Christiani published *Scandinavian Elements of Finnegans Wake*,[64] culling Scandinavian words and echoes out of the text in a Glossary and listing Danish, Norwegian, and Swedish words as well; in 1967 both Helmut Bonheim's *A Lexicon of the German in Finnegans Wake* and Brendan O Hehir's *A Gaelic Lexicon for Finnegans Wake*[65] appeared, adding their words to the cornucopia. In addition, the *Newslitter* has periodically been supplying esoteric lists (in Albanian and Malay and Dutch and Kiswahili —the latter even causing a tempest that momentarily disturbed the tea leaves). The net result has been minimal: the lexicographers have succeeded in providing a handful of identifications that we can now note in the margins of the *Wake* (and for which we are grateful) but they have only brought us imperceptibly closer to some sort of basic comprehension. It is painful to tell someone who has spent thousands of hours in wordhunts that his final effort now only provides him with a tool with which to begin work. For unless there is a *concept* developed on the significance of the language in the *Wake* (why do we find Chinese in these particular instances in the book? what connotations do Chinese and China have for *Finnegans Wake*?), the word-hoarder is offering us very little. Once it was suspected that the ideal reader for the *Wake* was a polyglottal European, the reader with the linguistic head start. Perhaps the ideal reader still is the English-speaker for

whom idiomatic English reverberates naturally within his head—and probably an English-speaking Irishman at that

The single most useful implement has been Clive Hart's *A Concordance to Finnegans Wake*,[66] which because of its completeness and thoroughness has changed the nature of *Wake* studies. Not only are the words in *Wake* alphabetized and paginated, but Hart includes sections on Syllabifications (the inner parts of compound words) and Overtones (where the ear makes the association although the eye sees variant spelling). With this sort of apparatus at hand, the Wakean need no longer trust to his rusty memory or crusty notes (more often memory, since it's difficult taking notes on afterthoughts). Since 1963 then, we have had every reason to assume a new burst of energy among *Wake* pursuers and indeed a new generation of Wakeans. But the possession of masterly tools does not create a master craftsman, and instead there seems to be a serious liability to concordance-conceived scholarship. Many an article now reads as if only the *Concordance* and not the *Wake* was used to advantage, that tracing an idea or a motif through the book can be shortcut by looking it up alphabetically and conjecturing from there. Considering that *Finnegans Wake* is a book that very few could claim to have *read*, there are some who have written on it who have read it far less than others.

With the publication of Hart's *Structure and Motif in Finnegans Wake* (1962) [67] *Wake* criticism came of age and the era of optimism began. Instead of reading the *Wake* in sequential progression and pointing out oddities and entities along the way (à la Guide and Key), Hart discusses the book as a whole, analyzing its structural elements and its basic themes and motifs. My book, *Joyce-again's Wake*,[68] three years after, also attempted to present approaches to the totality of the *Wake*, Joyce's attitudes toward Church and State, the poetics of his prose, the epic scope, and the philosophic thrusts. Although we were all aware that a great deal still needed to be done, and although we retained uncertainties about the rashness of some of our speculations, we nonetheless felt that

64. Dounia Bunis Christiani, *Scandinavian Elements of Finnegans Wake* (Evanston, Ill.: Northwestern University Press, 1965).

65. Helmut Bonheim, *A Lexicon of the German in Finnegans Wake* (Berkeley and Los Angeles, Calif.: University of California Press, 1967): Brendan O Hehir, *A Gaelic Lexicon for Finnegans Wake* (Berkeley and Los Angeles: University of California Press, 1967).

66. Clive Hart, *A Concordance to Finnegans Wake* (Minneapolis, Minn.: University of Minnesota Press, 1963).

67. Clive Hart, *Structure and Motif in Finnegans Wake* (Evanston, Ill.: Northwestern University Press, 1962).

68. Bernard Benstock, *Joyce-again's Wake: An Analysis of Finnegans Wake* (Seattle, Wash.: University of Washington Press, 1965).

the field was now very much open to further investigation. The possibilities were infinite but the rocky road had already proved treacherous: with skill and determination J. Mitchell Morse avoided most of the pitfalls in examining Joyce's "Catholicism," particularly as it resurfaces in the *Wake,* in *The Sympathetic Alien* (1959),[69] but that same year Frances Motz Boldereff stumbled painfully through an investigation of Joyce's Irishry in *Reading Finnegans Wake.*[70] In his opening sentence Morse warns that "if we find a genius at all sympathetic, we tend to re-create him in our own image,"[71] and this is just the sort of irreversible error that Boldereff commits; although the "Idioglossary" of Irish allusions is definitely of value, the book is rendered worthless by the personal and illogical involvement of the commentator with Joyce's text, not to mention the arcane irrelevancies. Almost a decade later her second book on the *Wake, Hermes to his Son Thoth, Being Joyce's Use of Giordano Bruno in Finnegans Wake,*[72] is the same kind of disaster.

Two collections of essays and short pieces, *Twelve and a Tilly* and *A Wake Digest* (1966 and 1968),[73] have added to the storehouse of explications, discussed the notebooks and the manuscripts in relation to the text, argued with the state of the printed text itself, offered word lists galore, and instructed on the possibilities of teaching *Finnegans Wake.* Of particular value to all practitioners, hard-core and tyro, is Clive Hart's "The Elephant in the Belly: Exegesis of *Finnegans Wake.*"[74] Reprinted from the *Newslitter* and having evolved from controversies regarding reading, overreading, and misreading the *Wake,* it is a cautionary note, a setting of ground rules, and a delineation of the rights and responsibilities of the Wakean commentators and explicators. The logic of Hart's dicta would apply as well to any work of literature requiring precise explication, but with the *Wake* it becomes necessary to restate them with emphasis: that every element of a word or phrase must be accounted for if an exegesis is to be of value; that planes of meaning must be established and a priority set among them; that the book is composed of *meaningful* components, each of which must function within any explanation.

Discounting Anthony Burgess's *A Shorter Finnegans Wake,*[75] the exact purpose of which (despite an explanatory introduction) eludes me, there have been only two important books on the *Wake* of late, and both of those were unveiled in 1969: William York Tindall's *A Reader's Guide to Finnegans Wake* and Margaret Solomon's *Eternal Geomater: The Sexual Universe of Finnegans Wake.*[76] Tindall's new Guide expands from the scant sixty pages devoted to the *Wake* in the earlier to more than five times the size. By avoiding the writings of others on the *Wake* Tindall remains a pure "reader" (with a little help from his friends). He offers his reader what he knows and what he has learned, assuming that those items explained are necessarily the ones that require explanation, that those bits and pieces dredged up are indeed the essence of the treasure. His choices then are arbitrary and his method—for all of the nuggets it reveals—is the chapter-by-chapter read-through. Margaret Solomon, more of a systematizer, has been doing her homework with diligence and has profited from the decades of *Wake* criticism. In addition, she insists upon taking the work as a whole and investigating in terms of a basic theme and its associative corollaries. The difference between the two 1969 contributions to *Wake* knowledge is primarily the difference between generations.

The two approaches—sequential reading and thematic analysis—will probably continue to track each other in *Wake* scholarship as they have with *Ulysses.* But the greater advantage for the future comes with the thematic approach despite the inherent danger, as can be seen in *Eternal Geomater,* of overstress. (Whereas it is admittedly germane to every part of the *Wake,* sex is no more the single essence of the book than food or war or nocturnal encounters; by her exhaustive study of the human bodily functions Solomon has blurred the

69. J. Mitchell Morse, *The Sympathetic Alien: James Joyce and Catholicism* (New York: New York University Press, 1959).

70. Frances Motz Boldereff, *Reading Finnegans Wake* (Woodward, Pa.: Classic Nonfiction Library, 1959).

71. *Sympathetic Alien,* p. ix.

72. Frances M. Boldereff, *Hermes to his Son Thoth: Being Joyce's Use of Giordano Bruno in Finnegans Wake* (Woodward, Pa.: Classic Nonfiction Library, 1968).

73. Jack P. Dalton and Clive Hart, eds., *Twelve and a Tilly: Essays on the Occasion of the 25th Anniversary of Finnegans Wake* (London: Faber & Faber, 1966); Clive Hart and Fritz Senn, eds., *A Wake Digest* (Sydney: Sydney University Press, 1968).

74. *Digest,* pp. 3-12.

75. Anthony Burgess, *A Shorter Finnegans Wake* (New York: Viking Press, 1966).

76. William York Tindall, *A Reader's Guide to Finnegans Wake* (New York: Noonday Press, 1969); Margaret Solomon, *Eternal Geomater: The Sexual Universe of Finnegans Wake* (Carbondale, Ill.: Southern Illinois University Press, 1969).

peripheral vistas that she acknowledges are infinite.) *Finnegans Wake* commentary requires both the encyclopedic inclusiveness and the single focus, yet rarely does a work of *Wake* scholarship attempt to combine both.

From the vantage point of 1973 the state of *Wake* investigation is not so encouraging as it was a decade earlier. Not only has the amount of publishing on the subject diminished in the past few years, but the possibility of a "major breakthrough" has also fallen by the wayside. I was still rather sanguine in my pessimism in 1965 when I wrote:

> It does not seem too soon to predict that *Finnegans Wake* will never be fully read by any reader (no matter how ideal he may otherwise be). Fragments will be chipped away, brought into the glare of the sun, polished to a high gloss and admired. Conversely, generalities and broad statements will be made about the *Wake,* and in many cases fairly well documented. But the replacement of piece after piece into a reconstructed mosaic fully indicating the lines of the book's ideas and material will probably never take place.[77]

Now I feel somewhat more pessimistic about my pessimism. A forthcoming book on the *Wake,* a pair of solid monographs by Grace Eckley and Michael Begnal,[78] indicates generally what can be expected from the new generation. Both authors are thorough in their examinations of a single motif or a narrative thread and argue their cases well: yet neither monograph does more than polish a fragment or document a statement, and the modesty of the monograph size attests to the scope of the insights. And this volume may well be the first book on *Finnegans Wake* in four years, marking the 70s as the period of recession compared to the boom years of the 60s. Perhaps we can take solace from the generally healthy state of the Joyce Industry with record production chalked up in *Ulysses* approaches and rising productivity in "early Joyce," even if the industrious Wakeans are lagging a bit behind.

Bibliography of Works Mentioned

Adams, Robert M. *Surface and Symbol: the Consistency of James Joyce's Ulysses.* New York: Oxford University Press, 1962.

77. *Joyce-again's Wake,* pp. 40-41.
78. *Narrator and Character in Finnegans Wake* (Lewisburg, Pa.: Bucknell University Press, 1975).

Atherton, James S. *The Books at the Wake: a Study of Literary Allusions in James Joyce's Finnegans Wake.* New York: Viking Press, 1960.

Baker, James R. and Staley, Thomas F., eds. *James Joyce's Dubliners: a Critical Handbook.* Belmont, Calif.: Wadsworth, 1969.

Beck, Warren. *Joyce's Dubliners: Substance, Vision, and Art.* Durham, N.C.: Duke University Press, 1969.

Begnal, Michael and Eckley, Grace. *Narrator and Character in Finnegans Wake.* Lewisburg, Pa.: Bucknell University Press, 1975.

Benjamin, Judy-Lynn, ed. *The Celtic Bull: Essays on James Joyce's Ulysses.* Tulsa, Okla.: University of Tulsa Department of English Monograph Series, 1966.

Benstock, Bernard. "The James Joyce Industry: an Assessment in the Sixties," *Southern Review* n.s. 2 (Winter 1966), pp. 210–228.

————. *Joyce-again's Wake: An Analysis of Finnegans Wake.* Seattle: University of Washington Press, 1965.

Blamires, Harry. *The Bloomsday Book: a Guide Through Joyce's Ulysses.* London: Methuen, 1966.

Boldereff, Frances M. *Hermes to his Son Thoth: Being Joyce's Use of Giordano Bruno in Finnegans Wake.* Woodward, Pa.: Classic Nonfiction Library, 1968.

————. *Reading Finnegans Wake.* Woodward, Pa.: Classic Nonfiction Library, 1959.

Bonheim, Helmut. *A Lexicon of the German in Finnegans Wake.* Berkeley and Los Angeles: University of California Press, 1967.

Brandabur, Edward. *A Scrupulous Meanness: a Study of Joyce's Early Work.* Urbana, Ill.: University of Illinois Press, 1971.

Brown, Homer Obed. *James Joyce's Early Fiction: the Biography of a Form.* Cleveland, Ohio: Case Western Reserve University Press, 1972.

Budgen, Frank. *James Joyce and the Making of Ulysses.* New York: Harrison Smith and Robert Haas, 1934.

Burgess, Anthony. *A Shorter Finnegans Wake.* New York: Viking Press, 1966.

Campbell, Joseph and Robinson, Henry Morton. *A Skeleton Key to Finnegans Wake.* New York: Harcourt, Brace, 1944.

Christiani, Dounia Bunis. *Scandinavian Elements of Finnegans Wake.* Evanston, Ill.: Northwestern University Press, 1965.

Connolly, Thomas E. *James Joyce's Scribbledehobble: the Ur-Workbook for Finnegans Wake.* Evanston, Ill.: Northwestern University Press, 1961.

————, ed. *Joyce's Portrait: Criticisms and Critiques.*

New York: Appleton Century-Crofts, 1962.

Dalton, Jack P. and Hart, Clive. eds. *Twelve and a Tilly: Essays on the Occasion of the 25th Anniversary of Finnegans Wake*. London: Faber and Faber, 1966.

Deming, Robert H. *A Bibliography of James Joyce Studies*. Lawrence, Kans.: University of Kansas Libraries, 1964.

––––––, ed. *James Joyce: the Critical Heritage*, vol. 1. London: Routledge and Kegan Paul, 1970.

Duff, Charles C. *James Joyce and the Plain Reader*. London: Harmsworth, 1932.

Ellmann, Richard. *Ulysses on the Liffey*. New York: Oxford University Press, 1972.

––––––. *James Joyce*. New York: Oxford University Press, 1959.

Envoy 5 (May 1951), Dublin, Ireland. (Special Joyce issue.)

Epstein, Edmund L. *The Ordeal of Stephen Dedalus: the Conflict of the Generations in James Joyce's A Portrait of the Artist as a Young Man*. Carbondale, Ill.: Southern Illinois University Press, 1971.

Fiedler, Leslie. "Bloom on Joyce; or, Jokey for Jacob," *Journal of Modern Literature* 1 (1970): 19–29.

Garrett, Peter K. *Twentieth-Century Interpretations of Dubliners*. Englewood Cliffs, N.J.: Prentice-Hall, 1968.

Gifford, Don. *Notes for Joyce: Dubliners and A Portrait of the Artist as a Young Man*. New York: Dutton, 1967.

Gilbert, Stuart. *James Joyce's Ulysses: a Study*. London: Faber and Faber, 1930.

Glasheen, Adaline. *A Census of Finnegans Wake: An Index of the Characters and Their Roles*. Evanston, Ill.: Northwestern University Press, 1956.

––––––. *A Second Census of Finnegans Wake: an Index of the Characters and Their Roles*. Evanston, Ill.: Northwestern University Press, 1963.

Gogarty, Oliver St. John. "They Think They Know Joyce," *Saturday Review* 33 (18 March 1950): 8–9, 35–37.

Goldberg, S. L. *The Classical Temper: a Study of James Joyce's Ulysses*. London: Chatto and Windus, 1963.

––––––. *James Joyce*. Edinburgh: Oliver and Boyd, 1962.

Golding, Louis. *James Joyce*. London: Thornton Butterworth, 1933.

Gorman, Herbert S. *James Joyce: His First Forty Years*. New York: B. W. Huebsch, 1924; reprinted as *James Joyce*, New York: Rinehart, 1940; revised, 1948.

Hanley, Miles L. *Word Index to James Joyce's Ulysses*. Madison, Wis.: University of Wisconsin Press, 1937; revised, 1965.

Hart, Clive. *A Concordance to Finnegans Wake*. Minneapolis, Minn.: University of Minnesota Press, 1963.

––––––. *James Joyce's Ulysses*. Sydney: Sydney University Press, 1968.

––––––. *Structure and Motif in Finnegans Wake*. Evanston, Ill.: Northwestern University Press, 1962.

––––––, ed. *James Joyce's Dubliners: Critical Essays*. London: Faber & Faber, 1969.

Hayman, David. *A First-Draft Version of Finnegans Wake*. Austin, Tex.: University of Texas Press, 1963.

––––––. *Ulysses: the Mechanics of Meaning*. Englewood Cliffs, N.J.: Prentice-Hall, 1970.

Herring, Phillip F., ed. *Joyce's Ulysses Notesheets in the British Museum*. Charlottesville, Va.: University Press of Virginia, 1972.

Higginson Fred H. *Anna Livia Plurabelle: the Making of a Chapter*. Minneapolis, Minn.: University of Minnesota Press, 1960.

Hodgart, Matthew J. C. and Worthington, Mabel P. *Song in the Works of James Joyce*. New York: Columbia University Press, 1959.

Hyman, Louis. *The Jews of Ireland: From Earliest Times to the Year 1910*. Dublin: Irish University Press, 1972.

Joyce, James. *Giacomo Joyce*. Edited by Richard Ellmann. New York: Viking Press, 1968.

––––––. *Letters of James Joyce*. vol. 1. Edited by Stuart Gilbert. New York: Viking Press, 1957.

––––––. *Letters of James Joyce*. vols. 2 and 3. Edited by Richard Ellmann. New York: Viking Press, 1966.

Kain, Richard M. *Fabulous Voyager: James Joyce's Ulysses*. Chicago: University of Chicago Press, 1947. New York: Viking Press, 1959.

Kenner, Hugh. *Dublin's Joyce*. London: Chatto and Windus, 1955.

Levin, Harry. *James Joyce: a Critical Introduction*. Norfolk, Conn.: New Directions, 1941.

Litz, A. Walton. *The Art of James Joyce: Method and Design in Ulysses and Finnegans Wake*. London: Oxford University Press, 1961.

Magalaner, Marvin. *Time of Apprenticeship: The Fiction of Young James Joyce*. New York: Abelard-Schuman, 1959.

––––––, and Kain, Richard M. *Joyce: the Man, the Work, the Reputation*. New York: New York University Press, 1956.

Morris, William E., and Nault, Clifford A. Jr., eds. *Portraits of an Artist: a Casebook on James Joyce's*

A Portrait of the Artist as a Young Man. New York: Odyssey Press, 1962.

Morse, J. Mitchell. "Molly Bloom Revisited." *James Joyce Miscellany*, 2. Carbondale, Ill.: Southern Illinois University Press, 1959. Pp. 139–49.

_____. *The Sympathetic Alien: James Joyce and Catholicism.* New York: New York University Press, 1959.

Mosaic 6 (Fall 1972). (Special Joyce issue.)

Moynihan, William T., ed. *Joyce's The Dead.* Boston: Allyn and Bacon, 1965.

O Hehir, Brendan. *A Gaelic Lexicon for Finnegans Wake.* Berkeley and Los Angeles, Calif.: University of California Press, 1967.

Prescott, Joseph. *Exploring James Joyce.* Carbondale, Ill.: Southern Illinois University Press, 1964.

Ryan, John, ed. *A Bash in the Tunnel: James Joyce by the Irish.* Brighton (England): Clifton Books, 1970.

Scholes, Robert and Kain, Richard M. *The Workshop of Daedalus: James Joyce and the Raw Materials for A Portrait of the Artist as a Young Man.* Evanston, Ill.: Northwestern University Press, 1965.

Schutte, William M. *Joyce and Shakespeare: a Study in the Meaning of Ulysses.* New Haven, Conn.: Yale University Press, 1957.

_____. *Twentieth Century Interpretations of A Portrait of the Artist as a Young Man.* Englewood Cliffs, N.J.: Prentice-Hall, 1968.

Senn, Fritz, ed. *New Light on Joyce from the Dublin Symposium.* Bloomington, Ind.: Indiana University Press, 1972.

Solomon, Margaret. *Eternal Geomater: the Sexual Universe of Finnegans Wake.* Carbondale, Ill.: Southern Illinois University Press, 1969.

Smith, Paul Jordan. *A Key to the Ulysses of James Joyce.* New York: Covici, Friede, 1927.

Staley, Thomas F. and Benstock, Bernard. *Approaches to Ulysses: Ten Essays.* Pittsburgh, Pa.: University of Pittsburgh Press, 1970.

Steinberg, Erwin R. "A Book with a Molly in it," *James Joyce Review* 2 (Spring-Summer 1958): 55–62.

_____. *The Stream of Consciousness and Beyond in Ulysses.* Pittsburgh, Pa.: University of Pittsburgh Press, 1972.

Sultan, Stanley. *The Argument of Ulysses.* Columbus, Ohio: Ohio State University Press, 1964.

Thornton, Weldon. *Allusions in Ulysses: an Annotated List.* Chapel Hill: University of North Carolina Press, 1968.

Tindall, William York. *James Joyce: His Way of Interpreting the Modern World.* New York: Scribner's, 1950.

_____. *A Reader's Guide to Finnegans Wake.* New York: Noonday Press, 1969.

_____. *A Reader's Guide to James Joyce.* New York: Noonday Press, 1959.

Wilson, Edmund. *Axel's Castle.* New York: Scribner's, 1931.

_____. "H. C. Earwicker and Family: a Review of *Finnegans Wake*," *New Republic* 94 (28 June and 12 July 1939).

Part III

SAMUEL BECKETT

Photographs by Kathleen McGrory

Samuel Beckett. Etching by Jack Coughlin. *Courtesy of Mr. Coughlin.*

Cooldrinagh, Foxrock. Former home of Beckett Family. *Photo by McGrory.*

"Turning this and cognate anxieties over and over in his mind he came at length to the southern limit of the Gallops and the by-road that he had to cross to get into the next list of fields . . . In the ditch on the far side of the road a strange equipage was installed: an old high-wheeled cart, hung with rags. . . . Squatting under the cart a complete down-and-out was very busy with something or other. . . . Now Belacqua could see what he was doing. He was mending a pot or pan." ("Walking Out," *More Pricks Than Kicks,* p. 111)

Tinker's van on Murphystown Road near Croker's Gallops (former Boss Croker estate) between Leopardstown Racecourse and Foxrock. *Photo by Mc-Grory.*

Grosvenor Hotel, Westland Row, opposite Pearse Station. *Photo by McGrory.*

". . . scarcely had Chas been shed than lo from out
the Grosvenor sprang the homespun Poet. . . ."
("A Wet Night," *More Pricks Than Kicks,* p. 57)

"Emerging, on the particular evening in question, from the underground convenience in the maw of College Street . . . he squatted, not that he had too much drink taken but simply that for the moment there were no grounds for his favouring one direction rather than another, against Tommy Moore's plinth." ("Ding-Dong," *More Pricks Than Kicks,* p. 41)

Statue of Thomas Moore, College Street, facing Bank of Ireland. *Photo by McGrory.*

Dental Hospital, Lincoln Place, between Dublin
Chess Club and Trinity College, within sight of
estate agency firm of O'Dwyer, Beckett, Collier, Ltd.
(Horner Beckett, cousin of Samuel Beckett). *Photo by
McGrory.*

"It was raining bitterly when Belacqua, keyed up
to take his bearings, issued forth into the unintel-
ligible world of Lincoln Place. But he had bought
a bottle, it was like a breast in the pocket of his
reefer. He set off unsteadily by the Dental Hospital. As a child he had dreaded its façade, its sheets
of blood-red glass. Now they were black, which was
worse again. . . ." ("A Wet Night," *More Pricks
Than Kicks,* p. 75)

"Thus, she having a friend, he his heart, in Portrane, they agreed to make for there. . . . The place was as full of towers as Dun Laoghaire of steeples . . . . 'This absurd tower' he said, now that he had been told, 'is before the asylum, and they are before the tower.' . . . The tower began well; that was the funeral meats. But from the door up it was all relief and no honour; that was the marriage tables." ("Fingal," *More Pricks Than Kicks*, pp. 28–31)

Portrane. Round tower with mental hospital towers in background. *Photo by McGrory.*

Portrane. Main gate, Saint Ita's mental hospital. *Photo by McGrory.*

"They could all three meet at the main entrance of the asylum in, say, an hour. . . . Thus they were all met together in Portrane, Winnie, Belacqua, his heart and Dr. Sholto, and paired off to the satisfaction of all parties. Surely it is in such little adjustments that the benevolence of the First Cause appears beyond dispute. Winnie kept her eye on the time and arrived punctually with her friend at the main entrance. There was no sign of her other friend. 'Late' said Winnie 'as usual.' In respect of Belacqua Sholto felt nothing but rancour. 'Pah' he said 'he'll be sandpapering a tomb.' ("Fingal," *More Pricks Than Kicks*, pp. 32–33)

" 'The Lovely ruins' said Winnie 'there on the left, covered with ivy.' Of a church and, two small fields further on, a square bawnless tower. 'That' said Belacqua 'is where I have sursum corda.' . . . Abstract the asylum and there was little left of Portrane but ruins. . . . 'In that case' said Winnie 'maybe you can tell me what the ruins are.' 'That's the church' he said, pointing to the near one, . . . 'and that' pointing to the far one, ' 's the tower.' 'Yes' said Winnie 'but what tower, what was it?' 'The best I know' he said 'is Lady Something had it.' This was news indeed. 'Then before that again' it all came back to him with a rush 'you might have heard tell of Dane Swift, he kep a'—he checked the word and then let it come regardless— 'he kep a motte in it. . . . A motte' he said 'of the name of Stella.' " ("Fingal," *More Pricks Than Kicks,* pp. 30–34)

Portrane. Ruins of church, churchyard, with Dean Swift's square tower visible on left. *Photo by McGrory.*

"When he came to the bridge over the canal, not Baggot Street, not Leeson Street, but another nearer the sea, he gave in. . . . Gradually the pain got better." ("A Wet Night," *More Pricks Than Kicks,* pp. 87--88)

Grand Canal, Mount Street Bridge with Baggot Street and Leeson Street bridges in distance. *Photo by McGrory.*

10

Ireland / The World: Beckett's Irishness

Vivian Mercier

SAMUEL BECKETT is an Irishman but not an Irish writer. Years ago I put this in a different way: "Beckett might be described as *in* the Gaelic tradition but not *of* it." Elsewhere in *The Irish Comic Tradition* I tried to explain why Beckett and Swift produced work that was continuous with the Gaelic tradition though "in neither case was this continuity the result of conscious imitation." There were, I suggested, Gaelic elements in the oral culture of English-speaking Ireland that Beckett and Swift picked up unconsciously. I still think there may be truth in this view: structuralists might well be able to show relationships between Gaelic and Anglo-Irish texts that are superficially quite dissimilar, though I doubt if these findings could ever be verified. But I have to admit that I was engaged in special pleading: an Irish comic tradition that found no room for Beckett and Swift would hardly have been worth writing about. In the present essay I want to emphasize another aspect of Beckett: when we remember that he is a special kind of Irishman—Protestant, middle-class, raised and educated mainly in what is now the Republic of Ireland—the special kind of universality he has achieved becomes a great deal more understandable.

I first put forward this idea in a *New Republic* article in 1955, only to have it dismissed by Martin Esslin in these words:

It has been suggested that Beckett's preoccupation with the problems of being and the identity of the self might have sprung from the Anglo-Irishman's inevitable and perpetual concern with finding his own answer to the question "Who am I?" But while there well may be a grain of truth in this, it is surely far from providing a complete explanation for the deep existential anguish that is the keynote of Beckett's work and that clearly originates in levels of his personality far deeper than its social surface.[1]

But indeed I wasn't talking about "social surface": I can't profess to know for certain what goes on at the deeper levels of my own personality, let alone Beckett's, but something very deep-seated must have prevented me from taking American citizenship during my 29 years in the United States. Only half in jest, I keep saying that my Irish passport is the best proof of my Irishness and, because somebody of my background has such difficulty getting accepted as Irish, I can't afford to give it up. I was pleased to learn, on the authority of Francis Warner,[2] that Beckett has kept his Irish passport up-to-date too. The less religion means to me, the more vital it becomes to my psychic health that I should identify with Ireland—not so much the political nation as the cultural entity. Perhaps, if I had stayed in Ireland, I would not have needed to impatriate myself: I might not have learned Old Irish in my thirties or written *The Irish Comic Tradition*. Although—or perhaps because—my Huguenot ancestors came to Ireland over two hundred years ago, I might have spent my life in Ireland teaching French language and literature.

1. Martin Esslin, *The Theatre of the Absurd* (Garden City, N.Y.: Anchor Books, 1961), p. 1.
   This essay was written while the author was a Fellow of the John Simon Guggenheim Foundation, to which grateful acknowledgment is made.
2. Francis Warner, "The Absence of Nationalism in the Work of Samuel Beckett," in *Theatre and Nationalism in Twentieth Century Ireland*, ed. Robert O'Driscoll (London: Oxford University Press, 1971), p. 179.

Expatriation—whether physical or spiritual—is easy for people of Beckett's and my background, the so-called Anglo-Irish, whom I prefer to call Southern Irish Protestants. Historically viewed, we are an intelligentsia as Toynbee defined it: a minority group that draws its ideas and general culture from outside its native country. Furthermore, our ancestors came to Ireland as colonists, so that we find it hard to shake off the wariness and mistrust of the natives proper to a foreign garrison. That mistrust has the effect sometimes of making conservatives among us take up liberal positions—against censorship and for birth control—in order to stress their difference from Catholics. Because we are colonials, the idea of return to the mother country, Great Britain, must always hold an attraction for some of us, including the kind of writer who wants a big readership and the power to influence public opinion over a wide area. However, since we live so close to her, we have fewer illusions about the mother country than do New Englanders, Canadians, New Zealanders, or Australians.

I have said enough to make it clear that Beckett's Irish background offered him at least three choices: expatriation, impatriation, and return to the mother country. A fourth choice was simply to stay put, as his father and mother and many of his Protestant contemporaries did, without much soul-searching about their Irishness. Beckett grew up—happily, as he insists—in Foxrock, then one of the more distant and exclusive Dublin suburbs. His neighbors were mainly well-to-do professional people, many of them Protestant, living in comfortable houses set in their own grounds. Golf was part of their way of life at a time when Irish golf clubs were less democratic than they are now. The males and some of the females of the family took the train every weekday to office, school, or college in Dublin. In all these places they were likely to be associating almost exclusively with fellow Protestants—as Beckett did at Earlsfort House School and later at Trinity College. Irish Catholics, rich or poor, played walk-on parts in their lives. The females who stayed at home spent their leisure time with other Protestant ladies, though their maids and gardeners were usually Catholic. If one preferred to think of oneself as English, there was really no reason not to. Gaelic was not compulsory at Protestant private schools—Beckett was too old to have been exposed to it anyway—so that even that rather factitious element of Irishness was missing.

Staying put, however, was never really a valid option for anyone self-conscious enough to become a writer, especially a creative one. Before the establishment of the Irish Free State, now the Republic, in 1922, it was certainly possible to return to the mother country or become an expatriate without anguish. Oscar Wilde and Bernard Shaw seem to have gone off to England more or less on the spur of the moment. On the other hand, it did cost Synge in particular a great deal of time and energy to impatriate himself. Interestingly, he first tried expatriation, hoping to earn a living by writing critical articles on European literature for periodicals in English-speaking countries. Eventually, as we know, he moved in the opposite direction, impatriating himself at the core of Gaelic folk culture in the Aran Islands. The resulting creative explosion—in nine years from his first visit to Aran in 1898 he had completed *The Playboy of the Western World* and three other plays still in the international repertory—suggests that for years previously he had been undergoing an identity crisis. Yeats, on the other hand, seems to have consciously chosen Irishness without a struggle.

John Hewitt, the Ulster poet, whose *Collected Poems* appeared in 1968, has given a very explicit account of his impatriation.[3] He begins by making the same point about the Northern Ireland Protestant that I have been making about his counterpart from the Republic:

> In my experience, people of Planter stock often suffer from some crisis of identity, of not knowing where they belong. Among us you will find some who call themselves British, some Irish, some Ulstermen, usually with a degree of hesitation or mental fumbling.

Given this triple choice, he rejected Irishness because he was neither Gaelic in speech nor Catholic in religion; Britishness was no more satisfactory, so he made up his mind that he was an Ulsterman. For many of the Protestants in Northern Ireland, who outnumber the Catholics there two to one, this might have seemed no more than staying put; Hewitt, however, adopted a more positive attitude:

> I set about deepening my knowledge of Ulster's physical components, its history, its arts, its literature, its folklore.

---

3. John Hewitt, "No Rootless Colonist," *Aquarius* (Benburb, Co. Tyrone), no. 5 (1972), pp. 90-95.

Ulster is to him a Region—"smaller than the nation, larger than the family"—and he hoped that "in this concept might be found a meeting-place for the two separated communities" of Northern Ireland. This seems a vain hope, but Hewitt's best poems, including long ones like "The Colony" and "Conacre," are based on his exploration of what it is to be an Ulsterman.

Did Beckett undergo a similar crisis of identity? It seems certain that he did, and that it was painful and prolonged, lasting from about 1930, when he returned from his two years' teaching at the École Normale in Paris, until at least 1937. In a deeper sense, as Esslin suggested, Beckett's identity crisis has been lifelong, but during the years 1930 to 1937 he oscillated between Dublin on the one hand and London, Paris, Germany on the other before finally settling in Paris. Lawrence E. Harvey describes Beckett's predicament at this period as follows:

> Caught between the two impossibilities of domestication and exile and unfailing in filial devotion, he found return and departure almost equally painful —and equally desirable—alternatives.[4]

Harvey's "domestication" is what I have termed "staying put," and in his view the only valid alternative was expatriation. When Beckett gave up his post as lecturer in French at Trinity, after only four terms (quarters), at the end of 1931, he was probably also rejecting the Foxrock world—of which Trinity was in many ways a continuation—at least at the unconscious level. But, after a vain attempt to support himself in Paris and London, he went back to Foxrock before the end of 1932. In June 1933 his father died, quite unexpectedly, after a brief illness. Beckett's elder brother then allowed him £200 a year for the goodwill of his interest in the family firm. Beckett, now independent though poor, spent three unhappy years in London and some six months in Germany before returning to Paris in October 1937. He was settling there for good, though he probably did not know this at the time. The way was opening to a self-discovery in expatriation as startling as Synge's in impatriation—the spate of fiction and plays that he wrote in French between 1946 and 1950.

Why was it that Beckett never seriously considered the possibility of impatriating himself? I think there may have been several reasons. One was surely that he had never lived in or even visited, perhaps, any part of Ireland where he was conscious of a minority or alien status. (Portora, of course, was virtually an all-Protestant school.) He had never walked, as I did every day in Clara, Offaly, past a row of half-doors over which stared ironic Catholic eyes—not those of romantic peasants but of sharp-tongued women and boys, the wives and children of factory workers, who knew more about me and my family than I would ever know about them. Another reason was that Beckett's true intellectual awakening took place after he went to Paris to teach English at the École Normale in 1928 and became a member of James Joyce's circle. No one has yet found any undergraduate contributions by him to *T.C.D.*, the College weekly, run like a secret society very much on the lines of *Punch*. Although his academic record was excellent, he must have spent a good deal of his time playing cricket and rugby and golf and going about with undergraduates for whom these activities were the chief interest of college life. When he did adopt the intellectual life, he went at it with sudden enthusiasm, producing the remarkable essay on *Work in Progress*, full of dogmatic assertions about aesthetics but also crammed with erudition. Hard on its heels came the poem *Whoroscope*, a pastiche of Eliot and Pound, larded with quotations and recondite allusions that had to be explained in notes. Usually a poet begins by imitating the classics of his language; Beckett, though, was *avant-garde* at the first leap. Doubtless Joyce encouraged him to experiment with form, forgetting the slow, painful way in which he himself had progressed from *Chamber Music* and the early *Dubliners* stories to the formal virtuosity of the later episodes in *Ulysses*. Joyce forgot, too, that his own hoard of Irish experience was virtually inexhaustible, whereas Beckett had brought from his carefully insulated suburban community very little that was usable and durable. Foxrock deliberately avoided much of Irish popular culture while providing regrettably little English culture, high or low, to put in its place. "A Wet Night" seems to boast how cosmopolitan and cultivated is the Dublin Beckett knows, yet the conversation never for a moment becomes interesting, whereas that of the half-educated native Dubliners in Joyce's "Grace" or "Ivy Day in the Committee Room" fascinates us. Beckett learned a lot in those first two years in Paris, and in the prewar years gen-

---

4. Lawrence E. Harvey, *Samuel Beckett: Poet and Critic* (Princeton, N.J.: Princeton University Press, 1970), p. 67.

erally, that he had to unlearn later. No wonder so much of his later work seems a continuous process of stripping, peeling, paring away.

One could argue that the banning of *More Pricks Than Kicks* in 1934 was crucial in alienating Beckett from Ireland. Harvey quotes an unpublished essay, "Censorship in the Saorstat [Free State]" that dates from 1936, in which Beckett denounces both censorship and the prohibition of birth control, saying that "sterilization of the mind and apotheosis of the litter suit well together." He was particularly indignant at the banning of books as "in general tendency indecent or obscene" by a censorship board that read only marked passages in works submitted to them. At one point in *Murphy* he writes: "This phrase is chosen with care, lest the filthy censors should lack an occasion to commit their filthy synecdoche [taking a part for the whole]."

But even before the order prohibiting his book had been made by the Irish Free State Minister for Justice, Beckett had gone on record once for all as rejecting the artistic canons of the Anglo-Irish literary revival: "the *Gossoons Wunderhorn* of that Irish Romantic Arnim-Brentano combination, Sir Samuel Ferguson and Standish O'Grady. . . ." In the special Irish issue of *The Bookman* for August 1934, he published an essay on "Recent Irish Poetry" that somehow escaped the notice of Federman and Fletcher but was reprinted in *The Lace Curtain*.[5] Here he divided contemporary Irish poets into "antiquarians and others," rejecting the antiquarians. In order not to be an antiquarian, one must recognize "the breakdown of the object":

> The artist who is aware of this may state the space that intervenes between him and the world of objects. . . . A picture by Mr. Jack Yeats, Mr. Eliot's "Waste Land," are notable statements of this kind. Or he may celebrate the cold comforts of apperception. He may even record his findings, if he is a man of great personal courage.

He reproaches the poets of the Revival and after for their "flight from self-awareness."

> At the centre there is no theme. . . . But the circumference is an iridescence of themes—Oisin, Cuchulain,

Maeve, Tir-nan-og, the Táin Bo Cuailgne, Yoga, the Crone of Beare—segment after segment of cut-and-dried sanctity and loveliness.

Except for Cuchulain, whose statue receives some attention in *Murphy*, these staples of the Gaelic tradition are totally absent from Beckett's creative work—indeed, without this article, we would not be sure that he was sufficiently aware of them to reject them. The phrase "sanctity and loveliness" from "Coole Park and Ballylee, 1931," indicates a familiarity with Yeats's poetry not to be guessed at from Beckett's creative work either. Elsewhere in the essay, too, he shows a knowledge of Yeats in the process of rejecting him. Beckett clearly enjoys his own iconoclasm: he implies that Synge was "a creative hack," and Stephens a "beauty expert," while George Russell ("A.E.") "enters his heart's desire with such precipitation as positively to protrude into the void." Younger poets like Austin Clarke, F. R. Higgins, and Monk Gibbon are also chided for their antiquarianism.

The poets of whom Beckett approves include Thomas MacGreevy—whom he calls "an existentialist in verse"—Blanaid Salkeld, Percy (Arland) Ussher, Lyle Donaghy, and Geoffrey Taylor. Naturally he saves his strongest commendation until the end of the essay:

> Mr. Denis Devlin and Mr. Brian Coffey are without question the most interesting of the youngest generation of Irish poets . . . they have submitted themselves to the influences of those poets least concerned with evading the bankrupt relationship referred to at the opening of this essay—Corbière, Rimbaud, Laforgue, the *surréalistes* and Mr. Eliot, perhaps also to those of Mr. Pound—with results that constitute already the nucleus of a living poetic in Ireland.

Unfortunately, none of those recommended poets except Denis Devlin produced a large enough body of genuinely original work to be accepted by that international audience for whom they were writing. Beckett's own poetry, except for "Enueg I," I find a sad mixture of pseudo-Pound and ersatz Eliot. Yeats was right: in cutting themselves off from a native tradition, the Irish poets of the thirties condemned themselves on the whole to pastiche, while Austin Clarke by persisting in his Irishness eventually became, like Yeats before him, a model for poets fifty years his juniors.

Beckett had natural gifts as a writer that would probably in the end have triumphed over any con-

---

5. Samuel Beckett, "Recent Irish Poetry," *The Lace Curtain* (Dublin), no. 4 (Summer 1971), pp. 58-63. Published under the pseudonym Andrew Belis in *The Bookman* 86 (Aug 1934): 235-36.

vention in which he chose to write. *Murphy,* for all its self-conscious cleverness, its pedantry, its cosmopolitan eclecticism, contains passages, especially in chapter 6 (on Murphy's mind) and chapter 13 (the last), that deal existentially with the human condition. But the true source of strength in Beckett's later works is his total acceptance of expatriation. Alienated, however unconsciously, from the majority of his fellow citizens of the Free State, he made alienation into a way of life: first in London during the unhappy years that produced *Murphy,* then in Paris. His wartime experience pushed him still farther along the path of alienation. As Alec Reid puts it, "For . . . two and a half years Beckett's life and Suzanne's depended literally on his ability to pass himself off as a French peasant. . . ."[6] He became estranged from his native tongue to the point where, like Nabokov, he could not merely write in a foreign language but be recognized as an inimitable—though often imitated—stylist in it. Circumstances had combined to make him an alienated artist: his own genius was to make him a fit laureate for an age of alienation. By the end of the war he must have realized that a man of his caliber could not be content—as I, a critic, can be—with a mere identification of himself as an Irishman or a Frenchman. Identity lay far deeper than identification: I am a man, yes, but what do I mean by "I" or "man"? *The Unnamable,* a novel about the impossibility and yet the necessity of saying "I," represents, I think, the final stage possible in that search for identity. Beyond lies annihilation, the loss of all being: Beckett looked at it in *Endgame* but could not accept it.

Endgame was not merely the logical end of Beckett's search for identity: it was the end of his creativity in French for perhaps four years. (*Fin de partie,* the original of *Endgame,* was finished by June 21, 1956; *Comment c'est,* his next major work in French, was published January 9, 1961.) Having come to an *impasse,* he decided to turn back—back all the way to Ireland, to Foxrock railway station and the adjoining Leopardstown Racecourse. Beckett himself said of *All That Fall* (1957), "It is a text written to come out of the dark." The play is set entirely in Ireland and includes some Anglo-Irish dialect, characteristics it shares with only two previous works, *More Pricks Than Kicks* and *Watt* (finished 1945).

6. Alec Reid, *All I Can Manage, More Than I Could,* 2nd ed. (Dublin: The Dolmen Press, 1969), p. 14.

For after all, as I said at the beginning, Beckett is an Irishman. He knows Foxrock, he knows the streets of Dublin, especially those near Trinity ("Ding-Dong," "A Wet Night"); he knows the Dublin mountains, west and southwest of Foxrock ("Love and Lethe," "Walking Out"); he knows north County Dublin ("Fingal," the Gaelic name for the area). He also knows the lower-class Dublin dialect; in *Watt* and *All That Fall* it is mainly used by the railway-station staff, but other users of it occur in *More Pricks Than Kicks*—especially the pedlar woman in "Ding-Dong" and the maid, Venerilla, in "A Wet Night." Oddly enough, the only work by Beckett written entirely in this dialect is an adaptation from the French: *The Old Tune* (1960), his version of Pinget's one-act play, *La Manivelle.* In the many plays written first in English rather than French after *Fin de partie*—*All That Fall, Krapp's Last Tape, Embers, Happy Days, Play*—it is hard to judge whether there is anything distinctively Irish about the speech of the middle-class characters. They do not use Dublin dialect words or Gaelic syntax, but I can't help feeling that Winnie in *Happy Days* might have gone to Alexandra School and College, Dublin, like my own mother and countless other Protestant young ladies down the years.

About Beckett's own English there is no doubt: although he uses no dialect, it has a distinct Dublin quality of the kind often called a Trinity accent, though neither Joyce nor Shaw, who both also spoke with it, went to Trinity. Most Trinity men in fact don't have this accent: properly speaking, it is that of the middle-class Dublin South Side, hard to acquire unless you or your parents grew up in the Georgian squares or the red-brick suburbs. Yeats hadn't it: his speech was that of Sligo, an odd mixture of western and northern Irish sounds.

Three other great Irish writers besides Beckett have made their home in Paris for shorter or longer periods, been much influenced by French literature, and received much admiration from the French: Oscar Wilde, John Synge, James Joyce. Beckett has something in common with all of them, but the differences in him are more important.

Wilde came from the Dublin professional class, went to Portora and Trinity, and wrote a play in French for the Paris stage. He seems a typical expatriate dilettante, trying to imitate the French *avant-garde* of his day, but succeeding only superficially. *The Picture of Dorian Gray* is a vulgarization of Huysmans' *À rebours;* Wilde's attempts at *symboliste* poetry are Swinburne and water; *Salomé* may be decadent, but it is still melodrama. None of this is any better than Beckett's early poems or *Murphy,* and there is nothing to suggest that if Wilde had lived longer he would have gone deeper. His best work was done for the London stage in the tradition of Congreve and Sheridan—a colonist returning to the mother country. It is Wilde the man rather than Wilde the artist who has achieved universality.

Synge, like Beckett, came from a more puritanical, less sophisticated Protestant home than Wilde. Unlike Beckett, he was lonely at Trinity. After some years of expatriation, Synge, as we have seen, impatriated himself. He did not, as Beckett implied in "Recent Irish Poetry," fly from self-awareness to an Aran idyll: on the contrary, Aran helped him confront himself and the human condition existentially in at least three plays— *Riders to the Sea, The Well of the Saints,* and *The Playboy of the Western World.* Act II of *Well,* properly understood, is the grimmest confrontation of all: Martin Doul literally *sees* that life is nasty, brutish, short. Synge found his universality where he looked for it, in folklore and folk life.

Joyce managed to have it both ways: he was an expatriate *avant-garde* artist who imagined that he was casting aside his family, his nationality, and his religion;[7] but, just as he brought one of his brothers and two of his sisters to Europe to live with him, so he kept his country and his church in his baggage too. The universality of *Ulysses* at least, and probably that of the other works, depends on parochialism. A glance at the names and addresses in the visitors' book at the Martello Tower in Sandycove ought to convince anyone who doubts this. People come from all over the world to visit a military relic at a suburban bathing place because a young Dublin man once spent a few days there and stamped its image forever upon the opening pages of his greatest work.

It seems unlikely that there will ever be a holy place of pilgrimage like Yeats's tower or Joyce's tower in any posthumous Beckett cult. The "necessary house . . . on the right as one goes down into the pit" has disappeared with the rest of the old Abbey Theatre, while the "breakdown of the object" in Beckett's own work almost guarantees that no other place less suited to subjective reverie is likely to capture the imagination of his readers. Cooldrinagh, Foxrock, his birthplace, lacks charisma in itself and has had none bestowed on it by his works. Nor are the places where he lived in Paris and London likely to attract the crowd. Dublin, London, Paris all lie on the circumference; as Beckett made clear in 1934, the center is what counts. While Beckett still lives, his mind is the center; after his death it will be found in his books. He has traveled farther than most men toward the center of his own being; more important still, he has been able to come back and "record his findings." We who read his books and watch his plays have been able to recognize ourselves in this part or that of his findings and thus are or ought to be prepared to take the rest on trust. Beckett's universality, in the last analysis, does not depend on impatriation or expatriation, on Irishness, Frenchness, or cosmopolitanism: it depends on the paradox of a unique self that has found its bedrock in our common human predicament.[8]

---

7. "I will not serve that in which I no longer believe, whether it call itself my home, my fatherland, or my church. . . ." Stephen Dedalus in *A Portrait of the Artist As a Young Man,* chap. 5.

8. I wrote this essay before rereading *Mercier et Camier* (Paris: Minuit, 1970), which I had first read in typescript a number of years ago. Of all the works written originally in French, this is the one most unmistakably set in Ireland. True, no Irish place-names are mentioned nor is there to my knowledge a Saint-Ruth Square in any Irish city, but Marshal St. Ruth died in Ireland at the battle of Aughrim, as every Irish schoolboy knows. Many of the surnames—Madden, Conaire, Joly, Hamilton—are common in Ireland. As for the names of the title characters, Beckett must have known E. D. Camier at either Portora or Trinity and by 1946 was probably aware of me as a Portora and Trinity alumnus; in that year, too, I praised *Murphy* in Cyril Connolly's *Horizon.* The coins and the drinks—stout, J.J.—are Irish too, but the clinching details come on pp. 165-68 of the French, where Mercier and Camier are walking along the old Military Road (*l'ancien chemin des armées*), see the city below them, and notice a simple cross out in the bog. They can't remember why it's there, but the narrator tells us that a patriot was executed there by the enemy, or at any rate his body was left there. "*Il s'appelait Masse.*" Irishmen with longer memories than Mercier and Camier will recall that his name was Lemass and that his family, though Catholic, was of Huguenot descent. I often passed his monument on walks over the Dublin Mountains; Beckett must have done so even more frequently.

11

Spirals of Need: Irish Prototypes in Samuel Beckett's Fiction

Sighle Kennedy

SAMUEL BECKETT, in commenting on the work of other Irish artists, has insisted that their achievements cannot be measured in terms of national background, but must be appreciated according to what he calls "the autonomy of the imagined."[1] Of painter Jack Yeats, whose Irish subject matter often attracted more attention than did his art, Beckett noted dryly: "The national aspects of Mr. Yeats's genius have I think been overstated, and for motives not always remarkable for their aesthetic purity."[2] Of Dennis Devlin's poetry, he declared even more emphatically that it must not be viewed through the biased lenses of nationalism or pedantry, but must be "free to be derided (or not) in its own terms and not in those of the politicians, antiquaries (Geleerte) and zealots."[3]

Almost every introduction to Beckett's work lists the dates and locations of his Irish birth, upbringing, and schooling.[4] But these chronic and geographic facts—even literary discussions of Beckett's distinguished Irish predecessors, Swift, Sterne, Yeats, and Joyce—do not seem to shed much light on the out-landish personages and situations that constitute the world of Beckett's novels and dramas. Is there any use then in approaching Beckett's work through its Irish elements, if these remain only a superficial aspect (however entertaining) of his art? In such a case, the answer must, of course, be No.

But Beckett's continued and varied use of Irish materials—a usage persisting through more than forty years of his residence abroad—seems to point to some deep involvement of this material with the central working of his genius. Why should he continue to introduce into his novels and plays Irish dialect forms, patronyms, place-names, historic and literary references, turns of thought, turns of phrase, cadences of speech? Why do central characters, in settings obviously not Hibernian, continue to bear the names of Murphy, Kelly, Moran, MacMann, Malone? How does the aged Krapp happen to remember the singing of old Miss McGlome of Connacht?[5] Why does the hero of "L'Expulsé" remember the first line of Thomas Moore's song on Sarah Curran (beloved of Robert Emmet), a line Beckett studiously renders into French as *"Elle est loin du pays où son jeune heros dort"*?[6] Why, in what is perhaps the most famous single passage from any of Beckett's

1. "An Imaginative Work!" review of *The Amaranthers*, by Jack Yeats, *Dublin Magazine* 11 (July-Sept. 1936): 80.
2. "McGreevy on Yeats," review of *Jack B. Yeats: An Appreciation and Interpretation*, by Thomas McGreevy, *Irish Times*, August 5, 1945, p. 2.
3. Review of *Intercessions*, by Dennis Devlin, *Transition*, April-May, 1938, p. 289.
4. Some well-known examples: John Fletcher, *Novels of Samuel Beckett* (London: Chatto & Windus, 1964), pp. 13-14; William York Tindall, *Samuel Beckett* (New York: Columbia University Press, 1964), pp. 3-4; Lawrence Harvey, *Samuel Beckett: Poet and Critic* (Princeton, N.J.: Princeton University Press, 1970), pp. 75, 153-54.

5. *Krapp's Last Tape* (New York: Grove Press, 1958), p. 15.
6. *Nouvelles et Textes pour Rien* (Paris: Editions de Minuit, 1959), p. 34.

works—Lucky's tirade in *Waiting for Godot*—
does the author introduce not only the little-
known Irish sport of camogie, but (in the English
version at least) the Irish philosopher, Bishop
Berkeley; and—as the last, thrice-repeated place-
name in Lucky's ruined mind—that desolate
rocky strip of Ireland's northwest coastland, Connemara?[7]

So persistent are the Irish usages in Beckett's
work that they go beyond the superficial "national
aspects" that he felt were overstressed in Jack
Yeats's paintings. The Irishness in Beckett's work
seems part of its vital core: that element which
he himself sees as constituting, in any work of art,
its "condensing spiral of need." Beckett further
asserts that literary comment is useful only as it
succeeds in tracing throughout such works, the
unique "type of need" embodied therein: "the energy, scope, adequacy of expression, etc." of each
work's creative spiral.[8] This article will attempt to
show the ways in which a handful of Irish references seem to indicate in three of Beckett's novels
(*Watt, Malone Dies,* and *The Unnameable*)
deeper spirals than those which have so far been
traced.

Only one Irish scholar, so far as I know, has
suggested a basically Irish source of energy for
Beckett's plays and novels. Vivian Mercier, in his
pioneering study, *The Irish Comic Tradition,*[9]
asserts that the most distinctive feature of Beckett's work is its creation of laughable-horrible figures; he cites Hamm, Clov, Watt, Arsene, Estra-
gon, Vladimir, and many others. These "grotesque-macabre" characters, as Mercier calls
them, have usually been regarded as a modern,
perhaps decadent, element in Beckett's work. Instead, Mercier suggests, they are much more closely akin to the stark archaic figures found in ancient
Irish art: its carvings, manuscript illustrations, and
mythic tales (pp. 48–49). So remarkable are the
specific parallels drawn by Mercier that it seems
surprising this line of study has not been followed
further. Perhaps two difficulties that for some
time delayed my own progress have also deterred
other scholars from following his proposal.

In the first place, Mercier insists on a very limited interpretation for the grotesque-macabre ele-

ment in Irish art, both in Beckett's work and in
early prototypes. He ascribes, as its sole motive,
the wish to "help us *to accept death and belittle
life*" (p. 49; Mercier's italics). The "macabre"
element is merely "a defense mechanism against
the fear of death"; the "grotesque," a defense
"against the holy dread with which we face the
mysteries of reproduction." Most Irish critics
have declined to accept such sweeping summaries
—summaries that Mercier himself has admitted
are "oversimplifying" (p. 49).

In a review sympathetic to Mercier's scholarly
efforts as a whole, Conor Cruise O'Brien gives his
grounds, historic as well as literary, for disagree-
ment with this thesis:

> [Mercier] accepts the notion, dear to so many
> Irish intellectuals, that "hatred of life" is a perma-
> nent and distinctive element in the Irish charac-
> ter. . . . One can, of course, find such symptoms if
> one looks for them: disgust and fear seem to be con-
> stant and universal elements in human existence,
> and in all "comic" traditions. The very ancient and
> beautiful Gaelic nature poetry, and the later and
> more "European" Gaelic love poetry, testify to the
> fact that in the Irish tradition, as in others, disgust
> and fear do not exclude all other emotions.[10]

O'Brien also points to another aspect of Mercier's proposal that has been questioned by Irish
scholars. Mercier includes in his "grotesque-macabre" tradition several authors for whom he can
cite no actual association with Irish modes of art.
Samuel Beckett is among these. As Mercier can-
didly notes,

> Beckett's relationship to the Gaelic tradition seems
> tangential indeed. . . . I should be surprised if he
> had any direct contact with Gaelic either at Portora
> Royal School in Northern Ireland or at Trinity Col-
> lege, Dublin. . . . We have the peculiar case here of
> an Anglo-Irishman who, like Swift, seems to fit com-
> fortably into the Gaelic tradition yet has almost no
> conscious awareness of what that tradition is. (pp.
> 75–6)

The supposition of such a purely mystical link between Beckett and the Irish tradition has been

---

7. *Waiting for Godot* (New York: Grove Press, 1954), p. 29.
8. Review on Devlin, *Transition,* April-May 1938, p. 290.
9. This study was first published in 1962 (New York: Oxford
   University Press). All quotations in this article are taken,
   however, from the second edition, 1969.

10. "Our Wits About Us," *The New Statesman,* Feb. 15, 1963.
O'Brien's opinion is similar to that expressed by most
reviewers in Irish scholarly journals: e.g., D. K. in the
Journal of the Royal Society of Antiquaries of Ireland 94
(1964): 74-75; E. G. Quin, *Hermathena* 97 (1964): 114;
Alf MacLochlainn, *Studia Hibernica,* no. 3 (1963), pp.
219-21.

treated with skepticism. O'Brien's review again is typical in expressing scholarly reserve:

> The idea that there is "an Irish mind" continuing with its own peculiar quirks, not shared even by other Europeans, from medieval times to the days of Samuel Beckett, seems to me implausible.

But Mercier's insight into the Irish quality of Samuel Beckett's work has stronger biographical grounding than he seemed to realize when, in 1961, he first put forth his theory.[11] At that time, data on Samuel Beckett's literary development were almost uncoordinated. Only later, as bibliographic studies appeared (notably those by John Fletcher in 1964 and 1970),[12] did it become obvious that Beckett's relationship to the Gaelic tradition was by no means tangential, and that—whether or not Beckett adopted this tradition for his own work—he had full conscious awareness of what that tradition is.

Even if Samuel Beckett received no formal training in Irish studies, very soon after graduation from Trinity College he became immersed in a most intense, informal program of this kind. In 1928, soon after arriving in Paris to teach at the *École Normale Supérieure,* Beckett became a member of the literary circle gathered around James Joyce. By June 1929, Beckett had published an essay that is recognized as the best early commentary on *Finnegans Wake.*[13] Joyce was so impressed with the young man's erudition, as well as his literary sense, that he encouraged Beckett to supervise translation of *Finnegans Wake* into French. An initial portion of this translation—the Anna Livia Plurabelle segment—was published in 1931.[14]

That Samuel Beckett was, in his early twenties, acknowledged by James Joyce as competent to interpret and, soon afterwards, to supervise translation of a work so full of Irish mythic references as *Finnegans Wake* seems proof enough that Beckett has been long equipped with an extensive knowledge of early Irish art and literature. Mercier, in connecting *Finnegans Wake* with its Irish sources, provides a concise summary of the range of Irish mythic art that Beckett must have mastered as background for his close and prolonged study of Joyce's work:

> In *Finnegans Wake* [Joyce] made ample use of the Finn Cycle in particular, besides referring to a number of figures in other cycles, as Adaline Glasheen's *A Census of Finnegans Wake* conveniently documents. . . .The individual references are less important than the new, almost Yeatsian, attitude to the Irish myth and folklore which is implicit throughout Joyce's last book. Like the myths and folklore of other peoples, they were used by Joyce as keys to dreams and to prehistory because they preserved the mental processes of primitive levels of consciousness and primitive eras of culture. Because the dream of human history which is *Finnegans Wake* was dreamed in Ireland, Irish keys possessed a peculiar value for Joyce. (pp. 243–44)

Beckett's essay on the *Wake* reveals his knowledge, not only of "the myths and folklore of other peoples . . . as keys to dreams and the prehistory," but also of the "peculiar value" that Irish myths possess, not only for Joyce, but for any modern Irishman—including Beckett himself.

Beckett also discusses Joyce's use of Giambattista Vico's cyclic theory, which traces *all* stages of

---

11. "Samuel Beckett and the Sheela-na-gig," *Kenyon Review* 23 (Spring 1961) : 299-324.
12. Professor Fletcher's initial bibliography, assembled with the cooperation and encouragement of Samuel Beckett, first appeared in *The Novels of Samuel Beckett,* pp. 234-48 (see also n4). Beckett's full bibliography through 1966 now appears as the first section in *Samuel Beckett: His Works and Critics,* by Raymond Federman and John Fletcher (Berkeley, Calif.: University of California Press, 1970), pp. 3-109.
13. "Dante. . .Bruno. Vico. . .Joyce," *Transition,* June 1929; also published in 1929 as the first essay in *Our Exagmination Round His Factification for the Incamination of Work in Progress* (Paris: Shakespeare & Co.). Quotations in the present study are taken from the edition published in New York by *New Directions Press* in 1933 (pp. 3-22). Richard Ellmann voices this favorable opinion of the article in *James Joyce* (New York: Oxford University Press, 1967), p. 626.

14. *Nouvelle Revue Francaise,* no. 212 (May 1931) , pp. 633-46. Adrienne Monnier makes clear in her collection, *Dernières Gazettes et Écrits Divers* (published posthumously in Paris by *Mercure de France* in 1961), that most of the credit for the published version was due to Beckett and his friend Alfred Peron. She writes of a decision by James Joyce that has somewhat clouded the matter of credit for this translation. Joyce later decided that, instead of leaving the work in the hands of only two young men, he would like to refer to his "Septante" in memory of other great French predecessors. He therefore arbitrarily increased the number of aides credited as working on the published version of the translation to seven. Mlle Monnier says of this change of plan: "À mon avis, la revision de Joyce était fort désirable, étant donnée son genie du language et sa connaissance de français, mais il ne me parut ni utile ni juste d' adjoindre à ceux qui avaient fait presque tout l'ouvrage—et magnifiquement, je vous assure—cinq personnes dont certaines, moi par example, n' étaient là que pour la figuration" (p. 19) .

literature and history back to their original evo-
lution from primitive myths. The young critic
then moves from general discussion to cite specific Irish examples of myth in Joyce's work: "It is
the old myth, the two washerwomen on the banks
of the river." Both washerwomen and the river
itself intermingle in the person of Anna Livia,
Joyce's titular heroine of this section and mythic
embodiment of Ireland's chief river, the Liffey.
Her daughter, in Joyce's twentieth-century myth,
is Isolde, reincarnation of the Irish princess whose
love for Tristan has become part of the entire European mythic heritage. In the *Wake,* as Beckett's
essay points out, Isolde represents more than an
individual heroine; she is "any beautiful girl." Her
mother ("Anna Livia herself") is "mother of Dublin, but no more the only mother than Zoroaster
was the only oriental stargazer" (p. 17). Creation
of archetypal personages like Isolde and Anna
Livia has always constituted, wrote the young
Beckett, an essential phase in man's primal effort
to understand himself and his experience: "The
first men . . . barbarians incapable of analysis and
abstraction, must use their fantasy to explain what
their reason cannot comprehend. . . .Hieroglyph-
ics or sacred language . . . is the common necessity of primitive people" (p. 11).

Beckett's interest in mythic expression did not
cease with his tracing of its operation through the
wide and varied flow of human types in *Finnegans Wake.* His subsequent critical statements
show that this interest continued to grow in assur-
ance and subtlety. The monograph *Proust* (1931)
praises especially this aspect of the French novelist's achievement: the courage with which Proust
pierced the surface of everyday experience to
reach and re-create the elemental forms beneath
it. Beckett notes that Proust's characters transcend
everyday proportions, becoming instead fabulous
shapes that are "neither created nor chosen": figures that can only be "discovered, uncovered, ex-
cavated, pre-existing within the artist, a law in his
nature." Beckett here ascribes to such art the essential function of assisting modern man to understand himself and his experience, declaring:
"the only reality is provided by the *hieroglyphics*
traced by inspired perception" (my italics).[15]

A year later, Beckett publicly took a personal
step forward: no longer did he merely praise the
mythic expression of other writers; he avowed his
own intention to work in this mode of art. By

signing the manifesto "Poetry is Vertical" in 1932,
he declared that his ultimate artistic aim would
be "the construction of *a new mythological reality*" (my italics).[16] In view, therefore, of Beckett's
repeated expressions of interest in mythic art, as
well as his specific mention of Irish examples, Vivian Mercier's proposal that the spirit of Beckett's
novels and plays "fits comfortably" into a Gaelic
mythic tradition seems deserving of a careful re-
examination.

Throughout Beckett's comments on myth, however, we notice one major point of divergence
from the spirit ascribed to his work by Mercier.
Among the many advantages presented by mythic
utterance, Beckett especially admires its vast inclusiveness. He takes pains to quote Vico's report
that "every need of life, natural, moral and economic" finds embodiment in the "30,000 Greek
divinities." So varied are the figures provided by
mythic expression that they offer to preliterate
peoples an entire span of language to express their
sense of reality. This primal human universe—
where every object finds embodiment in an ani-
mist personage—constituted, Beckett reports,
"Homer's language of the gods." The few examples that Beckett cites from Irish myth show that
he considers Irish examples akin to those of other
peoples. The two female figures discussed in his
essay are both beautiful: Isolde, "any beautiful
girl," and the matronly Anna Livia, noted for her
lovely hair (p. 17).

Mercier, on the other hand, immediately
shrinks the entire scale of Irish mythic expression
to the dimensions of a single type: the "grotesque-
macabre." Among female embodiments, he notes
only the *Sheela-na-gig:* a life-in-death figure characterized by skull-like head, skeletal ribs, and
twisted posture emphasizing genital parts. The arbitrary nature of Mercier's proposal concerning
Irish myth becomes more apparent if one phrases
a similar proposal concerning Greek myth. Can
it be seriously suggested that the entire Greek
pantheon would be adequately represented by
any one of its female figures: for example, by its
famous "grotesque-macabre" Medusa?

Watt is the Beckett novel that Vivian Mercier
discusses in most detail. His choice is a logical one.
Watt is well recognized as Beckett's most Irish
novel: every one of its four sections introduces material whose source may be labeled "from Eire."
In Section One, the geography of south Dublin

15. *Proust* (New York: Grove Press, n.d.), p. 64.

16. *Transition,* March 1932, p. 199.

with its contemporary train-and-tram connections, as well as its landmarks of a well-known race-course and mental home, is included. In Section Two, Mr. Knott's impressive suburban house and grounds are cared for by a variety of Hibernian attendants, from the Gall family members (father and son) who come to "choon" the piano, to the extensive Lynch family who are commandeered *in toto* to provide the services of a series of scavenging dogs. Section Three devotes at least half its span to Ernest Louit's research trip to the County Clare, together with an account of the sad fate of his dog, O'Connor, and the scholarly debut of Mr. Thomas Nackybal of Burren (the latter serving as exemplar for Louit's dissertation, *The Mathematical Intuitions of the Visicelts*). The fourth and final section of *Watt* introduces a convocation of railway officials, all of whose speech (as Niall Montgomery, an Irish critic, has remarked) "is accurate Dublin."[17]

If, therefore, Samuel Beckett is creating in his own work fictional "hieroglyphics," *Watt* is the novel where one might expect to find him drawing most widely on Irish prototypes. Mercier, however, sees in the complicated patterns of this novel the spirit of only one of its character groups. He limits the expressivity of *Watt* to the women of the Lynch family, and the bitter spirit of the *risus purus,* a laugh defined by Watt's disillusioned predecessor, Arsene, as "the laugh that laughs . . . at that which is unhappy."[18]

There can be little doubt that the Lynch ladies *do* present a painful/laughable hieroglyphic of human fertility at its most diseased and irrational level. Three full generations are catalogued: from that of elderly Kate ("covered all over with running sores of an unidentified nature but otherwise fit and well") through matronly Liz ("fortunate in being more dead than alive as a result of having in the course of twenty years given Sam nineteen children") to the oncoming generation: "two innocent little girlies [Rose and Cerise] bleeders like their papa and mama" (pp. 101-3).

Granted, however, that the Lynch family presents a stark outline of human fertility gone wild, how is this single type related to the many other "hieroglyphic" figures that appear in all of *Watt's* four sections? Here, I propose, is the point where a broader mythic interpretation is demanded. The Lynch family in *Watt* (like the *Sheela-na-gig* figure in Mercier's discussion of early carvings) is too narrow a sampling of the novel to provide an adequate base for analyzing the whole work. The most distinguished modern critic of early Irish art, Françoise Henry, describes the many, varied Irish mythic figures that constitute in ancient carvings and manuscripts "the decorative words of a mystical language."[19] (This phrase closely parallels Beckett's view of mythology as a "language of the gods.") Yet a language can hardly be construed with only one letter for its alphabet.

If *Watt* is visualized as a single vast design whose individual characters are "decorative words of a mystical language," certain broad outlines become apparent. Watt, the central seeker, integrates all four segments of this interlocking unit; other characters appear only as they are somehow related to his primal "hieroglyphic." The Lynch family, for example, is significant because Watt ponders long and painfully the possible meanings of its diseased and degenerating cycle of life. The narrator of *Watt* is at pains to stress that the ultimate significance of all these series of repeating incidents and objects must be found—not in any single one of them, but in *"the possible relations between such series* as these, the series of dogs, the series of men, the series of pictures, to mention only these series" (p. 136; my italics).

At first glance, the only relation between *any* of these series seems to be their mutual inconsequentiality. However, I suggest that in the case of the Lynch family (which indeed provides a hieroglyph for one type of human fertility), sev-

---

17. "No Symbols Where None Intended," *New World Writing,* no. 5, 1954, p. 326.

18. *Watt* (New York: Grove Press, 1959), p. 48. All quotations in the present article are taken from this edition.

19. *Irish Art in the Early Christian Period* (to 800 A.D.), (Ithaca, N. Y.: Cornell University Press, 1965), p. 205. It is at this point that Mercier's estrangement from the main current of scholarship on ancient Irish art becomes most noticeable. In the Spring 1968 issue of *Hermathena,* the scholarly journal published by Trinity College, Dublin, G. F. Mitchell sums up the achievement of Françoise Henry: "With the appearance of Mlle Henry's doctoral thesis, *La Sculpture Irlandaise* in 1932, a new era in the study of our carvings, manuscripts and metalwork began. In this new era, Dr. Henry has continued to lead the way, producing a steady stream of books, articles and notes" (p. 67).

Donal O'Sullivan, Director of the Irish Arts Council, in *Studies* 57 (Summer 1968), wrote of her major three-volume work, which has also been acclaimed in Switzerland, England, and the United States, as an achievement "magnificently done and no one living could do it better." Dr. Henry he describes as "the distinguished French scholar who has made us Irish so aware of our heritage" (pp. 204-6).

eral relations seem apparent with another cycle observed by Watt: that of the Magrew family. Several generations of the Magrew ladies, like the Lynches, are introduced. The basic stages of their lives are presented as deftly as are stages of the Lynch family's existence. Yet the spirit of the Magrew story is quite different from that in which the Lynch family is presented.

This *Magrew type* of humor, very light and almost gentle, is one that has been nearly ignored in Beckett's novels and plays. Such humor, however, is the only type that Beckett, in his own criticism, has singled out for admiration. In writing of Jack Yeats's novel *The Amaranthers*, Beckett praises its achievement of an irony so "slight" and "fitful" that "the face remains grave, but the mind has smiled." This produces (not "the bitter, the hollow, the mirthless" laughs so usually regarded as Beckett's essential notes) but a silent savoring of reality. Such humor is evocative, Beckett tells us, of "the profound *risolino* that does not destroy."[20] A study is yet to be made of the far-ranging use of the Italo-Irish *"risolino"* in Beckett's drama and fiction.

Watt encounters the fertile Magrew ladies as he is on his way to the house of Mr. Knott. He lies down to rest himself and, while at ease in the ditch alongside the path, he hears the voices, "indifferent in quality, of a mixed choir" (p. 33). These voices sing—in four parts—a round composed of a series of questions, each of which represents a stage in the life of the Magrews. The soprano voice first inquires:

> Greatgrandma Magrew,
> How do you do?
> Blooming, thanks and you?
> Drooping, thanks and you?
> Withered, thanks and you?
> Thanks, forgotten too.
> And the same to you.
>   (pp. 34–35)

The alto traces the same history in the life of Grandma Magrew; the tenor, of Mama Magrew; while the bass foretells an identical future for Miss Magrew. All four generations are simultaneously recorded as blooming, drooping, withering, and vanishing. The final line reminds the hearer that his own round of life will be the same as that of these musical ladies.[21]

This four-part song does indeed raise a *risolino*, a mental smile, at the inevitable cycle of life, but it seems to evoke none of the fear and little of the revulsion that Mercier implies is the sum of Beckett's attitude toward the human condition. The blooming, drooping, and withering of the Magrew ladies is—I suggest—as affable a reminder of mortality as Herrick's song: "Gather ye rosebuds while ye may,/Old Time is now aflying."

Watt, as central character of the novel, is shown, therefore, between two contrasting "hieroglyphics" of human fertility: the harmonious Magrews, lyrically presented, and the degraded Lynches, rendered in the most brutal prose. It seems obvious that the hero's experience is intended to be mythically broad enough to envelop awareness of human fate as a whole, not only its suffering, self-destructive aspect, but also its tolerably harmonious, sempiternal extent.

To anyone of Irish background, the very names of these two families bespeak their contrasting fates. Beckett appears to be adopting, in terms of his Irish background, the primitive practice of "type-names" expounded in his early discussion of myth. Primitive man (like every child in every age) extends the names of familiar things "to other strange objects in which he is conscious of some analogy" (p. 11). Beckett cites Joyce's almost invariable use of type-names (in the *Wake*, for example: Isolde, Earwigger, Anna Livia). So, in Beckett's modern tale of *Watt*, the surname "Magrew" seems Irishly expressive of the normal process of "blooming, drooping, withering"; its first syllable is a softening of the prefix "Mac," meaning "son of" in Gaelic. The second syllable ("grew") expresses that spontaneous expansive faculty of all living things.

The name of Lynch is as evocative, in Irish lore, of the opposite concept of family relationship. Padraic Colum quotes, in his *Treasury of Irish Folklore*,[22] an account of the notorious Judge Lynch of Galway, who in 1493 made his name

---

20. Review of *Amaranthers, Dublin Magazine* (July-Sept. 1936), p. 80.

21. That this round of existence is intended as a prototype is confirmed by the second verse, which tells of life "series" of Mr. Man, Mrs. Man, Master Man and Miss Man.

22. *A Treasury of Irish Folklore* (New York: Crown Publishers, 1954), pp. 349-50.

archetypal for a fanatical, self-destructive sense of family responsibility:

> James Lynch . . . traded largely with Spain, and sent his son on a voyage thither. . . . Young Lynch, however, spent the money entrusted him, and . . . conceived the idea of concealing his crime by committing another, having seduced or frightened the crew into becoming participators. The youth [a young Spaniard sent back with Lynch to collect money for the debt] was thrown overboard. . . . Later when his father learned of his crime, young Lynch was tried, found guilty, and sentenced to execution—the father being the judge.

Nor was this the end of the Lynch story. The young man's relatives and friends felt the sentence so severe that they threatened revolution; the executioner refused to carry out the penalty. "Their outcrys for mercy," we are told, "would have shaken any nerves less firm than those of the Mayor of Galway." But the father-judge was not to be swayed:

> Finding all his efforts fruitless . . . he, by a desperate victory over paternal feeling, resolved himself to perform the sacrifice which he had vowed to pay on the altar. . . .Still retaining hold of his son, he mounted with him by a winding stair . . . to an arched window overlooking the street, which he saw filled with the populace. Here he secured the end of a rope . . . and after taking from [the son] a last embrace, he launched him into eternity. The intrepid Mayor expected instant death from the fury of the populace, but the people seemed as much overawed or confounded by the magnanimous act. . . . They returned slowly and peaceably to their several dwellings. The unhappy father . . . is said to have secluded himself during the remainder of his life. . . . His house still exists in Lombard Street, Galway, which is yet known by the name of Dead Man's Lane.

The draconian literalness with which Judge James Lynch of Galway interpreted his function in life—exacting from his inexperienced son the full toll of maximum adult crime—has made the name of Lynch synonymous in Ireland with that arbitrary, self-righteous severity which so often passes for religious fervor.

Lynch, as an Irish "type-name," is already familiar to readers of Joyce's first two novels. In *A Portrait of the Artist as a Young Man*, as well as in *Ulysses*, Lynch is the name of the author's closest—but treacherous—ally. Richard Ellmann records Joyce's lasting indignation with the original

of this personage (Vincent Cosgrave) who "stood by, hands in pockets, while his friend was knocked about." Joyce, he notes, "determined upon the fictional name of Lynch for Cosgrave, because Lynch as mayor of Galway had hanged his own son, and in *Ulysses* he shows Lynch leaving Stephen in the lurch. Cosgrave did not like the name!"[23] Beckett—it is proposed—assigned the name of Lynch to his irresponsible, dog-raising clan as a similar stigmatic "type-name" in *Watt*.

But if Beckett's naming of the Lynch family recalls Joyce's use of this "hieroglyphic" Irish name, his "Magrew" family evokes as striking a precedent from the pages of W. B. Yeats. No critic, so far as I know, has pointed out that, in *Watt's* meeting with the Magrews, Beckett has adapted an incident from W. B. Yeats's collection, *Irish Fairy and Folk Tales*.[24]

Watt, walking through the dark night on his way to Mr. Knott's house, relives the experience of the good-natured Irish hunchback, Lusmore, who also lay in a ditch at night, hearing "a wild strain of unearthly melody." The narrator of his legend describes the musical effect of these fairy voices in terms that fit perfectly the later singing of the Magrew ladies: "Many voices, each mingling and blending with each other so strangely that they seemed to be one, though all singing different strains." Yeats provides in his footnotes the music of the tune his fairies sang (*Folktales*, pp. 344–45); Beckett, not to be outdone in imaginative exactitude, also provides the melody of the Magrews' song, adding *his* footnote on the very last page of *Watt* (p. 254).

The lyrics of Yeats's fairies express the same theme as the twentieth-century verses heard by Watt: the unceasing passage of time. The earlier Irish chorus voices its theme, however, in a more naive, concrete way than *Watt's*: merely chanting over and over (in Gaelic) the names of the first two days of the week: *"Da Luan, Da Mort"* (Monday, Tuesday). Watt's choristers reveal their more sophisticated concept of time, interspersing their account of the blooming and drooping of the Magrew ladies with the "wild strains" of two

23. *James Joyce* (New York: Oxford University Press, 1965), pp. 156-57.
24. "The Legend of Knockgrafton," by T. Crofton Croker, in *Irish Fairy and Folk Tales* (New York: Boni & Liveright, n.d.), pp. 44-48.

interminable series of numbers. The first runs:

> Fifty-two point two
> eight five seven one four two;

and the second:

> Fifty-one point one
> four two eight five seven one.

These ever-recurring decimals are typical of the irrational numbers that result whenever calendar-makers attempt to establish any regular pattern to record the passage of time. The digits of *Watt's* first chorus represent the number of weeks in a leap year (whose arbitrary total of 366 days is merely another attempt to make up for the fact that there is no exact ratio between the time of earth's rotation on its axis [a day], and the time of its revolution around the sun [a year]).[25] The unsatisfactory results of time-reckoning as measured by the movements of both sun and moon, the most obvious celestial markers in earth's sky, may account for the orderly minded Watt's antipathy to both planets. The reader is told (on p. 33): "If there were two things that Watt disliked, one was the moon, and the other was the sun."[26]

Perhaps the most striking similarity between the singers in *Watt* and those in Yeats's Irish folk-tale is their relaxed acceptance of this ultimate irrationality in all human attempts at time reckoning. Watt's voices create a song from the monotony of modern astronomic statistics. Lusmore's fairy chorus is even more carefree, seemingly content to lilt forever the names of the first two days of the week.[27] This alert but uncensorious attitude, visible in both groups, presents a sharp contrast to that which rules the destiny of the wretched Lynch family.

Instead of accepting and even creating an artistic expression for the natural round of mortality, the Lynches make their lot ever more unfortunate, both by their acquiescence in Mr. Knott's exploitation of their poverty, and by their own over-imaginative fabrications. Onto the neutrally turning cycles of time, the Lynches load arbitrary burdens of their own. First they accept, without protest, Mr. Knott's assumption that the most profitable use of their days is to rear a series of famished dogs to consume his leftovers (pp. 98–100). Next (as if to protect themselves from admission of this grim situation) they guide their lives by another insensate proposition. The Lynches are convinced that their fate will be transformed—immediately and forever—if only they can bring the total of all their ages to equal exactly one thousand years (pp. 103–10). Mercier concisely summarizes this Lynch family travesty of the millennium: "This mad race between creation and destruction never seems quite to work out: the latter consistently wins by a short lead" (p. 74). Instead of "blooming, drooping, withering" like the Magrews, the Lynches (with their apocalyptic insistence on a hoped-for perfect existence) intensify all the destructive possibilities of mortality. Their disregard for the human cycle of life blights each of its members through all life's seasons. Even new blossoms, such as Rose

---

25. In their monographs on Samuel Beckett, both Hugh Kenner (p. 104) and William York Tindall (p. 20) have commented on the significance of this first chorus sung by Watt's voices.

　　The digits of the second chorus contain one typographical error. Beckett's orginal version of the song (in the third of his manuscript notebooks of *Watt*, now at the Humanities Research Center of the University of Texas) reads:
> Fifty-*two* point one
> four two eight five seven one.

This represents the number of weeks in a year of usual length; the error slipped into Beckett's own manuscript copy of the song in the succeeding notebook (4), and has been carried along in all versions since that time.

26. The wide variety of expedients resorted to by Greek astronomers, in their efforts to establish harmony between the cycles of the moon and the round of the seasons (dependent on the sun), has been summarized by Thomas Heath in *Aristarchos of Samos* (London, 1913), pp. 287 ff.

27. Lusmore wins their friendship, and has his hump removed, when he harmoniously adds another phrase ("*Augus da Dardeen,*" which means in English, "And also Wednesday") during a pause in their song. But the fairies' gratitude to Lusmore is due to his tactful harmony, rather than to his logical expansion of their lyrics, as is proved by their reverse reaction to a later, ill-timed addition. Jack Madden, a bad-tempered hunchback, who hopes to imitate Lusmore's good fortune by breaking in, inharmoniously with the phrase "*Augus da Hena*" ("And also Thursday"), learns how little they prize mere quantity of addition. The fairies not only give him a beating, but nail Lusmore's old hump on top of his own.

　　This Irish folk-tale centering on two contrasting hunchbacks may also cast light on the obscure relation between Watt and the bad-tempered hunchback, Mr. Hackett. A porter, at one point, curses the mild-tempered Watt: "The devil raise a hump on you" (p. 24); and Mr. Nixon remarks to Mr. Hackett on the occasion of Watt's first appearance: "The curious thing is, my dear fellow. . . that when I see him, or think of him, I think of you, and that when I see you, or think of you, I think of him" (p. 19).

and Cerise, are doomed to be "bleeders" like their elders.

This contrasting relationship between "the series" of the Magrews and "the series" of the Lynches ("to mention only these series") illustrates the way in which Beckett weaves material from his Irish heritage into the broader novelistic patterns he is creating in *Watt*.[28] These two hieroglyphic groups show him adapting to his central theme incidents from Irish folklore and local history, as well as the overtones that these incidents have acquired from their appearance in the work of Beckett's two great Irish contemporaries, W. B. Yeats and James Joyce.

The examples of Irish mythic usage that Mercier has proposed as existing in *Malone Dies* are as stimulating as those he pointed out in *Watt;* but, for this reader, they too fall short of the insights they seem to open.[29] He focuses on the explicit account of tragi-hilarious lovemaking between the moribund Moll and MacMann, citing this as illustrative—to an unprecedented extent—of the grotesque-macabre tradition in Irish comedy. Moll seems simply another embodiment of the *Sheela-na-gig;* MacMann, a male equivalent of the Dagda, that ancient Irish earth god whose virility and gluttony are parodied in the heroic narrative *The Battle of Moytura*. Incidents in this tale depict the Dagda as an ur-Gargantua (created hundreds of years before Rabelais dreamed of that hero's enormous capacities). After eating a meal so large that no man-made container can hold it, the Dagda attempts to have intercourse with an ominous female magician, the enemy king's daughter. (For various reasons, translators have declined to translate this passage verbatim.) Shortly afterward, the Dagda makes love again, this time to that most repulsive and fearsome of all Irish goddesses: the Mor-rígu, embodiment of battle slaughter.

Moll and MacMann; Mor-rígu and the Dagda —these personages, if considered in the spirit of modern realistic fiction, might well be termed "grotesque and macabre." In such a light they are forcefully interpreted by Vivian Mercier as representing the climactic phase of this tradition: "The love affair of Moll and MacMann on the brink of the grave in *Malone Dies,* is calculated to undermine the reverence for life, and awe before the reproductive processes of all but the most wholesome personalities" (p. 76). This judgment ignores, however, not only the mythical mode of storytelling, but even an essential criterion for all literary interpretation: it focuses on these individual incidents in isolation from their fictional contexts. The result does not do justice either to Irish mythic tales or to an essential, complex incident in one of Samuel Beckett's most powerful (and most profoundly moral) novels.

The figure of the Dagda, in its original mythic presentation, must actually remain unknown to the modern reader. The story, as we now have it, is a much later version, preserved but adapted by medieval tale-bearers who were as obviously aware of its incongruities as we are today. Mlle Marie-Louise Sjoestedt comments on the gluttony and love-making of the Dagda:

> While the redactors delighted in emphasizing the grotesque obscenity of this double episode, one can recognize it as a ritual manifestation of the powers of voracity and sexual vigour which are attributed necessary to the prestige of a barbarous chieftain. (p. 57)

Proinsias MacCana's volume *Celtic Mythology*[30]

28. Although only a few of *Watt's* Irish references can be noted here, mention should be made of Beckett's bow to Oscar Wilde, his fellow alumnus at both Trinity College and Portora Royal School. Ernest Louit explains the disappearance of data on his dissertation by taking a leaf from *The Importance of Being Ernest*, adapting on his own behalf Miss Prism's account of her loss of "an infant of the male sex": "He [Louit] had the misfortune to mislay . . . between the hours of eleven and midday, in the gentlemen's cloakroom of Ennis railway-station, the one hundred and five loose sheets closely covered on both sides with shorthand notes" (*Watt*, p. 173).

29. This alternately stimulating and frustrating aspect of Mercier's comments on Irish myth is noted by David Krause in his article "The Hidden Oisin" in *Studia Hibernica* 6 (1966). After praising Mercier's discussion of Ossianic poetry, Krause adds that the implications of the points Mercier raises "remain innocuous and unexplored" (p. 17).

30. *Celtic Mythology* (London: Hamlyn, 1970), pp. 66-67. All standard historians agree that the Dagda, although an earthy force himself, is consistently allied with gods that represent man's highest qualities, such as Lugh (figure of beauty, intelligence, order), and Aengus, god of romantic love, who is the son of the Dagda. When the gods of the Tuatha are finally driven underground, it is the Dagda who provides them with a refuge. For other sources, see: Thomas F. O'Rahilly, *Early Irish History and Mythology* (Dublin, 1946) p. 314; Miles Dillon, *Early Irish Literature* (Chicago: University of Chicago Press, 1948), pp. 59-60; Alvyn and Brinsley Rees, *Celtic Heritage* (London: Thames & Hudson, 1961), pp. 35-38.

brings out the significance of these incidents even more clearly. The Dagda, he notes, is a god protective of all manifestations of life. (His name means "the good god.") Dagda is using his virility in a way that every primitive man and woman would approve: to beguile two deathly forces that intend destruction to his whole people. The first, an enemy king's daughter, is a feared magician. The second, the goddess Mor-rígu, is an even more notorious death-figure: the "dread female who is seen before a battle washing the mangled heads and limbs of those who are destined to die." Sympathetic laughter would therefore be justified in the original myth by these sexual conquests of the Dagda because, in them, the elemental life force is outwitting two "hieroglyphic" figures of death. As MacCana makes clear, this incident constitutes obvious justification for the Dagda's respected status: "By his physical union with her [the Mor-rígu] he ensures victory and security for his people. Nothing could more clearly underline his role of father figure among the gods" (pp. 66–67).

The incident of the love-making of MacMann and Moll in Beckett's novel, *Malone Dies*,[31] presents much the same jolting fusion of primal wish for survival, with detached subsequent parody, that is noted by scholars in the medieval retelling of *The Battle of Moytura*. Like that earlier incident, the pathetic-ridiculous *affaire de* Moll and Macmann becomes known to the reader only through the words of an intrusive storyteller. In Beckett's tale, this narrator is Malone, central figure of *Malone Dies*. He is whiling away the time —as he waits for death in an asylum—by telling himself stories. After several brutal incidents (which he discontinues), Malone decides to concentrate on the figure of MacMann, the creature who seems most successfully to distract his thoughts from himself. MacMann is intended to be a persona as unlike Malone as possible and, up until the time when MacMann meets Moll, he fulfills this wish of his creator: he presents the appearance of a completely passive individual.

MacMann's relations with Moll at first follow a line that is also the precise opposite of Malone's own. Malone has reported that since his own entry to the asylum he has refused all offers of personal help; in particular, he has rebuffed the assistance of an old woman (p. 8). MacMann, how-

ever, accepts assistance. When Moll first offers to take care of him, he bewilderedly allows her; he soon comes to rely on her in a passive, childlike way.

In the initial stages of this incident Malone seems gratified at the the lively turn his narrative is taking: "I pause to record that I feel in extraordinary form. Delirium perhaps" (p. 86). But MacMann suddenly forsakes his former passivity. The discovery that his entry into the institution has entailed discarding his disreputable clothes brings him to his first act of complete revolt:

> He at once began to clamour loudly for his clothes . . . he cried, My things! My things!, over and over again, tossing about in the bed and beating the blanket with his palms.

When Moll comes to realize the depth of her charge's distress—observing that he continues to cry out, "notably for his hat"—she leaves him, and manages to retrieve the hat from a rubbish heap.

In the course of this scene wherein Moll shows courageous compassion for her helpless charge, MacMann becomes aware, for the first time in his fictional existence, of the possibility of a loving human relationship. The incident seems, to this reader at least, not only extremely touching, but rendered without irony. (There seems in this telling at most a *risolino*.) Moll appears at MacMann's bedside,

> holding with the tips of her fingers the hat in question . . . for it was fringed with manure and seemed to be rotting away. And what is more, she suffered him to put it on, and even helped him to do so, helping him to sit up in the bed and arranging his pillows in such a way that he might remain propped up without fatigue. And she contemplated with tenderness the old bewildered face relaxing, and in its tod of hair the mouth trying to smile, and the little red eyes turning timidly towards the recovered hat, and the hands raised to set it on more firmly and returning to rest trembling on the blanket. (pp. 87–88)

There seems little wonder that Moll begins to assume in MacMann's eyes an appearance as glowing as that of the beautiful heroine Celia, who in Beckett's first novel, *Murphy*, also comes to brighten the bedchambers of Murphy and Mr. Kelly.

But Malone, the storyteller, now breaks in on the situation he has created. The story is not progressing as he planned and he confesses himself

---

31. *Malone Dies* (New York: Grove Press, 1956), p. 8. All references are to this edition.

uneasy at "this extraordinary heat . . . which has seized on certain parts of my economy. . . .And to think I was expecting rather to grow cold, if anything" (p. 88). Malone is startled, not only by the measure of vitality his characters have assumed, but by his own resentment at their independence of his mood. He acquires new insight into the brutal incidents he has created in his earlier stories: "My notes have a curious tendency, as I realize at last, to annihilate all they purport to record."[32]

But this measure of self-knowledge does not change Malone's destructive vein; instead, he deliberately sets out to demolish the relationship between MacMann and Moll—coldly trying to strip them of any sympathy they have gathered for the reader and for each other. Malone abruptly shifts the course of his narrative, proceeding to mock, on every level, the ineptitudes of the helpless pair. Moll, in particular, becomes Malone's target: he mocks not only her sexual ardors and her ugliness, but her sentimentality, her pietism, her letter-writing, and her excruciating taste in jewelry. Nevertheless, although this storyteller does his utmost to turn MacMann and Moll into creatures of ridicule, the reality of their belated affection remains—for each other, and for Malone himself—unshakable. When Malone tries to force his imagination into depicting MacMann and Moll tiring of one another ("A few words in conclusion on the decline of this liaison"), he is forced to stop. He admits: "No, I can't" (p. 93). Malone then cuts off his narrative to compose a threnody—not for MacMann and Moll—but for himself:

> Weary with my weariness, white last moon, sole regret, not even. To be dead, before her, on her, with her, and turn, dead on dead, about poor mankind, and never have to die any more, from among the living. Not even, not even that. . . . Not even, not even that, and die, without having been able to find a regret. (pp. 93–94)

Malone agonizes at being driven to the admission that a fictional pair he himself has created—ugly, stupid, senile, and physically impotent—still possesses a power that he himself lacks. By no means does Malone feel that the ability of MacMann and Moll to love "on the brink of the grave"

can be made contemptible. In his own eyes, Malone is forced back on the only tactic left to the morally vanquished: he resorts to sheer physical destructiveness. He begins the next section: "Moll. I'm going to kill her." And in the narrative of *Malone Dies* he proceeds to do just that. After Moll's destruction, Malone puts MacMann into the hands of the self-beating ax-murderer, Lemuel.[33] The final chapter of his saga concludes in an explosion of text, through which the creator-destroyer Malone disappears along with the scattered remnants of his last creative-victim.

If Samuel Beckett is employing in *Malone Dies* a fictional method akin to that of Irish mythology (and I agree with Mercier that he is), can any relationship be traced between the three central, closely associated "hieroglyphic" figures: Malone, MacMann, and Moll? There seems indeed a spirit at work here "to belittle life and to accept death." But that spirit is, I suggest, centered in the figure of Malone, and not in those of his ridiculed victims, MacMann and Moll. Ultimately, Malone dies as the embodiment of his own death-dealing nature.

Ancient Irish literature does present "hieroglyphics" of the same coldly destructive type as Malone, but these are not deities of life and fertility like the Dagda; they are gods who represent dangers to all human values, both physical and spiritual. The Dagda is set, in every struggle, on the side most sympathetic to humanity. He not only wins over to its aid the female fury, the *Morrigu*, but he is powerful in the crucial struggle to overcome that even more destructive male figure: Balor of the Evil Eye. Lady Gregory describes the cold malice of Balor's look: "There was a power of death in one of his eyes, so that no one could look at it and live." Balor's destructiveness was universal, threatening all living things. Had the Dagda not assisted Lugh, the Irish sun god, in overthrowing Balor, "the whole of Ireland," we

---

32. William York Tindall's monograph *Samuel Beckett* points out this basic distinction between Malone's scabrous presentation, and Beckett's obviously sympathetic intention as author of the novel: "Malone's outrageous humor, whether scrupulous neutrality or disgust, cannot hide Beckett's good will to slobs" (p. 27).

33. Beckett's use of the name Lemuel, as drawing from *Gulliver's Travels* for MacMann's brutal keeper has been noted, but not accounted for. Although Beckett recurrently cites and refers to Swift's work in his novels, his only direct critical comment compares its use of allegory unfavorably to the more integrated spirit of Jack Yeats's fiction. In the latter narrative, there is "no allegory, that glorious double entry . . . but the single series of imaginative transactions. The Island is not throttled into Ireland, nor the City into Dublin. . . . There is no satire. Believers and make-believers, not Gullivers and Lilliputians; horses and men, not Houyhnhnms and Yahoos; imaginative fact, beyond the fair and the very fair." (For source, see n1).

are told, "would have been burned in one flash."[34]

The marked Irishness of the names of the three characters who dominate the last half of *Malone Dies* (Malone, Moll, MacMann) has been noted by many critics. So far as I know, however, no one has traced in these names anything but a random choice on the part of the author. Yet, following the theory of mythic "type-names," the name of "MacMann" is obviously an Irish equivalent for "son of man." This significance is jeeringly commented on by Malone, who uses it as equivalent for an Irish version of Everyman: MacMann, he tells us, is "no more than human, than the son and grandson and greatgrandson of humans" (p. 68). Later, he adds a further gibe in the same vein: "The MacManns are legion in the island and pride themselves, what is more with few exceptions, on having one and all, in the last analysis, sprung from the same illustrious ball" (p. 88). MacMann's position as a helpless victim (one who, moreover, retains the ability to love in spite of utmost deprivation) seems to entitle him to the biblical, sacrificial overtones of this title: Son of Man.

The name "Moll" reveals similar ranges of meaning if looked at as an Irish "type-name." Its source is Mary, name of the Virgin-Mother of Christ. In Ireland, devotion to Mary evolved the softer everyday form of Moll for use as an affectionate pet name. But over the centuries (perhaps as so many Irish women distressfully emigrated overseas), this pet name took on aggressive, even lawless, connotations: Molly Pitcher, Moll Flanders. Today, "moll" is recognized as a common noun, found in every English dictionary, endowed with the meaning of "unmarried female companion of a thief, vagrant or gangster."[35] MacMann's kind-hearted protectress in *Malone Dies* seems to embody all the varied overtones of her name: from unselfish devotion, and reminiscence of Christ's crucifixion, to a cool courage in ignoring rules of the establishment.

And what about the central name in this novel —Malone? A number of critics have sensed that the name of the principal figure in a narrative so superbly intense as *Malone Dies must* be of significance. Yet, as a "type-name," there seems to be no outstanding precedent in Irish lore to ac-

count for its use here. In the absence of immediately obvious signification, however, another warning from Beckett's statements on mythic expression may be pertinent. He asserts the need for a reader to "apprehend" (not merely encounter) such poetic wording, adding that: "It is not to be read—or rather it is not only to be read. It is to be looked at and listened to" (p. 14).

When the name of this malicious, malevolent, maleficent storyteller is "looked at," and especially "listened to," another pronunciation of the letters in "Malone" suggests itself. May not the second syllable of the name be "apprehended"—not with its customary long "o"—but as in the more usual way of pronouncing the word: "one"? Then the name of this self-demolishing hero would indeed take on the stature of a "type-name."[36] His title—Mal One—would express this Evil One's position in the cosmos of his own making: a hieroglyphic expressing all that is destructive in man's thoughts and wishes.

The strange narrative that follows *Malone Dies* to complete Samuel Beckett's trilogy presents a protagonist with so little "oneness" of character that he seems rightly named *The Unnamable*. Only a single aspect of this personage will be considered here: the mixture he presents of Irish references from his past and French landmarks of his present destiny. John Fletcher has annotated many of the latter. The "chop house" in front of which Mahood, an amputee without arms or legs, stands in a jar may be identified with a Parisian restaurant called *The Ali Baba*, which used a similar figure of a man in a jar to hold its daily menu. Mahood gazes out at a statue (actually existing some distance away in Paris), which was erected as a memorial to the Parisian who popularized horsemeat in French cuisine.[37]

---

34. Lady Augusta Gregory, *Gods and Fighting Men* (New York: Scribner's 1904), pp. 28, 59.

35. E.g., *American College Dictionary* (New York: Random House, 1956).

36. A well-known precedent for such a shift in this vowel sound can be noted in the verb "atone," now pronounced with a long "o" although originally pronounced as the two separate words that compose it: "at one." James Joyce plays on its shifts of meaning and sound in *Ulysses*: it embodies his theme of the atonement/*at-one-ment* of the Son and the Father (New York: Modern Library Edition, 1961), pp. 18, 729.

Professor John Unterecker has also suggested that the same significance is derived from the name Malone, and "without distorting pronunciation by spelling it *Mal-own*: Evil itself, or more literally yet, *possessed of essential sickness*." In both readings (which Beckett may well have intended simultaneously) *Malone* is apprehended as a type-name, or hieroglyphic title, of its destructive possessor.

37. *Samuel Beckett's Novels*, pp. 184-85.

In spite of this precision in the novel's Parisian references, an Irish critic, Niall Montgomery, points out that the narrator's consciousness keeps wandering far beyond the borders of France; it periodically settles on "the island," a locale sometimes associated (unflatteringly) with Ireland:

> I was under the impression I spent my life in spirals round the earth. Wrong, it's on the island I wind my endless ways. The island, that's all the earth I know. I don't know it either, never having had the stomach to look at it.[38]

But this "island," so deeply engraved on the narrator's consciousness, retains some connection, however painful, with visibility. In recounting the physical equipment need for future progression, he notes detachedly of his corpus:

> the eye, let's leave him his eye too, it's to see with . . . it's to weep with, it's to practice with, before he goes to Killarney. (p. 101)

Montgomery also points out that when in the words of the English version the narrator envisages the truly macabre possibility that Mahood may "emerge from his urn, and make his way towards Montmartre, on his belly," he thinks of him as singing a line from "The Lily of Killarney."[39]

The reader cannot help wondering what stimulus revives these Irish memories of *The Unnamable*—even while such a reader keeps in mind Beckett's insistence on his principle of "the autonomy of the imagined." Why should Mahood, in the midst of his ghastly predicament in Paris—an existence that provides a most telling symbol of the intellectual, spiritual, and physical disasters that have overtaken modern man—why should Mahood persist in linking his plight to references so peculiarly Irish?

Here again, a prototype from Beckett's Irish past suggests a precedent for this savage "hieroglyphic" of modern reality, a precedent as familiar to anyone of Irish background as Finn McCool, or Galway's Judge Lynch. For almost two hundred years, a famous Dublin ballad has engraved this war-blasted figure on the Irish imagination. Padraic Colum wrote that the song: " 'Johnny I Hardly Knew Ye' is masterly in its cynical acceptance of the woes of war for the poverty-stricken slum-dweller. There's nothing before the maimed

private soldier but beggary. . . . In 'Johnny,' a soldier has come home and his girl sings of what the wars have done to him."[40]

The details of Mahood's physical disaster seem close to Johnny's. We are told of Mahood's body that "only the trunk remains (in sorry trim), surmounted by the head." This latter appendage is "a great smooth ball . . . featureless but for the eyes, of which only the sockets remain" (p. 23). At one point, Mahood wonders detachedly whether his ball of a head may have the shape of "an egg, a medium egg?" (p. 24). In any case, he feels sure that his head and trunk are "stuck like a sheaf of flowers in a deep jar, its neck flush with my mouth, on . . . a quiet street near the shambles" (p. 55). Here, Mahood's remaining organic functions as well as his physical deprivations are turned to good economic account. Organically, he provides manure for the landlady's kitchen-garden and visually, his bare, diseased head, rising above the rim of the jar, serves as a prop and an advertisement (p. 55).

The Irish ballad of the returned war hero, Johnny, reveals the same basic situation, as is told through his "landlady's" questions and exclamations. After asking him in vain, "Where are your eyes that looked so mild?" and "Where are the legs with which you ran?" and noting that he is now "doubled up head and tail," she breaks into the lament:

> You haven't an arm and you haven't a leg,
>   hurroo, hurroo!
> You haven't an arm and you haven't a leg,
>   hurroo, hurroo!
> You haven't an arm and you haven't a leg,
> You're an eyeless, noseless, chickenless egg,
> You'll have to be put in a bowl to beg:
> Och, Johnny, I hardly knew ye![41]

Johnny's proprietress is named Peggy; Mahood's chief caretaker is given the name of Marguerite. As if to further identify Johnny and Mahood, Beckett's narrator refers to his "vice-exister" as a "billy in a bowl" (p. 37).

The dominant quality shared both by Beckett's twentieth-century protagonist and by Dublin's eighteenth-century Johnny is their extraordinary ability to accept life—even at unspeakable nadir

---

38. *The Unnamable* (New York: Grove Press, 1958), p. 84. All quotations are from this edition.
39. "No Symbols," pp. 325-26. (See also n17).
40. *A Treasury of Irish Folklore*, p. 589.
41. *Ibid.*, p. 606. Since completing this essay, I have seen Marilyn Gaddis Rose's comment on this same likeness in "Irish Memories of Beckett's Voice," *Journal of Modern Literature* (Spring 1971), p. 130.

points. Dublin's Peggy has no doubt that Johnny will accept his future with her—bowl and all. Marguerite of Paris never questions that Mahood will accept life on the elemental terms she can offer. The last three jolting clauses in *The Unnamable*'s unbroken course show a human spirit persisting through its ultimate, unalleviated spiral of need: ". . . you must go on, I can't go on, I'll go on" (p. 179).

When Vivian Mercier presented his study of *The Irish Comic Tradition,* he warned his readers that this work made "no claim to be the last word on its subject; it is much closer to being the first one" (*Preface,* p. vii). This article closes with a similar disclaimer: the hoped-for scholarly study that will adequately relate "the Irishness of Samuel Beckett" to the multiplicity of other factors in his artistic spiral cannot be expected until a far distant future. In the meantime, however, "the national aspects" of Beckett's genius—unlike those he felt were overstated in Jack Yeats's work—have hardly been stated at all. Interim studies, such as the present, must be offered tentatively, subject always to revision in the light of Beckett's "autonomy of the imagined." At the present time, one can only suggest that an author's imagination, in its autonomy, may well turn to the resources of its land of origin.

A report given by Harold Hobson, the English critic, of his conversation with Samuel Beckett in 1956 (when the latter received an award as "dramatist of the Year") calls attention to this persistent "Irishness" in Beckett's work as well as his personality. Hobson alludes to the fact that Beckett, although born in Ireland, had been many years away from that country. He quotes himself as noting (rather obliquely): "You have lived a long time in France." Beckett's answer is as little direct as Hobson's remark; he replies: "Yes, but I still have my green Eire passport."[42]

Future scholars will gauge with greater sensitivity the degree of "Irishness" in Samuel Beckett's work. It seems, however, that entry to certain spirals of his art will continue to require the possession (in sympathy at least) of a "green Eire passport."

42. *International Theater Annual, 1956* (London: John Calder & Co.), p. 153.

12

The Deterioration of Outside Reality in Samuel Beckett's Fiction

Rubin Rabinovitz

AT THE BEGINNING of his career, Samuel Beckett used a dense, learned style unlike that of his more famous later works. In his first published books Beckett at times imitates, and more often parodies writers like James Joyce and T. S. Eliot. The allusiveness in Beckett's early works is a pedant's paradise; the vocabulary, a lexicographer's purgatory; the syntax, a grammarian's inferno ("I see main verb at last," a poem of this period announces). Beckett was ultimately to deplore this cultured showing off; his later books use simpler words, fewer allusions, shorter sentences. But these works are complicated in another way: the visible world of his early fiction—a Dublin salon, a London rooming-house—fades and the furniture of mundane reality disappears.

Beckett's early novels, with their learned references and conventional settings, display an interest in outside reality that betrays their heroes' announced desire to withdraw into themselves. In the later novels, however, geographical locations are unspecified; settings are spare and strange; and a desire to achieve verisimilitude is replaced by an emphasis on inner verities.

The early collection of stories, *More Pricks Than Kicks* (1934), still presents time and place in a conventional manner. In *Murphy* (1938), Beckett uses hyperbole to parody conventional descriptions of locale: the narrator's compulsive notation of place and date for the most trivial events is a counterpoint to Murphy's desire to escape

from time and space. In the works after *Murphy* this prodigality ceases and the chronology and geography become indistinct.

In *Watt* (published in 1953, but written about ten years earlier), the narrator is often vague about dates and seasons: "It was summer, he thought, because the air was not quite cold."[1] Even the time of day is in places omitted:

> Could you tell me what time it was, said Watt. It was as he feared, earlier than he hoped (p. 228).

Normal chronological sequence is violated in word order (Watt's inversions), sentences (the conclusion of a paragraph on page 237 appears on page 164), and in entire sections (Part IV chronologically precedes Part III). The hypnotic and stagnant quality of repetitious passages makes it seem that the novel's internal chronology will supersede the reader's perception of time outside the book.

The deterioration of chronology contributes to a larger sense of timelessness in *Watt*. Unlike

1. *Watt* (New York: Grove Press, 1959), p. 215; references to the novel given in the text are to the same edition. Other works by Beckett used for this essay were all published by the Grove Press in New York: *Poems in English* (1961); *More Pricks Than Kicks* (1970); *Murphy* (1957); *Proust* (n.d.); *Waiting for Godot* (1954). References to these works in the text are again to these editions. I should like to thank the Columbia University Council on Research in the Humanities for a grant that assisted me in the completion of this study.

books that are meant to be read only once, the most intense perception of a passage in the novel does not necessarily occur at the moment it is before the reader. The significance of many segments—Arsene's speech is an example—is altered and heightened by successive rereadings, as indistinct relationships between various parts of the novel become perceptible. Beckett's later fiction is like music in this respect; the cumulative effect of repeated exposure to the work may overshadow the impression created by a single passage apprehended at a given moment. As the linear quality of the work diminishes, its parts are in a sense experienced simultaneously and its temporality is reduced.

A vagueness in *Watt* about locale, like the vagueness about time, helps to remove the novel from the fixity of a concern with physical reality. It also helps to universalize the action; Beckett has no desire to write another great novel about Dublin. Hence, for example, the reader is never told where Mr. Knott's house is located. A number of critics have concluded from internal evidence that it is probably in Foxrock, a suburb of Dublin; but the narrator makes it clear that this sort of information must be withheld. On the train, Spiro asks Watt about his destination:

> Where do you get down, sir?
> Watt named the place.
> I beg your pardon? said Mr. Spiro.
> Watt named the place again.
> Then there is not a moment to lose, said Mr Spiro (p. 28).

Watt, Spiro, and presumably the narrator all know the name of the place; but the reader will not.

As the descriptions of time and space grow hazy, Beckett's style becomes simpler. In his early work the idea that stylistic elegance should be valued for its own sake is rarely questioned. But the style of each book after *More Pricks Than Kicks* becomes plainer as Beckett begins to feel that reality's complexity is concealed beneath a deceptively simple surface.

In the works after *Watt*, written in French, Beckett simplified his style by eliminating embellishing devices. The result is a stylistic poverty that matches the existential poverty he describes. Beckett's comment that he began to compose his

books in French because it made writing without style easier is an indication of this transition.[2]

In *Murphy* and *Watt* Beckett had not entirely abandoned his ornate style; he sought instead to overcome its deleterious effect by using it in a seemingly inappropriate manner. In these novels elegance appears where one least expects it: in a description of Watt blowing his nose, for example (234–35). Like cosmetics, the stylistic elegance that usually heightens beauty may transform undistracting homeliness into a grotesque eyesore. Existence for Beckett is often grotesque; the style is more appropriate than it first appears.

Along with unnecessary effusiveness in style, Beckett avoids emotional effusiveness. Any pathos in his later works is implied; sentimentality is mocked; joie de vivre is suppressed. Irony, parody, understatement, and obscurity are his favorite tools for this purpose.

The chief device for limiting emotional feeling in the early works is comic hyperbole. A trickle of bubbling emotions in "The Smeraldina's Billet Doux" (a story in *More Pricks Than Kicks*) is quickly transformed into a geyser of steaming passion, so as to diminish the possibility for bathos. The later works are more subtle. In what may be a parody of Eliot's objective correlative, Beckett supplies the ingredients for a particular emotional response and then withholds the response itself:

> Mr Hackett decided, after some moments, that if they were waiting for a tram they had been doing so for some time. For the lady held the gentleman by the ears, and the gentleman's hand was on the lady's thigh, and the lady's tongue was in the gentleman's mouth. . . . Taking a pace forward, to satisfy himself that the gentleman's other hand was not going to waste, Mr. Hackett was shocked to find it limply dangling over the back of the seat, with between its fingers the spent three quarters of a cigarette (*Watt,* p. 8).

Mr. Hackett is not shocked—though the reader may have expected him to be—by an open display of what Beckett elsewhere calls oyster kisses. Similarly, the narrator's clinical tone hardly seems appropriate to the circumstances. Other love scenes in *Watt* and *Murphy*, like the one with Mrs Gor-

---

2. Quoted in Niklaus Gessner, *Die Unzulänglichkeit der Sprache* (Zurich: Juris-Verlag, 1957), p. 32n. This early study of Beckett has a good discussion of his transition to an impoverished style.

man or the Wylie-Counihan liaison, are written in the same mechanical style.

This anaphrodisia is not the result of a desire to mollify the puritanical reader, or even the puritanical nonreader. Taking the second category first, Beckett inveighs against "the filthy censors" and "their filthy synecdoche" in *Murphy* (p. 76). As for literate puritans, during a love scene in the same book ("Miss Counihan had never enjoyed anything quite so much as this slow-motion osmosis of love's spittle") the narrator says "The above passage is carefully calculated to deprave the cultivated reader" (pp. 117–18).

In *Watt* the inappropriately austere sexual descriptions are juxtaposed against the stylistic triumphs of the nose-blowing scene. Perhaps Beckett feels that a public jaded by literature's obsessive concern with sexual organs is ready at last to acknowledge an unwarranted neglect of the olfactory apparatus. Whatever his feelings about nose-blowing, in eliminating sexually arousing material, Beckett here illustrates a point he often reiterates: that the satisfaction of desire does not lead to happiness. As Arsene says in *Watt,* "the glutton castaway, the drunkard in the desert, the lecher in prison, they are the happy ones" (p. 44). Mary, who in the same book makes a heroic effort to satisfy her constant desire for food, is hardly an example of human felicity. In his mechanical descriptions of eating or of love-making, the narrator refuses to glorify an ultimately frustrating experience. Satisfaction of desire is momentary; it gives way to a renewed, more acute hunger. Seen in this light, a mechanical tone in describing sexual activity is a courtesy to the reader.

The traditional problems of lovers—jealousy, protective parents, and *Weltschmerz*—rarely trouble Beckett's characters. Their complaints are more fundamental. Sam Lynch is a paralytic; and of the two ladies whom Watt favors with his attentions, Mrs. Watson has had a leg amputated and Mrs. Gorman, a breast. Watt and Mrs. Gorman never go beyond kissing because "Watt had not the strength, and Mrs Gorman had not the time, indispensable to even the most perfunctory coalescence." The narrator comments on the sad circumstance "that a trifling and in all probability tractable obstruction of some endocrinal Bandusia, that a mere matter of forty-five or fifty minutes by the clock, should as effectively as death itself, or as the Hellespont, separate lovers" (pp. 141–42).

The Hellespont; Leander loving Hero, struggling through the waves; Byron, loving heroics, plunging through the foam—all this withers before Beckett's irony. A sentimental view of love is useless, even an encumbrance. Exaggerations of love's euphoria make the reality insufficient; love ends not with an operatic crescendo but in a humiliating diminuendo. Romantic exaggeration, ostensibly a distraction from the misery of life, only adds disappointment to the misery.

Nor is this misery alleviated by poetic rapture about the beauties of nature. Perfumed flowers, a bird's song, and the harvest moon are part of the same grand scheme that bequeathed typhus and bubonic plague to humanity. Beckett would rather describe rats and lice: with them one knows where one stands.

Most of the flowers that adorn the landscape in *Watt,* "the foxgloves, the hyssop, the pretty nettles, the high pouting hemlock" (p. 33) are poisonous. The moon, whose appearance would be compared "by some writers, to a sickle, or a crescent" (p. 222), is according to Beckett "of an unpleasant yellow colour" (p. 30). In a parody of biblical prose, Sam describes how he and Watt killed birds and gained the trust of their "particular friends," a family of rats. "And then we would sit down in the midst of them, and give them to eat, out of our hands, of a nice fat frog, or a baby thrush." Sometimes they feed a young rat to its relatives. "It was on these occasions," says Sam, "that we came nearest to God" (pp. 155–56).

The cruelty of God or nature in this pessimistic view of existence makes even tragic gestures futile. Beckett's dying heroes do not shake their fists heavenward in a final act of defiance: nature cannot be rebuked. Tragic literature suggests that suffering ennobles humanity; Beckett sees only spiritual poverty in its wake. Suffering is slow, unattractive, repetitive, impersonal; and Beckett's style has similar qualities when he writes about suffering. The deaths of Belacqua and Murphy; the tears of Kelly and Watt; the diseases of the Lynch family—all are described in a cold, remote tone. Each event, as in life, provokes whatever feeling it will; the narrator's mask prevents him from suggesting appropriate emotional responses to these visions of suffering.

Beckett goes to great lengths to maintain an impassive tone. In places where the reader might too easily be moved to pity, when the characters suffer, for example, entire passages may be deleted. The reader never sees Murphy at the moment he turns over in his rocking chair; although afterwards his bloody nose and awkward position are described, his pain is not. There are details about the events that lead up to Murphy's death, but his death itself is omitted. Watt is hit by a door, and later a bucket is dropped on him; using a variety of evasive tactics the narrator manages to avoid mentioning his pain (pp. 237, 241). The reader is distracted from these omissions by intrusive parentheses, " (Hiatus in MS) ," which spring up in the text between the two occasions where Watt is struck.

The distracting parenthesis is a tool Beckett often uses, either to dampen the emotional quality of a passage or to blur a meaning that might be too obvious. An example is the following sentence in which Arsene speaks of his frustration in an attempt to formulate a hard-earned bit of wisdom: that any attempt to define the ineffable is bound to fail.

> Why even I myself, strolling all alone in some hard earned suspension of labour in this charming garden, have tried and tried to formulate this delicious haw! and I may add quite useless wisdom so dearly won and with which I am so to speak from the crown of my head to the soles of my feet imbued, so that I neither eat nor drink nor breathe in and out nor do my doodles but more sagaciously than before, like Theseus kissing Ariadne, or Ariadne Theseus, towards the end, on the seashore, and tried in vain, notwithstanding the beauties of the scene, bower and sward, glade and arbour, sunshine and shadow, and the pleasant dawdling motion carrying me about in the midst of them, hither and thither, with unparalleled sagacity. (pp. 62–63)

Here the parenthetical statements diminish both the pathos and the clarity of the passage; but the humor of the parentheses is as important as the emotions and meaning that they obscure. If at its communicative level the passage is a diagnosis of intellectual despair, at its comic level it provides an analgesic. Much of Beckett's writing is like this; the pain he describes cannot be alleviated by commiseration, but it is somewhat diminished by laughter.[3]

The name Watt itself reflects this blend of seriousness and comedy. Watt's serious side is his role as what-man, a questioner constantly frustrated in his pursuit of meanings. But he also has a role as wattman—in French, a tram-driver. Beckett uses this word in *Proust* (p. 52) , and again in *Waiting for Godot* (p. 28) , when Lucky alludes to Puncher and Wattman, a punning reference to a ticket-taker and a tram-driver.

The tram is associated with a metaphor in a limerick Beckett quoted to Lawrence Harvey:

> There was a young man who said, "Damn!
> I suddenly see what I am,
> A creature that moves
> In predestined grooves,
> In fact not a bus but a tram."[4]

The tram metaphor as Beckett uses it is similar to the image of the Cartesian cyclist that is important in his earlier works.[5] Man is both body and mind, tram and driver. So long as he remains a prisoner in his body, man's freedom of choice is largely illusory: physical laws, like the tram's rails, rigidly direct his movements. The tram must remain on the rails and the body is trapped in time and space; but the mind may withdraw from physical reality just as the driver may descend from the tram.

When we first see Watt he has just descended from a tram: like Murphy, he seeks to liberate himself from the necessity of the physical world. Physical reality is always associated with trams and railroads in Watt: the novel's scenes of conventional people engaged in conventional activities all occur at tram-stops or railroad stations. Knott's house is at a distance from the tracks, but its corrosive nihilism is hardly an alternative to life on the tracks. In his last appearance Watt is remote from the tracks: he returns to his private mansion, a metaphorical place not unlike Murphy's little world. In Beckett's works, art, laughter, and a withdrawal into the inner self are the principal means for alleviating the harshness of physical reality. All of these elements are present in the wattman metaphor.

This intricate metaphor illustrates the complexity of the presentation of reality in Beckett's

---

3. See for example Arsene's comment on the three laughs, *Watt*, p. 48.

4. Lawrence Harvey, *Samuel Beckett: Poet and Critic* (Princeton, N.J.: Princeton University Press, 1970) , p. 242. Harvey attributes the limerick to Maurice E. Hare.

5. See Hugh Kenner, 'The Cartesian Centaur," a chapter in his book *Samuel Beckett* (Berkeley, Calif.: University of California Press, 1968) , pp. 117 ff.

writing—a complexity that one might feel is unwarranted when it seems to weaken the impact of Beckett's ideas. But actually, the complexity works to enhance both the aesthetic and the intellectual aspects of Beckett's fiction. *Watt* and *Murphy* are both stories of men struggling after a stubbornly elusive reality. Beckett's complex presentation of fictional reality creates for the reader a counterpart to the elusive reality Watt and Murphy pursue. If he is willing to contend with this complexity, the reader will find that he has been forced, in his own life, to undergo an experience very much like those which are described in the books before him.

13

Interview with Jack MacGowran

by Kathleen McGrory and John Unterecker,
April 20, 1971, at
Western Connecticut State College, Danbury, Conn.

NOTE: On April 20, 1971, Jack MacGowran appeared with John Unterecker and Kathleen McGrory at Ives Auditorium of Western Connecticut State College. He had consented to contribute to this book an edited transcript of the public interview that took place on that evening. He began by making a very long statement about Beckett and then answered questions from Mr. Unterecker, Miss McGrory, and members of the audience. The typescript of the interview was, however, not available before his death, so that revisions and editorial suggestions he might have made could not be incorporated in the final text. Because he was anxious to have his thoughts on Beckett presented, we have kept editorial correction to a minimum, less than he would probably have made, in the hope of preserving the flavor of a remarkable evening.

JU We might begin by talking about Beckett himself and something about his whole career. Could you start with that?
JM Yes. Well, Beckett's whole career would take me a long time to talk in full about. What I want to deal with initially are several misconceptions about Beckett's work. I'm sure that misconceptions have occurred about the work of many other

great writers who in their own times were superficially scanned by their readers or—if they were playwrights—badly produced by their producers. Certainly Beckett has suffered from his share of them.

At first, the public felt that this ogre of a man was best to stay away from because he was said to deal with matters so linked to human despair as to be impossible to bear. This was the first impression that came out about Beckett's work. And then he was misrepresented as being incomprehensible. Even the most knowledgeable of critics dismissed most of his earlier work, when they wrote about it, as utter rubbish and mumbo-jumbo. I suppose we can forgive them, in a way; for when Beckett finally became recognized, he seemed to emerge as a new form of writer with a new style of writing, a new pattern, a new way of using words. Above all, he is a man who is in love with the word itself and therefore his choice of words is very carefully made. In recent years the theater, to my mind, has lost the function of communication by words. Words were spoken— dialogues were written—by many writers; but the function of words as communication seems to have got lost. But Beckett has revived the proper use of the right word at the right time—for communication. This puzzles a lot of people. But it really should not. And the fact that he writes mainly about people in distress should not in any way deter people from exposing themselves to his work.

Mr. MacGowran died on January 30, 1973, during his appearance in Sean O'Casey's *The Plough and the Stars* at the Vivian Beaumont Theater in New York.

We are all, at one time or another in our lives, subject to some form of distress, but not to constant despair. Neither is Beckett. I mean, no matter how you approach Beckett, through his novels or his plays, no matter what setting he places his characters in for dramatic purposes, never will they give way to despair. But they will shake these off, for their ideal intention is to survive completely whatever situation they are placed in—in the hope that there may be some relief from that situation. Now in this context, Beckett turns out to be more a philosopher of hope than despair. In *Waiting for Godot,* which you are probably most familiar with, when the tramps at the end say, "Well, shall we go?" nobody moves. They don't move because deep down lurks the hope that tomorrow or the day after tomorrow or the day after that tomorrow or the day after that again, Godot—whatever or whoever he is—will arrive and relieve them from their situation. This is an aspect of Beckett I would like to stress—Beckett is *not* the philosopher of despair at all—he's not an unbeliever in what may happen. He's a very moral man and a very spiritual man. The key word in all his plays is the word "perhaps." As an intellectual—and he is one—he knows that very few of us are aware of what may happen where mysteries surround us, in an afterlife or during life. So the key word that runs through his novels and his plays is "perhaps." And therein lies a hope that there's a fifty-fifty chance of things going our way. And he also has a quality that a lot of earlier Irish writers had in their works—O'Casey being one of them—writers who arose during the Yeatsian period, the "Golden Era." They had a sort of double vision that saw human tragedy and comedy running side by side, and they gained power from the realization that laughter of a kind can be a release from the tensions of terrible tragedy—and can, in its own way, result in a subtle catharsis at the end, in which one feels purged rather than depleted by possible tragic circumstances.

But this aspect of Beckett was ignored by many writers and critics. Knowing the man closely for fourteen years, I began to feel angry at his mistreatment. Because he's a man who will rarely raise his voice in protest against what is said about him. For he's not concerned, as he said in a letter to someone, with success or failure. Neither means anything to him who has more often breathed in the revivifying air of failure. So that he is not worried about critical opinions. But I

took up the cudgels on his behalf—I wanted to prove such critics wrong. I wanted to present to the public at large a wide spectrum of Beckett's work—the whole range of his theater and fiction, which could bring to the public at large a view of Beckett that had become so narrow that one could not see beyond this gloomy, despairing, nihilistic aspect. He has a high comic sense, which arises out of a certain kind of boredom with life. And this comedy of a certain sort—it's not slapstick comedy that we may be used to in many ways—comedy falls into many categories—for the want of another word one could call it "black comedy" or "relief comedy." What I've tried to do as an actor is to make visible this complex comic vision of a man all too often dismissed as despairing.

That's enough on Beckett for a moment. I asked him why, when he was a professor at Trinity College, he suddenly decided to leave for France—because he was in a very big position at Trinity. And at this time he was very keen to meet Joyce with whom he had become acquainted through books, and wanted to meet him very badly. He was professor of French at Trinity College and with the birth of a real writer still lurking in him at this time, what he really wanted to be, I discovered, was a painter. But there you are—arts are married; if you don't do the one, you'll do the other! *I* am a frustrated writer. So he was lecturing one day at Trinity College when, he said, "Suddenly a flash hit and I wondered what on earth I was doing trying to teach students and why I was trying to teach something about which I knew nothing at all." So he left Trinity, made for Paris—but he got to London first, where he spent one year as an attendant in a mental home. And as a result of that experience he wrote his first novel, called *Murphy,* a highly comic novel in the narrative vein. He then went on to Paris, where he did become acquainted with Joyce, as a friend of the family, and helped Joyce to read at a time when Joyce was going blind. But then shortly after that, the war started, and being neutral and being Irish, he said, "I am not involved in this world war. I remain neutral as an Irish citizen, and I see no reason for myself to be involved in any way." But when the atrocities of Hitler began to show themselves in the gas chambers and all those other horrors, he said, "I can no longer stand by with my arms folded." And so he joined the French Resistance Movement and became one of its key men. And of course every

Nazi bullet was marked for him. And he was on the run. He escaped from a wood one time, where he had been trapped for five days by the Nazis who were surrounding the wood; when they invaded Paris, he had to flee with his wife Suzanne to an unoccupied zone of France, where he acted as a farm laborer during the day. And at night, by candlelight in this farmhouse, he wrote his second novel, called *Watt*.

Now you would imagine that the influence of where he was staying and what had happened might run through his novel; but not at all. He drew on Dublin—its characters, its locale—for most of the novel. And toward the end of it, if you have read the novel, you will notice a change of style, one that anticipates his trilogy, which took a greater form. The earlier part of *Watt* is in a narrative style—and I would like to read you the opening passage of *Watt*. And I—whether my sense of humor is oblique or peculiar—don't know how it might appeal to you. But this is how it goes:

(MacGowran here read the opening pages of *Watt*)

And that's just an idea of his observational capacity and of the humor he can see in the situation.

There are a few things I'd like to clear up about Beckett that have reached the world in many various ways: that he's a recluse, that he doesn't want to meet anybody, that he's an ill-tempered man, and all that. This is grossly untrue. Beckett is one of the most compassionate men I have ever found in my life. He is a very private person—which is a very different thing from being a recluse. He needs his private life very badly for the material he writes. Writing, he says, to him is agony. It's having nothing to express but the desire to express. He is so concerned with the world about him, with the human condition generally, that this becomes his main theme. He is a genuinely creative writer who writes because he has to say what he has to say. When he was offered the Nobel Prize in 1969, he wired them back saying, "I do not want this prize. I would rather you gave it to somebody else. Please do not give it to me." They would not accept his refusal. And he's not a man who will engage in a prolonged fight at all. When they forced it on him, he said, "All right, all right. I will accept it, but I'll not go to Stockholm to receive it." Nor did he go. He sent

his publishers. Because he could not bear the limelight it might shed upon him, and thus disrupt his private life. He also secretly felt, I think, the fact that Joyce had never been awarded the Nobel Prize, and he felt that he should have been. The fact that Joyce hadn't been given the Nobel Prize made Beckett feel that he was not entitled to it.

Beckett's life is lived on very simple terms. He has a collection of friends whom he is extremely loyal to. He is responsible for the success of many young painters in Paris, whose work he advanced and helped in every way. Any one of his friends who's in trouble has only to call on Beckett and he will be helped in every way possible. Helping human nature is one of his greatest virtues.

He is not a recluse. He does not hide away. He just does not like this glare of publicity, and he does not like being adored or lionized. And I think if he was, it might affect what he writes. He's now 65 years of age and a very fit man.[1] Contrary to what people might think of Beckett, he was a very fine athlete in his day. He was an expert cricketer, an expert rugby player, and a very good golfer. These activities all had to stop when his eyesight became poor. But he still walks like an athlete. He is spare of frame. He's about six-foot-one, he walks loosely, like an athlete. He does a lot of walking. He's kind—so kind, that you would not expect it from him.

He will discuss his work with many people, but he will not try to explain it as an abstract painter might try to explain an abstract painting. There was a time when I was with some people who tried to *force* him to explain many things in *Godot* that were in an area that was quite inexplicable. And he said, "I'm sorry that I can't help you in this case. What I have written is on the page. I would feel superior to my own work if I tried to explain it. If I knew who Godot was, I would have said so." He said, "it is not God." This was meant sincerely. So he does not like to be questioned deeply on areas of his work that are possibly unconscious in their origins or unconscious in their organization. But if you are working with him as an interpreter, or doing his plays, he will spend hours helping you on his work—hours. So that when you are actually going to involve yourself in his work, he will devote himself entirely to it.

---

1. "Now" is Spring of 1971, the date of the interview.

Here are a few more little facts about Beckett just to give you a pen-picture of the man himself. He has a great sense of humor. A very deep sense of sadness—not for himself, but for the world at large. And a certain Celtic melancholia that goes with us all. This is part of his heritage. But as he said to me, "You must not regard my work as in any way autobiographical—it may be in some various odd places. People have said to me that I must have had a very unhappy childhood, to be a writer like this." He said, "This is not true. I spent a very happy childhood. I came from a very upper-class, well-to-do family, in Stillorgen, County Dublin, where my father was a quantity surveyor and a very famous swimmer. I, by ordinary standards, had a very happy childhood. But by my nature I was more aware of unhappiness around me than of happiness." But he himself did not spend an unhappy childhood. There was one great gift that all members of the Beckett family shared: that was classical music. Which brings me to the point of how allied classical music and great literature are. There's not a great deal of difference. Beckett is a very brilliant musician himself, who plays classics brilliantly on the piano. All his relatives are in classical music—his nephew, who is chief flute player for the London Philharmonic Orchestra; his cousin, John Beckett, who is a composer for the harpsichord and one of the principal harpsichordists of the British Isles. Beckett's whole background is one of classical music. Now, on reading his work, particularly his later work, you become aware of this, because the work turns into word-music as if the whole basis of a sonata was running through his mind as he wrote it. Despite the fact that he wrote two novels that were narratives and two short stories that were narratives, his more developed work is that of a poet rather than a novelist—and a poet who is more musical than most. Poetry runs completely through his work. Just to confirm that Beckett was not without poetry, musical language, and a sense of humor, even in the most appalling circumstances, I'd like to render you a little piece from my show, which is taken from the novel called *Molloy*. If you don't mind, I'll have to stand for this.

(Reading from *Molloy*: "I took advantage of being at the seaside to lay in a store of sucking stones . . . etc.")

JU One of the things that interests me in your handling of that monologue is the breaks and pauses—did you work this out with Beckett or was this your own plan? Did you check it with him at all?

JM Well, it was partly my own timing, but I checked it with Beckett first, you know, so that he was satisfied with it. And there was also a certain emphasis required at certain times by pauses and timing; to allow the idea to get through to some degree I used these pauses myself and then tested them out on Sam Beckett.

JU And he agreed to them.

JM And he agreed.

JU Did you do very much work with him in which he had a director's hand?

JM Oh yes. We did a production of *Endgame,* which started off as an amateur production in Paris and which Sam rang me about and said, "I know you're interested in playing Clov again," which I had done before and felt I had not done properly. This was about eleven years ago. I had first played it with the late George Devine of the Royal Court in London, who played Hamm; George was too avuncular and nice a person to play Hamm. You needed a different kind of actor. He also directed the play, which he didn't handle very well. So night after night we were subjected to calls—"Get off the stage!" "Rubbish!"—banging of seats, everybody walking out. We plowed on, mercilessly, with the play and ended up night after night with about four people in the audience, two of whom were asleep. So after this, I felt we hadn't done justice to the play. I said, "Sam, some day this must be done properly, and I would really like to do it properly." Then he rang me about an amateur production that was going on in Paris, and would I play Clov? I said, "Yes, I will, but I would be very keen to know who will play Hamm." Because the dependence of one character on the other is so strong that it cannot be played without their being of equal degree. So I said, "If you can get an actor called Pat McGee, whom I know very well, to play Hamm, I'll be very happy to do it." I had to do all kinds of inveigling to get Pat McGee to do Hamm, because his agent didn't want him to play it. He said nothing would come of it. The fact that McGee is now one of the most respected actors in London came as a result of this show. So it shows I wasn't wrong anyway. But I did get McGee to play it and it turned out to be a professional production in the end. Sam directed the whole production for six weeks in London. There was a producer allotted to the show—a young boy who did not know much about Beckett. But Sam was kind to him and allowed his name to go down on the program because Sam would not go down on the program as director. Well, all of the direction came directly from Samuel Beckett and we worked very, very deliberately and very finely on the show for six solid weeks before we went to Paris. So that, in a way, it is the most definitive production of *Endgame* there has ever been. We ran for nine weeks in Paris, in English, which was a kind of record. The Royal Shakespeare Theatre became interested in the show, came over to see it, brought us back, and we played two seasons in the Royal Shakespeare, to crowded houses—the same show which we'd played to four people ten years before that.

JU In directing you, was Beckett's focus on characterization, or was he primarily interested in precision of action?

JM Characterization was very important to him. I knew this would automatically be, because he had written the characters. But what I didn't suspect was his natural feeling for movement, which he had by instinct. And he knew how to reduce certain moves to a simplicity which conveyed what they were meant to convey without any fussiness. His directions were deliberate and without a choice of this, that, or the other. He'd say, *"This* is the way *that* should go—the head should be turned to the right, or the head should be turned downward or turned upward. And the move should be in this direction or in that direction." And so precise were his directions, you know, that we never failed to find the pattern of simplicity working each night.

JU It was then almost an anti-Method approach to directing? What I'm trying to say is that you'd be *calculating* your stage presence in the kind of direction Beckett gave you?

JM Yes.

JU In so much Method directing, you evolve your performance. But it seems to me that his anti-Method approach would be quite in keeping with the kind of prose that he writes in the novels, the kind of thing he does in his poetry.

JM Yes, the precision that lies within his work he applies in every direction in the theater. He also is a great master of lighting in the theater, which has up to now, except in the hands of a few very select people, just been bashed on and left on as a light source. But he knew lighting had more of an effect than this. And he played with lighting as if it were a real actor. One has only to see that little play called *Play,* in which three people are in an urn and speak when the light hits them, and don't speak when there's no light on them— or reduce the intensity of their vocal speaking as the light dims or the light grows stronger. He allies light to performance in a very strong way and is very, very good at knowing how to light a play to its maximum effect.

JU What happened after opening nights? Did Beckett continue to work on his script and on the actors' interpretations? Did he work with you in this way?

JM Yes.

JU Was there much reworking?

JM Yes, there were slight reworkings, but not very much.

JU He knew what he wanted.

JM —Only in the sense that he realized that certain passages were literary and were only dulling an audience because of their literary quality rather than their dramatic quality, and he decided "We'd better cut this literary section out here and start from there and pick it up here where the dramatic value starts again. And let's lose anything that's of a purely literary value which, to an audience, can get very dull and boring. And he became more and more aware of what a theater means as he grew with it. He grew with the theater because he made many changes in his original plays as he went along from production to production. He changed lots of lines in *Endgame* that were in the first draft he had made when he became aware of what the theater meant as theater. He changed lots of lines.

JU Also, of course, he became aware of the possibilities of individual actors, didn't he? I'm thinking particularly of his writing *Eh, Joe,* for example, in which he was thinking of you as an actor.

JM Yes, if he felt that an actor was very devoted, or felt very strongly about his work, or knew how to interpret it in some way, even without explaining how he could do it, he immediately took an interest in that actor. And this was at a time when Beckett was hardly known. But when those few of us who became impassioned of his work could not leave it alone because of certain qualities in it, he respected us very much and knew that we knew somehow what he was trying to say. He gave us all the attention he could, and then wrote plays for us, which is a very happy thing to happen to an actor.

JU It's a very happy thing to happen to a writer, too.

JM It's a wonderful marriage to this degree—that one is born in a generation as an actor where a living writer of the calibre of Beckett can work hand in hand with that actor and so bring out the best in both. It rarely happens. And I feel lucky and fortunate to have been born of his generation and to have lived with him, and to have known him so long and deeply.

JU Don't you feel, too, that the same theatricality that's in the plays is also in the novels?

JM Oh yes, the novels are strongly dramatic and are meant to be read. I mean, the passages I read to you tonight were both from novels and not from plays. Beckett has said to me: "I know that my word on the printed page is difficult to read and assimilate and I know also that it gets added dimension when read and dramatized." Because his work in the novels has a dramatic quality which is borne out in being read.

JU We're all trained to read so fast. We take speed-reading courses. But the quality of Beckett's humor—and Beckett's sadness, too—comes through in terms of the human voice. A great deal of the power of Beckett is in your slowing down of the reading to the speed of a mind saying words out loud—and not too quickly, either.

JM Yes, the pace of the reading of Beckett is very important. I talked at great length with him about the pace at which his material should be read. And we talked about the pace and we decided upon the pace, for the simple reason that images can be lost if you speak too fast. People cannot catch up with the images that are created, cannot have a chance to assimilate them exactly. So the pace is dictated by the writing.

JU Kathleen, did you have a question?

KM Yes. I wondered, Jack, about your reading in New York: you seemed to speed up the pace of the Lucky soliloquy in *Godot*. Could you say why that's faster than the rest?

JM Yes, yes. The "Lucky," from *Godot*, is an attempt to speak on the part of a man who once was a very accomplished speaker, one who knew how to explain fully about life, but who's now so senile and so overcome by circumstances that he has lost track of what he was going to say. And in an effort to get back to his main subject, he began to get faster and faster in his speech, in the

hope that the speed would bring him back to his original idea. And all that resulted in it was a frantic quality in which everything became speeded up—his images of the world to come and what was happening now, and the world before, all became one; and he couldn't separate them, so he quickened them up to such a degree that they became just a quick succession of words unrelated to each other. For the relationship could have been followed from the earlier part of the speeches, in which he was reasonably coherent.

JU Let's move out to the audience now.

AUD I have a question that has maybe three answers.

JU You've got three people!

AUD Well, one person can answer. In Irish literature, there seems to be a part of the theologies we see in other literatures. But say, in reading Beckett or Joyce or Eugene O'Neill, you don't really see any Marxism. So you've got an ideology of Marxism: not in Beckett. You don't see the ideology of Freud in Beckett. You don't see the ideology of Existentialism in Beckett. What is it that Irish literature has or does that keeps it apart from all the rest of us?

JM Yes. Well, contemporary forms of existentialism you find in Beckett to some degree. You don't find them in Joyce or in O'Casey or many of the other writers because it was a subject that was akin to Europe alone—Central Europe—and never reached Ireland. I mean, many other things reached Ireland very strongly, like Jansenism, and hence begins the fight against Jansenism which resulted in a complete anti-Jansenistic attitude. But Irish writers differed completely from Continental writers in that existentialism as such did not come into their work. Except in Beckett, of course, and this is because he lived so long among French writers that he became aware of Existentialism. And to a degree he touches on the subject. But no other Irish writer does at all, because he's not aware of existentialism; he's not aware of it. There are many reasons for this. The basic faith of the country,—its heritage, its insular quality—has prevented existentialism from making many inroads into his writings.

JU But in a sense that's been one of the sources of power for the Irish writer—that instead of developing a drama of ideas or a literature predominantly of ideas, it becomes a literature built out of feeling—something which is almost unique in modern English literature and, until relatively re-

cent times, in America. We've had a very intellectual twentieth century, and I think one of the
things that gives Irish literature its very special
power is this focus on private feeling and on characterization. It's very, very strong in all Irish writing.

KM Well, in O'Casey's later works, Marxism is
very strong. *The Star Turns Green,* for example.

JM Oh yes, O'Casey I've forgotten. I beg your par-
don. Marxism is very strong, very strong. But
those plays are rather weak.

KM When they leave that primitive strain, whatever it is, they seem to lose something of their
Irishness and much of their power.

JM What O'Casey was, was anti-clerical to a
marked degree because the narrowness of Irish
Catholicism worried him terribly. Because he
thought, it took all the joy out of life. He thought
the people were brought up in the fear of God
rather than in the love of God. And the joyless-
ness was part of the gray, drab Irish countryside.
And this is why he veered toward the pagan in
the Irish—the feeling for joy and release and enjoyment of life. And to that degree, he called it
Communism. Knowing Sean as I did for many
years before he died, I don't think he was aware
very much of what Communism really meant. Once
I was sitting in the middle and there was a Hungarian girl on his right and I was sitting on his
left, and she was translating his work, or had come
to ask to translate his work into Hungarian. And
à propos of nothing at all, he turned to her and
said, "What religion are ye?" And she said, "Oh,
I'm a Protestant." And he turned to me and said,
"What religion are you?" I said, "I'm a Roman
Catholic." "Well thank God I'm a Communist!"

AUD Why do so many Irish writers have to leave
Ireland to write about it?

JM A very good question indeed. Although,
strangely enough, there are a handful of very good
writers who never left Ireland at all. Frank O'Connor, who's probably known to most of you as a
very good short story writer and who died recently, made a comment that every Irishman's private
life begins at Holyhead [point of departure for
Irish emigrés traveling to England] and London.
But the reason why a lot of them left the country was the repressive form of the official and un-
official censorship in the country that did not permit them the chance to expand the writing in the

way that they wanted to. They had to seek a place
where they could write freely. O'Casey's was a different case entirely, I think. He would have remained in Ireland indefinitely—he would not
have left but for his row with Yeats over *The
Silver Tassie.* Because here, I think, Yeats was
wrong. O'Casey wrote a realistic first act, a realistic third act, and a second act that was Surrealis-
tic—and very beautiful indeed. Yeats turned the
play down at the Abbey, much to O'Casey's surprise, telling O'Casey that he had fallen between
two stools, that the mixture did not work. But it
does work, and work beautifully. And therein
Yeats made a grave error in rejecting the play.
O'Casey, being a very sensitive person, was so hurt
by this that he left Ireland. And that was the reason O'Casey left. But in the end, I may happily
say that he and Yeats became very close friends,
and it was all forgotten. But once he left the country, he never came back. Nevertheless, O'Casey
held to the very end of his life a hope that Ireland might become a less joyless country and a
more gay country than when he saw it.

JU It's odd you say, "a less joyless country." But
of course it was joyless from his point of view.
And yet, who presented so much joy in his plays
as O'Casey?

JM Yes. You see, he manufactured joy in his plays
to a degree. He manufactured great joy, which
was a kind of a pagan joy—which cannot be dismissed, because before Ireland became Christian
it was pagan! And the qualities still lie very deep
in the Irish for enjoyment. They are very capable
of enjoyment. The narrow world in which O'Casey lived as a youth and the privations he suffered
in the slums certainly made for a gray world. But
there are many parts of Ireland, mostly outside
of Dublin itself, that are full of joy, full of gaiety,
full of laughter. I mean, I often say to myself,
"Where else in the world, in any Catholic country, will you find a goat crowned king every year!"
I mean, nothing more pagan can be thought of.
That's Puck Fair, a week's festival in which no
drinking-house shuts for twenty-four hours a day
—nobody is sober for a week, and a goat is
crowned king of Ireland!—even to this day.

KM Could you tell us briefly about the recent law
passed in Ireland to encourage artists?

JM Yes, I would like to see this expanded because
it is a move in a very great direction by the pres-

ent government in Southern Ireland—I *hate* to say "Southern Ireland"! I want to say "Ireland," meaning the whole country! The division of Ireland, to me, is a shame. And that division has brought about what we see now—unreasoning, barbaric bloodshed, which is going to go on for ages because nobody knows how to settle the question up North. But that would never have occurred if that country had not been divided—a small island such as—Well, I'm talking of Southern Ireland anyway. Two years ago a law was passed which was one of the best steps toward art that has ever been done in any nation. And it would be nice to see it repeated by many other nations. All creative artists, that is, musicians, writers, sculptors—creative artists of any sort, excluding actors—the reason becomes very clear for that, however—are tax-free. No matter what they sell in the way of paintings, literature, compositions, sculpture, et cetera, it's completely tax free. They live tax-exempt. Which means they can work in any country in the world and send their money back to Ireland completely free of taxation. Actors are not included, and actors bellyache about this to a terrible degree because, they say, "We are creative artists, too. Why are we not tax-free?" It is because most Irish actors are semi-professional, because the country cannot afford, outside the Abbey Theatre, to pay full rates to professional actors. So they work at other jobs and so they're semi-professional. You see, anyone who does even a commercial on T.V., once in a year, could go in and say, "I'm an actor," and claim tax-exemption. So Ireland would have hundreds, who weren't actors at all, claiming tax-exemption. But no matter how hard it is on actors, the step was a step in the right direction—that all creative art produced and sold in Ireland is at the moment tax-free.

AUD Joyce and Beckett seem to have got just about as far away from Ireland intellectually as they could, and yet we think of them both as being very Irish. Do you feel that Beckett's writing is really Irish, or is he writing about an Everyman of Everyplace?

JM No. Specifically, if you read his novels, you'll recognize the terrain, the language, the Celtic rhythms—it's all Irish, very, very Irish. His subjects are very international, because they involve the world and people in general. Joyce, who left

Dublin and said he was leaving forever, that he would use silence, exile, and cunning, you know, and that he would forge in the smithy of his soul the conscience of his race, wrote about nothing but Dublin. And to this extent, Beckett and Joyce have something in common. Although Joyce never came back to Dublin, anyone who came from Dublin Joyce was eager to know: Was such and such a shop still there? Was so and so still alive? Did Mrs. So-and-So still walk her dog at such an hour of night? You know he was preoccupied with Dublin. He wrote about Dublin the whole time, although he was removed from it. Beckett has the same obsession with what's happening in Dublin, though his writing is not so precisely about Dublin as Joyce's was. But you can recognize his Irishness very strongly. That was not escapable. The heritage has gone so deep that he has never really left Ireland, although he works in France, like Joyce. Joyce and Oliver St. John Gogarty, if you remember, battled out a terrible feud from the Martello Tower which they shared in the early days of their life—and Gogarty was a great surgeon, a great sportsman, a great writer, and a great man about town, a great physical specimen, and of the ladies much beloved. A very good-looking man, a very successful man, and a very monied man, and one given to practical jokes. And he grew up at the time that Joyce grew up, and he played jokes on Joyce. But Joyce was very humorless where a joke against himself was concerned, and he would not speak to Gogarty. Even years later, when Gogarty met him in the middle of Dublin and said, "Jimmy, let's end this stupid feud, whatever it's for, it was all in fun. Here's my hand—let's forget about it," Joyce ignored his hand and walked on. He would have nothing to do with Gogarty. Yet, on his deathbed in Zurich, there were two books on the bedtable: there was a dictionary and a book of Gogarty's called *As I Was Walking Down Sackville Street*. So he never left Gogarty, either.

JU Any other questions?

AUD There are two films I'd like to have you tell about. One is the film Beckett made in 1964 in New York, and the other one I would like you to tell about is the Peter Brooks film *King Lear* you played the Fool in. Has it ever been released?

JM Yes. The first one is rather strange. Because I had talked to Beckett at great lengths about mak-

ing a film about *Waiting for Godot*. But he is very
loath to change anything written for one medium
into another medium, and said, "How can you
photograph words?" I still see the possibility of
cinema in *Godot*. He doesn't see it yet. Nor will
he release it. "I'd rather study the technique of
film writing and write it myself." So he wrote
"Project One" or "Film" for me at the time. The
director was in Minneapolis and then phoned me
in excitement and said he could not make it for
six weeks after I had my tickets for the *Queen
Mary* to go over and start the movie. And he said
he could not do it for six weeks, by which time
I was contracted for the Royal Shakespeare and so
I could not do it. And I said to Beckett, "I'm
deeply distressed that I cannot do the movie for
you, due to the fact that it has been postponed."
Beckett asked me to suggest a replacement but I
said, "I don't know what to suggest." So the director came up with Buster Keaton. And Beckett,
who was a great lover of the silent movies said,
"Yes, yes, we'll do it." So it was an interesting experiment in movie-making in that it was concerned with the fact that man can escape from
everything except himself, as you know if you
have seen it. The whole movie is about man es-
caping from every watching eye. You never see
him from the front. You only see his back the
whole time, until the very end of the movie. Then
you realize that the one thing he cannot escape
from is himself.

I saw *King Lear* last week in a private showing and was very pleased with the result. I think
Peter Brooks has done quite a job with *King Lear*,
and I think it's going to be quite successful. And
will be released here in New York before the end
of this month—not here, this is Connecticut! Not
far away. It will be released in New York before
the end of the month. It was done under quite
terrifying circumstances up in the very northern-
most point of Jutland in Denmark, in midwinter,
where it was twenty degrees below freezing. And
I am not a lover of the cold. Give me any amount
of heat—I don't care how hot it is, but cold no.
And twenty degrees below freezing numbed me
within five minutes, and most of the movie was
shot out of doors, and I had the flimsiest costume
of the lot. So during the storm sequence, in which
Lear goes mad and chases across this icy, snowy
waste, with ice and wind, and I'm following the
whole time, the rain was drawn from a glacial lake
by a fire brigade, and poured on me for hours on

end. And it turned to ice as it hit me. It turned
to ice as it touched my costume. And literally I
don't know how I did it at all. It had sound problems. And also had print problems. There are
areas in the movie where the screen goes blank.
The voices carry on. This was an innovation of
Brooks, though not entirely deliberate. He had
shot it in light that was far too dark, and nobody
could see a thing!

AUD I noticed in the trilogy and in *How It Is*,
increasingly in the central character, a decay in
the traditional sense of the novelistic style and
what we call "the novel." I was wondering if this
was intentional?

JM In the trilogy generally? What was the essence
of the question? I'm afraid I've missed it.

AUD The Progression of the style, which itself
seems to follow the decay of the central character
—is this intentional?

JM Yes, I think it is. *Malone Dies* is set indoors,
where it's the last seconds of a man's death in
which he goes through everything that has happened in his life. *Molloy* is set, as you know, in a
strange out-of-doors world. *The Unnamable* is also in the outer world, but the character has
reached absolute silence, he is just at the point
before he will cease to be able to say words entirely. And this is a further decay of the individual as an individual. In the later novel *How It
Is*, you have a character struggling in mud and
mire, trying to make human contact with the next
person. Carrying a sack, as you know, that contains
all his belongings. For the intention is to try and
find human contact—not to be utterly alone. In-
terdependence is a very strong factor in Beckett's
plays, and even in *How It Is*, as they are crawling
through the mire and mud, the intention is to try
and reach out and find and touch something belonging to another human being—so that persons
make contact. It is a kind of logical development
of what happens to a man under circumstances
that weigh him down and down and down and
down.

JU The other thing that you were suggesting is
that there's a stylistic parallel to that kind of growing petrification toward the end of *The Unnamable*—as the central character is growing more and
more physically cramped. It seems to me very true
that you have a stylistic tightening of the novel as
it goes on, and an increasing franticness in *The
Unnamable*, so that the words are coming in a
kind of—

JM —They are, very fast—

JU —tumbled, pell-mell fashion.

JM They come in a very fast speech—they tumble out.

JU Right, more and more. Not incoherent. It isn't, it seems to me, but desperate. I think that the tone—

JM No, not incoherent at all, but the pace increases very rapidly because it's spoken in a rhythm that is very definite with quick breaths in between.

JU Yes. I think that the fascinating thing in *The Unnamable* and in all of Beckett is just what you were saying, Jack, that the passionate desire is communication, but circumstances are continually making that communication increasingly difficult—so that at the end of *Malone Dies* the central figure is left alone in bed with a pencil that keeps getting shorter and shorter.

JM And shorter.

JU Which becomes a marvelous parallel with the writer's situation. Because he's in a sense always writing himself out. And yet his need is writing—his need is communication. Similarly, all of the figures who are telling their stories to the central figure of *The Unnamable* are driven people—as is the central figure himself who, in turn, has to tell those stories. That drive is there, terribly. Those stories have to get told. And the reason one tells stories is not so much to convey knowledge but to assert the relationship between people. It's an idea I think that's very close to something in Martin Buber, when Martin Buber talks about the crucial human experience as dialogue, the exchange that's made between people. In Buber that reality consists not in the individual's solipsistic self, the private self that can't find an outlet, but reality comes when two people see each other in some intense fashion. And as Buber says, this can happen between strangers on a subway, for example, when two people happen to look into each other's eyes. Reality is that communication between those two people, or between people and a work of art, or, Buber would add, between a person and his God. It seems to me that Beckett's situation is about the desperateness of the need for that communication in a world in which that communication becomes increasingly difficult.

JM Difficult. You know if you apply it, you know, sincerely to ourselves, if we were placed in similar circumstances, our frantic desire would be to find something real and livable, near us, not to be alone in that quagmire. We would, ourselves, do

the same thing, because of our nature. It would dictate that we search around hopefully for another human being—*anything* living. Why do people keep cats and dogs, you know? Because they live. They are living things. They are needed. So man, alone—but no man is an island. Man alone, he cannot exist. He needs his fellow men. And when he gets to that situation you mentioned in *How It Is,* his need becomes desperate in a world where they seem to be disappearing completely. You know there's a great desperation in *How It Is.*

JU And yet, as we were saying in the car driving up, suicide is the one thing that does *not* happen in 98% of Beckett's work.

JM No, you would give up if you were given to despair over that situation, which many people might be. You would say, "To hell with it!" and just let death overtake you. But Beckett is so anti-self-destruction in himself that he determined, no matter what the circumstances are, his characters will survive until Nature calls them, or God calls them. They will survive. He will not have them kill themselves in any way whatever. If they happen to die en route, they die from natural causes. But they won't voluntarily—they won't commit their own death.

JU Let's make this a last question and then break.

AUD You mentioned progression several times and your concern with despair. I think it is strange that you applied this to Beckett's work as a whole. In both Beckett and Joyce I think everything is quite cyclic. You can't say "Next year it will be better," any more than last year or the year before. You seemed to invert that into hope.

JM I did. Basing it on the word "perhaps," which Beckett himself says is the key word in all he writes. Perhaps tomorrow it will happen or the next day. I mean there *is* an element of hope in that, for no one can be conclusive. I defy any politician to say today, in this country or in many other countries that I know, "Next year we will be prosperous and be great!" They can say, "Perhaps we will be prosperous and great," but we can't go any further than say "Perhaps we will be." And that's the only hope that's left for the ordinary man today, by those who govern and rule us. We've learned through experience in any country, in any government, that however good their promises are before they're elected, when politicians get elected, those promises never seem to take place. So we are left in the same situation as we were in the beginning. So that we can never say in truth that next year is going to be a *great* year. No more can the man in the vineyards say, "I will have a great crop of vine next year"— "Perhaps I will have a great crop of vine next year, perhaps next year will be good,": this is what he is saying. And this is the only element of hope I'm referring to. I don't think I referred to hope in Joyce. I didn't at any moment talk about Joyce and hope.

AUD I get this feeling generally—it's true of O'Neill. That implies something outside the eternal recurrence cycle you see in most great writers. But as for hope, there isn't much hope.

JM Yes, yes, yes.

AUD I don't know if even a "perhaps" comes in.

JM Well, Joyce had a reason, I suppose, to hope less than Beckett did, because he had a daughter called Lucia who was mentally disturbed from birth. She is in a rest-hospital at the moment, in England. And Joyce took on himself a terrible guilt about Lucia, to the degree that he thought she might have been conceived in drink, and so therefore it would have been his fault. As a result of that, he became acquainted with Freud and Jung, and deeply discussed her condition with them. But Jung and Freud did not hold out any hope for him at all as regards Lucia. There he lost hope completely. I don't believe a sense of guilt ever left him. But on the other hand, I think Beckett faces the grimness of the world very squarely and manages to make jokes in spite of it. That is, he sees a world in which there is death, and death of course has great finality. And he sees a bleak world, too. But facing that bleak world, his characters choose to stay. They don't quit and they do make jokes out of the bleakness. They have to, to survive, make jokes out of it. But he does see the world in its total reality. He would not draw back from truth one step—he would not create an illusion that is not true. Everything he writes about is absolute truth as he sees it, which makes it harsh at times. To make his dramatic statement, he has to put his characters in situations that we might not normally find ourselves in, though we do find ourselves in situations equally hard to cope with. But he does say this is the world you are living in—this is what you do to survive in it. He could not create a fairy-tale land, you know. This he could not do. He is utterly truthful to what he writes. And it's not easy for him, either. Because he himself has had to lose every illusion that was ever there in his mind, to face the true reality of life.

JU Without illusions, his characters go on.

JM Without any illusions whatever, they go on. Without illusions.

Chronological Bibliography of Works by William York Tindall

John Eichrodt and Kathleen McGrory

1. *John Bunyan, Mechanick Preacher*. New York: Columbia University Press, 1934.
2. "D. H. Lawrence and the Primitive." *Sewanee Review* 45 (1937) : 198–211.
3. *D. H. Lawrence and Susan His Cow*. New York: Columbia University Press, 1939.
4. "The Study of Contemporary Literature." *English Journal* 28 (1939) : 33–39.
5. "The Robert Bridges Collection." *Columbia University Quarterly* 33 (1941): 154–58.
6. "Scholarship and Contemporary Literature." *Columbia University Quarterly* 33 (1941): 20–33.
7. "The Trouble with Aldous Huxley." *American Scholar* 2 (1942) : 452–64.
8. "Literary Signposts." *American Mercury* 56 (1943) : 114–20.
9. "Felix Culpa," "The Section," "The Fleece" (Poems). *Accent* 5 (1944) : 28–29.
10. "The Navigation" (Poem). *Quarterly Review of Literature* 1 (1944): 163.
11. "Exiles: From Rimbaud to Joyce." *American Scholar* 14 (1945) : 351–55.
12. "Goliath" (Poem). *Rocky Mountain Review* 9 (1945).
13. "The Intruders" (Poem). *Quarterly Review of Literature* 2 (1945) : 106.
14. "The Shadow" (Poem). *Briarcliff Quarterly* 2 (1945) : 74.
15. "The Symbolism of W. B. Yeats." *Accent* 5 (1945): 203–12.
16. "Transcendentalism in Contemporary Literature." *The Asian Legacy and American Life*. Edited by Arthur Christy. New York: John Day Company, 1945.
17. "Felix Culpa," "The Section" (Poems), reprinted in *Accent Anthology*. New York: Harcourt, Brace and World, 1946.
18. *Forces in Modern British Literature, 1885–1946*. New York: Knopf, 1947.
19. "The Recantation of T. S. Eliot," *American Scholar* 16 (1947) : 431–37.
20. "The Sociological Best Seller." *English Journal* 36 (1947): 447–54.
21. "Many-Leveled Fiction: Virginia Woolf to Ross Lockridge." *English Journal* 37 (1948) : 65–71.
22. "The Poetry of Dylan Thomas." *American Scholar* 17 (1948) : 431–39.
23. *James Joyce, His Way of Interpreting the Modern World*. New York: Scribner, 1950.
24. Samuel Butler, *The Way of All Flesh*. Introduction by William York Tindall. New York: Harper, 1950.
25. "Dante and Mrs. Bloom." *Accent* 11 (1951) : 85–92.
26. D. H. Lawrence, *The Plumed Serpent (Quetzalcoatl)* Introduction by William York Tindall. New York: Vintage Books, 1951.
27. "Joyce's Chambermade Music." *Poetry* 80 (1952) : 105–16.
28. D. H. Lawrence, *The Later D. H. Lawrence*. Selected, with an introduction by William York Tindall. New York: Knopf, 1952.
29. "Rumer Godden, Public Symbolist." *English Journal* 40 (1952): 115–21.
30. "The Symbolic Novel." *A.D.* 3 (1952) : 56–68.
31. "James Joyce and the Hermetic Tradition." *Journal of the History of Ideas* 15 (1954) : 23–29.
32. James Joyce, *Chamber Music*. Edited, with notes, by William York Tindall. New York: Columbia University Press, 1954.

33. *The Literary Symbol.* New York: Columbia University Press, 1955.

34. *The Literary Symbol* (Japanese edition). Translated by Toshiko Soda. Tokyo: Shinozaki Shorin, Ltd., n.d.

35. "America's Gift to Ireland," *New Republic* 229 (June 25, 1956) : 18–20.

36. "The Ceremony of Innocence." *Great Moral Dilemmas,* edited by Robert MacIver. New York: Harper, 1956.

37. *Forces in Modern British Literature, 1885–1956* (revised edition of *Forces in Modern British Literature, 1885–1946*). New York: Vintage Books, 1956.

38. "In Search of Lawrence." *The Nation* (Feb. 4, 1956) , p. 97.

39. "Apology for Marlow." *From Jane Austen to Joseph Conrad,* edited by Robert C. Rathburn and Martin Steinmann, Jr. St. Paul: University of Minnesota Press, 1958.

40. "Beckett's Bums." *Critique* 2 (1958): 3–15.

41. James Joyce, *Chamber Music* (German edition). Introduction by William York Tindall. Translated by Johann Ulrich Saxer. Zurich-Stuttgart-Wien: Europa Verlag, 1958.

42. "The Criticism of Fiction." *Texas Quarterly* 1 (1958): 101–11.

43. *A Reader's Guide to James Joyce.* New York: Noonday Press, 1959. London: Thames and Hudson, 1960.

44. *Beckett's Bums.* (Privately printed.) London: Shenval Press, 1960.

45. *James Joyce* (Italian edition of *James Joyce, His Way of Interpreting the Modern World*) . Preface by Glauco Cambon. Bibliographical Guide by Umberto Eco. Milan: Bompiani, 1960.

46. *The Joyce Country.* (Photographs and text.) University Park, Pa.: Pennsylvania State University Press, 1960.

47. *Wallace Stevens.* Minneapolis: University of Minnesota Press, 1961. (University of Minnesota Pamphlets on American Writers, no. 11.) Second printing, 1966. London-Bombay-Karachi: Oxford University Press, 1961. Toronto: Thomas Allen, Ltd , 1961.

48. *Wallace Stevens* (Latin American edition) . Translated by Leopoldo Fontenelle. Sao Paolo, Brazil: Martin Press, 1960. (*Escritores norteamericanos.*)

49. *Wallace Stevens* (Arabic edition) . Beirut, 1962.

50. *The Literary Symbol.* (Reprinted.) Bloomington, Ind.: Indiana University Press, 1962.

51. *A Reader's Guide to Dylan Thomas.* New York: Farrar, Straus, and Cudahy, 1962. London: Thames and Hudson, 1962.

52. *Wallace Stevens* (Spanish edition). Madrid: Editorial Grecos, 1962. (*Tres escritores norteamericanos: Walt Whitman, Wallace Stevens, T. S. Eliot.*)

53. *John Bunyan, Mechanick Preacher.* (Reprinted.) New York: Russell and Russell, 1964.

54. *Samuel Beckett.* New York: Columbia University Press, 1964. (Columbia Essays on Modern Writers, no. 4.)

55. "Poet Behind the Desk." *Saturday Review* 49 (Nov. 19, 1966) : 42–43.

56. *W. B. Yeats.* New York: Columbia University Press, 1966. (Columbia Essays on Modern Writers, no. 15.)

57. *Guia para la lectura de James Joyce* (Spanish edition of *A Reader's Guide to James Joyce*) . Translated by Raquel Bengolea. Venezuela: Monte Avila Editores, C.A., 1969.

58. *A Reader's Guide to Finnegans Wake.* New York: Farrar, Straus and Giroux, 1969.

59. *The Poems of W. B. Yeats.* Selected, edited and with an introduction by William York Tindall. Drawings by Robin Jacques. New York: Thistle Press (Limited Editions Club), 1970.

60. *The Joyce Country.* (Photographs and Text.) Revised and enlarged edition. New York: Schocken Books, 1972.

61. "Mosaic Bloom." *Mosaic* 4 (1972) : 3–9.

Tindall Papers, 1938–1966. (Ca. 7000 items.) Columbia University Libraries, Special Collections. Correspondence, notes, manuscripts, and typescripts concerning Samuel Beckett, James Joyce, Wallace Stevens, D. H. Lawrence, Dylan Thomas, *The Literary Symbol.*

Modern Irish Literature: Essays in Honor of William York Tindall, edited by Raymond J. Porter and James D. Brophy. New Rochelle, N.Y.: Iona College Press, 1972.

(N.B.: With the exception of a few items listed above, book reviews are not included in this bibliography.)